THE
FABRIC
OF
INDIA

THE
FABRIC
OF
INDIA

edited by Rosemary Crill

V&A PUBLISHING

Published to accompany the exhibition
The Fabric of India at the Victoria and Albert Museum,
London, from 3 October 2015 to 10 January 2016

Supported by

With thanks to

First published by V&A Publishing, 2015

V&A Publishing
Victoria and Albert Museum
South Kensington
London SW7 2RL

Distributed in North America by Abrams,
an imprint of ABRAMS

ISBN: 978 1 851 77853 9

Library of Congress Catalog Control Number 2015934093

10 9 8 7 6 5 4 3 2 1
2018 2017 2016 2015

A catalogue record for this book is available
from the British Library.

Designed by Kathrin Jacobsen
Copy-edited by Lise Connellan
Index by Ann Barrett
New V&A photography by Richard Davis,
Jaron James, V&A Photographic Studio

Printed in Italy

V&A Publishing

Supporting the world's leading
museum of art and design,
the Victoria and Albert
Museum, London

Cover illustration: details of pl.173
Frontispiece: detail of pl.210

pp.14–15: see pl.8
pp.76–7: see pl.151
pp.180–1: detail of pl.230

CONTENTS

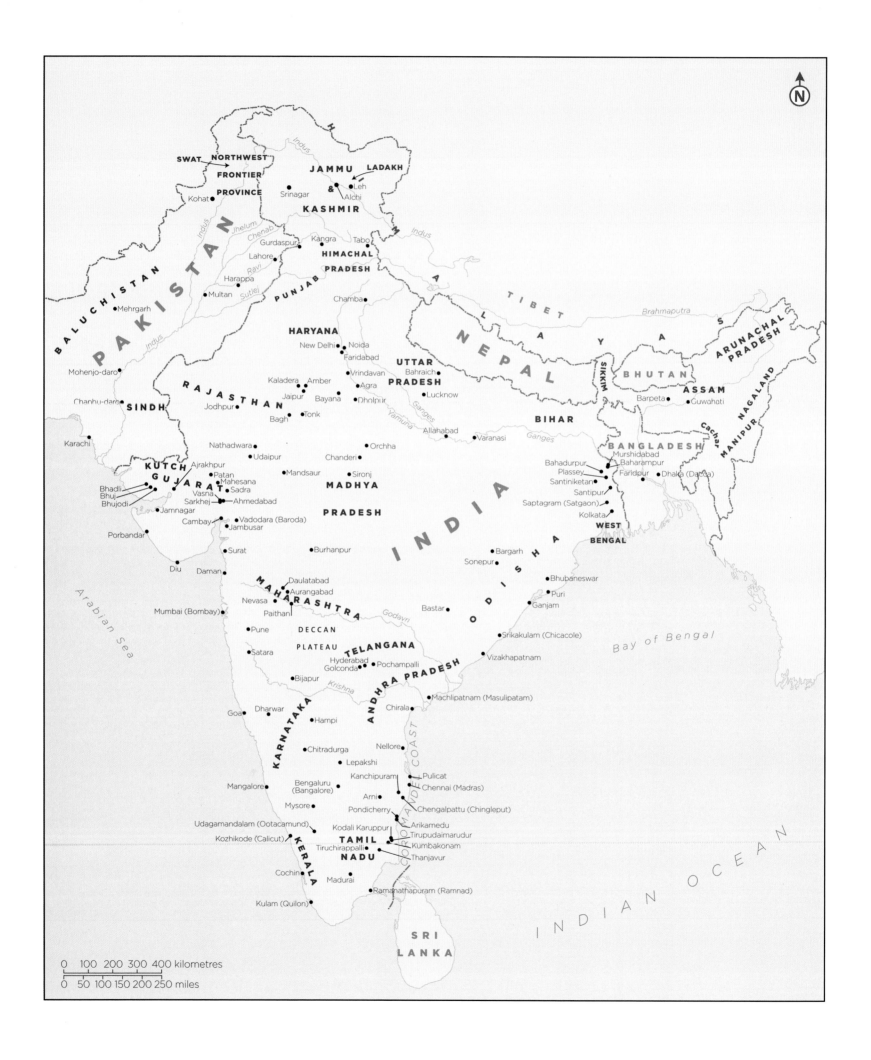

DIRECTOR'S FOREWORD

ndia's glorious textiles have been prized across the globe for centuries. The V&A is proud to hold the greatest collection of them in the world. Surprisingly, however, no major exhibition has ever been held at the V&A or elsewhere that focuses solely on the textiles themselves, nor has any book sought to provide an overview of this huge subject. This is what *The Fabric of India* exhibition and this accompanying book have set out to do.

Many of the pieces seen in both the exhibition and the book have been brought out of storage for the first time since they were acquired in the nineteenth century. These unseen treasures shed a new light on the way we perceive Indian textiles. They not only include the well-known examples of mirror-work embroidery or export chintz but encompass a huge range of beautiful and often utilitarian fabrics that demonstrate fully the artistry of India's craftspeople.

Much of the work shown here was collected from international exhibitions of the nineteenth century, starting with the original Great Exhibition held in London in 1851, in which the V&A has its origins. These nineteenth-century textiles underpin the exhibition and book, yet the historic scope of both is far greater. Pieces of over 1,000 years old or those reflecting the opulence of the seventeenth-century Mughal court can be freshly appreciated alongside contemporary works. Others show the huge impact of Indian textiles on cultures outside India's boundaries, whether in the villages of Indonesia or the drawing rooms of Europe. The political force of cloth is also made clear, especially in its key role as a focal point for India's movement towards independence, a goal achieved under Mahatma Gandhi in 1947.

Today, India's designers and makers are creating waves in international settings with exciting new ways of using traditional skills and materials. They are contributing to India's growing profile as a leading hub of contemporary design, as well as to its economy and its very identity as a nation. *The Fabric of India* shows how India's great tradition of textile-making has shaped the nation and the wider world, in the present as much as the historic past.

Martin Roth

INTRODUCTION

A Mughal painting of about 1590 (pl.1) shows the prophet Idris introducing mankind to the concept of wearing tailored garments in place of animal skins. The court artist who painted this imaginary scene shows Idris in the centre of the upper part of the page presenting bales of cloth to men dressed in furs. The lower half of the painting shows several stages in the production of cotton cloth. These vignettes of washing cotton, cleaning it with a bow, preparing the warp, and weaving the cloth on a pit loom are clearly not taken from ancient mythological sources but instead are accurate depictions of activities the artist had seen going on around him.

All of these processes are still carried out in India today, where, in spite of industrialization and the opening up of global markets, millions of people are still involved in making cloth by hand.[1] While the number of people involved in hand-weaving decreases from year to year, India's Ministry of Textiles' Annual Report for 2013–14 states that 'Handloom weaving is one of the largest economic activity [sic] after agriculture providing direct and indirect employment to more than 43 lakh [4.3 million] weavers and allied workers. This sector contributes nearly 11% of the cloth production in the country.'[2] The modern world of cheap mass-produced goods inevitably demands fewer handmade products than the pre-industrialized world did, and the position of the handmade in India has changed radically even over the past hundred years. But historically the richness of India's textile tradition is unparalleled, with a value that transcends mere economics. The cultural historian Stella Kramrisch has written:

> Textile symbolism in India is hallowed by tradition. In the Rig Veda and the Upanishads the universe is envisioned as a fabric woven by the gods. The cosmos, the ordered universe, is one continuous fabric with its warp and woof making a grid pattern. Hence the importance of wholeness, not only of the uncut garment, like the sari or the dhoti, but also of the cloth woven all in one piece, on which a sacred picture is to be painted. Whether as a cover for the body or as ground for a painting, the uncut fabric is a symbol of totality and integrity. It symbolizes the whole of manifestation.[3]

This kind of assimilation of cloth into myth could only take place in a culture in which weaving had occupied a central role for many centuries. The subcontinent's unique natural resources of textile fibres and dyestuffs have combined with millennia of ingenuity and innovation to create an astonishing array of fabrics. Almost every region developed its own textile specialities, whether in weave, dye, print or embroidery – and sometimes a combination of several of these. Many of these specializations were based on the availability of local materials, such as the dye root *chay*, which grows in coastal southeast India and helped to assure the supremacy of the dyers of that region, or the wild silks of the northeast or the pashmina goat-hair of the far north, both of which are used for highly distinctive local textiles. In addition to these natural resources, other factors such as the proximity of running water for dyeing, an appropriately damp climate for weaving fine muslin, a relatively stable political situation to provide patronage and a readily available market for the finished products all contributed to the evolution of a huge range of regionally specific manufactures. Some of these specialisms retained their unique local characteristics over time – ikat-dyeing in Odisha, shawl-weaving in Kashmir or block-printing in Rajasthan, for example – while others developed under the influence of textile makers from outside their region. Tie-dyed saris from Madurai in Tamil Nadu reflect the Saurashtran incomers to that area, and some Bengali woven silks may often be confused with those of the urban centres of Gujarat, whose weavers contributed to their development in Bengal.

Cloth has always been present at all the major life-cycle rituals in India, and is still visible in much of everyday religious observance and everyday custom. From a simple thread tied

1 (opposite)
Idris giving instruction to mankind in the art of weaving
Mughal, *c.*1590
31 x 18.3 cm
(page 41.5 x 28.5 cm)
British Library, London,
Johnson Album 8, no.5

around the wrist after *puja* (worship) to the gifts of elaborate saris at weddings, yarn and cloth are inextricably linked to religion and spirituality, especially in a Hindu context.[4] Cloth itself is imbued with significance, with silk the prime example of a fabric that is considered by many Hindus to be intrinsically pure and appropriate for all auspicious occasions. Pious Muslim men, on the other hand, are discouraged from wearing pure silk as it is considered excessively luxurious, and most vegetarians, whether Hindu or Jain, only wear silk made from cocoons from which the caterpillar has emerged naturally, rather than being killed by boiling or steaming in the degumming process. Loosely woven fabrics of any fibre were traditionally thought to be particularly vulnerable to potential pollutants, whereas tightly woven textiles with smooth surfaces were most effective at deflecting ritual pollution.[5] Certain colours too have traditionally been seen as particularly auspicious: red often signifies fertility and is associated with Hindu weddings, and also with the power of female deities, who are often dressed in red cloth; yellow is particularly associated with the god Vishnu, and yellow *pitambar* (from Sanskrit *pita*, meaning 'yellow') saris and dhotis are considered suitable garments in which to perform *puja*. A yellow-ground Varanasi silk dhoti in the V&A's collection, acquired from the Great Exhibition of 1851, is labelled in Roman script as '*Pethamba Zhurd beyldar*' (yellow *pitambar* with creeper pattern) and described in its original documentation as 'worn by men in mourning or at meals' – that is, on occasions requiring ritual purity (see pl.31). In Islam, green is associated with the prophet Muhammad and with the hajj (pilgrimage to Mecca), a green turban signifying that its wearer has completed this important ritual journey.

Textiles have always been a dominant part of gift-giving, whether religious or secular. A mid-nineteenth-century study estimated that as much as 80 per cent of India's cotton production was used as gifts, and of this a large percentage would have been donated to temples.[6] Secular tributes to ruling powers were often at least partially paid in cloth, such as the fine muslins of Bengal or the pashmina shawls of Kashmir. Rolls of cloth were among the tributes offered to the Emperor Akbar (r.1556–1605) – for example, by his former ally Asaf Khan, who wished to reingratiate himself with the emperor (pl.2) – and were among the precious birthday gifts offered to the young Prince Khurram in 1607.[7] Robes of honour (*khilat*)

were the favoured form of ceremonial gift from a Muslim ruler to an individual, although they were occasionally given out in great numbers, without the personal interaction that was customary between donor and recipient. In 1576, for example, Akbar gave the noble in charge of arrangements for the hajj an astonishing 12,000 robes to distribute among the pilgrims.[8] The practice of bestowing *khilat* was an ancient one that was current throughout the early Islamic world, and the Mughals immediately incorporated it into their protocol after Babur's defeat of the Lodhi sultan at the First Battle of Panipat in

2

***Akbar receiving trophies
of war from Asaf Khan***
(detail)
Mughal, by Miskina and
Bhagwan, *c*.1586–9
Page from an *Akbarnama*
manuscript
33.6 x 19.9 cm
V&A: IS.2:52–1896

1526. Two years later Babur was distributing fine robes to distinguished visitors to his court, robes that are likely to have come from the looted Lodhi storerooms at Agra.[9] While the *khilat* was essentially a symbolic gift, there is at least one Mughal painting in which the recipient, Da'ud Khan, the Afghan ruler of Bihar and Bengal, is seen not only accepting but energetically putting on the robe given by Akbar's commander as a token of his new allegiance (pl.3).

The tradition of giving *khilat* (or *sar o pa*, 'head and foot', as it is often known in India) continued well into the eighteenth century: the Mughal outfit of turban, robe and waist-sash owned by Captain John Foote and shown in a portrait of him by Sir Joshua Reynolds in 1761[10] is very likely an example of the basic set of clothes most often given as *khilat* (see pl.108). The highest grade consisted of garments that had been worn (or, more realistically, touched) by the emperor himself, called '*malbus-i khas*' (special or personal clothing). Rulers might on occasion remove the turban from their own heads and place it on the head of a favoured courtier as a special gesture of approval.

Today, textile hand-skills are gradually being lost and in many cases have completely disappeared from their traditional places of manufacture, a trend that has been evident since the middle of the nineteenth century, when British-made textiles started to replace local ones in the Indian domestic market (see pp.185–9). In spite of this, the importance of textiles as gifts has not disappeared: although today's gift to a temple, relative or employee might be a printed polyester sari rather than a hand-woven cotton or silk one, cloth is as vital an element of gift-giving as it has been for centuries.

Textiles have been used as markers of high status in India since the earliest times. Their use as prestigious gifts or as lavish furnishings to display wealth and impress visitors is clear both through surviving examples and written accounts. In a culture traditionally without solid furniture, fabrics can be suspended from the ceiling, spread on the floor and hung on walls to decorate rooms and can also serve as seats and tables as well as all-enveloping covers for piles of bedding that in other cultures might be stored in cupboards. This textural and multicoloured immersion in cloth has always impressed visitors to India, especially those from the West, and has helped to form an impression of the subcontinent as a uniquely colourful place.

3
Da'ud receives a robe of honour from Mun'im Khan
(detail)
Mughal, by Hiranand, *c.*1604
Page from an *Akbarnama* manuscript
23.8 x 12.3 cm
Freer Sackler Galleries, Smithsonian Institution, Washington, DC, F1952.31

Traditionally, one of the obligations of a ruler was to provide patronage for local artisans. This has ensured that regional textile types of the highest quality were used at local courts, and these have in some cases survived in museum and royal collections. The Mehrangarh Fort Museum in Jodhpur, the Maharaja Sawai Man Singh II Museum in Jaipur and the Chowmahalla Palace Museum in Hyderabad, for instance, have preserved remarkable examples of textile manufactures made for their local courts, both as dress and furnishing. While many textiles of the nineteenth and twentieth centuries are notable for their lavish materials and rich embellishments, rulers in earlier centuries, including the Mughal emperors, often prized fineness of cloth over ostentation. The love of diaphanous muslins and feather-light pashmina shawls is an example: worn by the emperors Akbar and Jahangir and their courtiers, these were minimally decorated but worn to show the discernment and connoisseurship implicit in an appreciation of such finely spun and woven fabrics. The same dedication to high-quality materials is found in some quarters today, with some discerning buyers – both male and female – prizing plain muslin and pashmina (or the even finer and softer antelope-hair fabric called *shahtoosh*) over lavish embroidery or gold-embellished velvet or silk.

The international exhibitions that followed on from the Great Exhibition of 1851 in London provided an opportunity for Indian manufactures of all kinds to be displayed in London and other European cities. Much of the V&A's present holdings of Indian textiles was acquired from these exhibitions, which at that time entered the collection of the India Museum, founded by the East India Company in the closing years of the eighteenth century.[11] While today we usually expect an exhibition, whatever the subject, to display carefully selected items, each telling a specific story, those of the nineteenth century were intended to show the complete range of manufactures of each country, represented in quantities clearly designed to astonish visitors. Exhibits sent from Madras to the Paris International Exhibition in 1855, for example, ranged from the lowliest 'iron bars made use of by burglars for making holes in the Walls of Houses'[12] to exceptional pieces like 'a gorgeous canopy or carpet of velvet, embroidered with gold by the Mahomedans of Triplicane, [which] will give the people of Europe some idea of the splendour with which the ceremonials of the people of this country are conducted'.[13] An embroidered panel (see pl.13) is an example of embroidery from Triplicane that was displayed in the same exhibition.

The objects displayed in these exhibitions varied immensely in both quality and rarity, and this breadth was carried over to the holdings of the India Museum and subsequently gave the V&A's Indian collection its distinctive character. While other museums throughout the world have

acquired objects – whether made for India's courts or for export – that may be as splendid as some in the V&A, it is the combination of such treasures with thousands of everyday pieces that makes the V&A's collection the greatest body of Indian textiles in the world. For the acquisition of the Museum's rarest historic pieces we have to thank perceptive scholar-curators such as K. de B. Codrington, who recognized an embroidered coat (see pl.111) as being 'of Jahangir's reign and ... among the few surviving early Mughal textiles'[14] after it had been rejected for purchase when first offered to the Museum in 1929, and C. Stanley Clarke, who purchased many world-class Mughal, Deccani and Rajput pieces, including the 'duck-shoot' floor-spread (see pl.132), from the dealer Imre Schwaiger in the 1920s.[15] But for the preservation of much that is particularly special about the collection – the thousands of everyday textiles that illustrate vanished skills – we are indebted especially to pioneers such as John Forbes Royle, who fought tooth and nail in the 1850s for space in which to house and display textiles and other manufactures from the exhibitions. It is mainly to unsung heroes like Royle that we owe the existence of these unique objects in the V&A today.

This book tells some of the story of these everyday textiles as well as the great masterpieces made for the Mughal court, for export markets and for religious use. It focuses on aspects of India's textile-making and history that have perhaps been less frequently told, together with the key milestones in this complex story. India's textile tradition stretches back to the Indus Valley civilization and its antecedents in around 6,000 BC and continues to the present day. Some aspects of this long tradition – for example, the continuous use of cotton in India and the wider world – form an unbroken thread, while others, such as the complex weaves of the Mughal court, appear and disappear at specific periods and places. Some regional specialities have remained localized, while others spread out to influence practice in other areas. Handmade textiles have been key to the development of modern India, and today are gaining a high profile in internationally acclaimed design studios. This is the story of the diversity of India's textiles and the astonishing technical mastery that made them.

1

MATERIALS AND MAKING

The unparalleled range of India's woven, dyed and decorated textiles would require several volumes of description and analysis to do it justice. Even a full summary of each topic remains difficult if not impossible to compile, for even if one possessed an encyclopedic understanding of all the literature in addition to a comprehensive knowledge of historic collections, lost aspects of India's textile history continue to be rediscovered through dye and fibre analysis, archaeology and the reinterpretation of early texts.

FIBRES

The range of raw materials from which Indian textiles are or have historically been made is itself immense. As well as a huge variety of plant and animal fibres, secondary materials such as metal-wrapped thread must also be considered. What follows is a brief historical overview of the main elements of this ancient tradition.

COTTON

One must begin with cotton (pl.4). Cotton (Sanskrit: *karpasa*) is the fibre most closely associated with the Indian subcontinent and it is not an overstatement to suggest that without its presence the entire history of India, and thus the world, would have evolved dramatically differently. One species, *Gossypium arboreum* ('tree cotton'), grew wild in the damp sandy tropical areas bordering the shores of southwestern India and further west along the coasts of the Red Sea, Egypt and the Horn of Africa. It was most likely first harvested by man in the Neolithic period for its seeds, as both a food and oil crop, but it was probably in India that its short hairy fibres were first collected, deseeded, spun into thread and woven into cloth.[1] Seeds and fibres of cotton from around 6000 BC have been excavated at the pre-Harappan site of Mehrgarh in Baluchistan and although no thread or cloth has survived, the presence of spindle whorls

4
Group of cotton textiles
(left to right)
Chanderi, Madhya Pradesh,
*c.*1867
377 x 151 cm
V&A: 5183 (IS)

Dhaka, Bangladesh, *c.*1872
94.6 x 95 cm
V&A: 8361 (IS)

Arni, Tamil Nadu, *c.*1855
619 x 91.7 cm
V&A: 8794 (IS)

at sites throughout the Indus Valley in the same period also implies that weaving took place.[2] The first actual traces of woven cotton on the Indian subcontinent were discovered at Mohenjo-daro, another Indus Valley site, and can be dated between the mid-third and the early second millennium BC.[3] That tiny sample was dyed red, an additional technical innovation requiring knowledge of the use of mordants (fixing agents).

The world's earliest surviving woven cotton fragment has been found not in India itself but at Dhuweila in Jordan, dating from around 4450–3000 BC.[4] This cotton cloth was almost certainly imported from Indus Valley settlements.[5] The wealth generated by such trade, combined with self-sufficiency in food crops, was the basis of the economy of northwestern India.[6] That wealth allowed the expansion of further settlements, which encouraged the development of local cultures. Without cotton domestication, cultivation and export, the art, culture

and history of India would necessarily have developed quite differently.

This early mastery of cotton cultivation and processing led to experimentation and cross-breeding with other varieties of cotton. *Gossypium herbaceum*, a shrubby type native to Arabia but probably first cultivated in Gujarat, was able to survive in more arid regions, eventually becoming the next dominant species grown throughout the subcontinent before being supplanted by *Gossypium hirsutum* in more modern times.[7] By the Roman period, many regions of India had already become famous for their types of cotton. Cotton from the Gangetic plain, especially eastern Bengal, could be spun into the thinnest threads, the Dhaka muslins and *jamdani* weaves of later times being their most famous products (pls 4, 52). The Deccan plateau, with its deep 'black cotton' volcanic soil (called *regur*), was another area long famed for exceptionally

high-quality cotton. Deogiri, modern Daulatabad, was a great centre for the weaving of fine muslin,[8] but hundreds of towns and villages across the subcontinent gained local reputations for their individual varieties of cotton, each possessing special characteristics. In addition, cotton subspecies, each of which thrives in different environments, display a wide range of colours – not just white, but off-white, yellow, pink and brown. Historically, all Indian cotton was hand-spun using a drop-spindle. The spinning wheel (*charkha*) was probably introduced

from Iran by the thirteenth century, allowing greatly increased production. Curiously, no matter where on the subcontinent or when during its long history, almost everyone hand-spinning cotton into thread tended to twist it in the same direction: anticlockwise, in the so-called 'Z' direction. Thus, confirming a 'Z' twist has always been the first step in establishing the provenance of historic Indian cotton textiles.[9] Other cotton-producing areas of the world may spin the yarn in either a 'Z' or 'S' direction, but in India the 'Z'-twist is always used.

5

Group of cotton towels
(left to right)
Extended plain weave
Chennai or Tamil Nadu,
*c*1862
380 x 88 cm (three towels)
V&A: 5587 (IS)

Extended plain weave
Nellore, Andhra Pradesh,
*c*1855–79
487 x 70 cm (six towels)
V&A: 5585 (IS)

Diamond twill weave
(*cheshm-i bulbul*)
Hyderabad, *c*1867
52 x 46 cm
V&A: 5594 (IS)

Extended plain weave
Agra Central Jail, Uttar
Pradesh, *c*1867
267 x 92 cm (three towels)
V&A: 5568 (IS)

On the textile label:

CLASS IV.
C. IV. FIBRES.
*Coloured Scarfs of
Mudar floss.*
No. 6699 *Shahpore*

BAST AND OTHER FIBRES

While cotton has dominated Indian textile history in terms of volume of cloth woven and exported, other more humble fibre-producing plants have also been woven into cloth for millennia and they, too, became important commercially. An extensive group of plants including hemp (*Cannabis sativa*), mallow (*Abutilon theophrasti*),[10] jute (*Corchorus olitorius*), flax (*Linum usitatissimum*), nettle (*Urtica dioica*), Nilgiri nettle (*Girardinia diversifolia*) and ramie (*Boehmeria nivea*) all contain bast fibres. These strong, hollow fibres can only be extracted after a lengthy, complicated process known as retting, which involves breaking down the outer stems and removing everything but the useful inner fibres. Like cotton, both hemp and linen were probably first cultivated in the ancient world for their oily seeds: such seeds dating from the time of the Harappan civilization were recovered from early archaeological sites in the Indus Valley and Gujarat. Within an Indian context, linen cloth woven from flax (Sanskrit: *kshauma* and *dukula*) never gained the dominance it achieved in the economies of Egypt, Mesopotamia or Eastern Europe, probably because of competition from the more widely available cotton. There is some evidence for linen-weaving in eastern India up to the eighteenth century but it seems to have died out after that.[11] However, linen has recently started to be reintroduced in small quantities in some areas, specifically for use in the production of fashion garments, although the fashion industry also uses imported linen.

Even though jute and hemp produce coarser thread than cotton, both resist rotting well and retain their strength much better when wet, making them excellent for rigging or any other rope or cloth used on ships. Cloth woven from jute became crucial to the economy of Bengal and has traditionally been used for inexpensive gunny sacks as well as matting. Although the materials discussed so far are the most economically important plant fibres used in India, others are known: for example, mudar floss (*Calotropis gigantea* – pl.6), which has been woven into cloth and even used as the pile in knotted carpets.[12]

6
**Length of mudar floss
fabric** (detail)
Shahpur Jail, Uttar Pradesh,
*c.*1862
56 x 50 cm
V&A: 6699 (IS)

SILK

The use of silk in India goes back to at least the third
millennium BC. This is not the fine, white mulberry silk
domesticated in China at approximately the same time, but
the yellow, golden or brown silks that derive from the native
moths of eastern India. The range of silk used in India is large
and its categorizations often confusing. Most modern accounts
of the Indian silk industry mention 'wild' silks, as opposed
to the 'domesticated' mulberry silk, but these terms require
clarification. 'Domesticated' silk is the product of the *Bombyx
mori* silk moth, which was subject to very early domestication
in around 3000 BC, as Chinese records confirm. This process
has resulted in a flightless insect that feeds exclusively on
mulberry leaves and that is able to produce lustrous, white,
uniform, round filaments. Though deriving from wild insects,
the *Bombyx mori* moth has been so selectively bred that it can
no longer survive in the wild and throughout its entire life cycle
must be carefully tended by humans.

Within India, several types of large Saturniid moths –
tasar/tussar (*Antheraea mylitta*), muga (*Antheraea assamensis*)
and eri/endi (*Philosamia cynthia ricini*), all native to India's
northeast – have long been extensively reared in what are now
Assam, Bengal, Bihar, Odisha and Andhra Pradesh in order to
produce economically important silk crops (pl.7).[13] Silk thread
from both muga and eri moths has recently been identified at
the very early Indus Valley sites of Harappa and Chanhu-daro,
dated 2450–2000 BC.[14] These discoveries dramatically push
back the date of what had previously been the earliest silk thread
discovered in India: filaments found inside a copper bead at
Nevasa in Maharashtra from around 1500 BC.[15]

Though 'wild' when compared to the rearing of Chinese
Bombyx mori moths, whose entire life cycle takes place within
sterile sheds, India's tasar, eri and muga moths have not been
completely wild or entirely domesticated for millennia either.
For example, as the muga's captive stock degenerates within a
relatively short time, wild seed cocoons must be collected from
the jungle every few generations.[16] Collecting the cocoons and
rearing new silkworms is still usually performed by tribal groups
in the jungles of eastern India. While stocks of muga and tasar

7 (opposite)
Group of woven silks
(clockwise from top left)   Tasar, with weft-ikat
Tasar   decoration
Odisha, *c.*1995   Nuapatna, Odisha, *c.*1988
128 x 271 cm   197 x 98 cm
Private collection   V&A: IS.4-1988
Eri   Muga
Cachar, Assam, *c.*1855–79   Guwahati, Assam, *c.*1855
170 x 92 cm   325 x 92 cm
V&A: 5513 (IS)   V&A: 5520 (IS)

silkworms are traditionally left *in situ*, eri worms are now raised entirely in special sheds in the villages, and dedicated farms for tasar and muga cultivation have also been developed. Female tasar and muga moths are individually tied to tree branches or trays of leaves to prevent their escape during mating and egg laying, and they are carefully guarded from natural predators. Of the three main Indian Saturniid moths, eri moth sericulture is closest to the Chinese model, as eri moths never leave their enclosures, but none of these moths is either entirely 'wild' or entirely domesticated.

When compared to the even and lustrous filaments of Chinese mulberry silk, tasar silk threads are much thicker (pl.8), flatter and more irregular in diameter and come in shades of brown. Muga has a natural golden colour, while eri tends to be white or brown. Another crucial feature of traditional eri silk production, which differentiates it from the others, is that only the eri moth is allowed to emerge from its cocoon alive. This makes its silk suitable for use by those Hindus, Jains and Buddhists who avoid other silks on religious grounds, knowing that the insects have been killed in their making. Unlike the cocoons of the caterpillars producing tasar, muga and mulberry silk, the eri cocoon is not one long continuous filament; it is irregular, made up of shorter segments and open at one end, so eri fibres can never be continuously reeled but always have to be treated as

short fibres and spun into thread. When those spun threads are woven into cloth, the fabric is correspondingly less glossy and smooth than if it had been woven from continuous reeled silk.

We do not know when mulberry silk moths (as opposed to 'wild' types) were first commercially raised in India, but it is not impossible for it to have occurred as early as the third century BC. Chinese *Bombyx mori* eggs could easily have reached India via Iran or Central Asia along the famous Silk Road, which stretched from northern China to the Mediterranean. There were also earlier land and sea routes passing south through Yunnan in western China and on to Burma, with one branch crossing by sea to the ports of eastern India and the other continuing over the mountains into Assam's Brahmaputra Valley and from there into Bengal. This southeastern 'silk road' is a strong contender for the most probable route for the transmission of *Bombyx mori* sericulture from China to India during the early centuries AD (pl.9).[17]

The ancient oral traditions of India, some composed early in the first millennium BC (though not written down until centuries later), contain many Sanskrit words for fibres, filaments and cloth. Panini's famous grammar of around the fourth century BC uses *kauseya* for silk, as do other primary texts dating from the late centuries BC to the early centuries AD.[18] Even in these very early documents, a distinction is already made between indigenous silk and imported Chinese silk. In the period from the third century BC to the third century AD both the *Arthashastra* and the playwright Kalidasa refer to *chinapatta* and *chinamsuka*, which have both been translated as 'Chinese silk', while the *Mahabharata* just uses the term *pattaja*. *Paat* and its regional variants are still the most common modern terms in India for local mulberry silk.[19]

There are so many thousands of references from the first millennium and following half millennium AD describing local silk production in different parts of India that it must have been a relatively common activity at the time.[20] Whether woven from local or imported silk – and, if local, whether mulberry silk, eri, muga or tasar – remains unknown. However, by the time Abu'l-Fazl compiled *A'in* 32 of his *A'in-i-Akbari* in the mid-1590s, his list of the types of silk available to the Mughal court included examples imported from Europe, Egypt and Iran as well as local productions from Gujarat and Lahore.[21] With very few exceptions, all of the earliest surviving silks of the Mughal

8 (top)
Group of silk skeins
(left to right)
Mulberry silk waste (*fesua*);
eri; muga; muga *ghicha*;
tasar *ghicha*; tasar *jhurri*;
tasar *nassi*; tasar *katia*

Madhya Pradesh and
Assam, 2015
58 × 15 cm (max.)
V&A: IS.16-23-2015

9 (bottom)
**Group of
mulberry-silk skeins**
Bengal, *c.*1817
23 × 6.5 cm (max.)
V&A: IS.57-1990

10
Part of a shawl (detail)
Varanasi, Uttar Pradesh
(acquired from Burhanpur,
Madhya Pradesh), c.1855
Silk and metal-wrapped
silk thread
340 x 68 cm
V&A: 0675:2 (IS)

period are woven entirely of mulberry silk.[22] Earlier records
note that Indian weavers imported mulberry silk from Iran, the
Ottoman Empire, Central Asia and China, when available and
affordable, but one can deduce that they mostly worked with
Indian silk: an examination of the earliest surviving Indian silk
textiles confirms this suspicion as the threads show slightly
less processing and more irregularities of diameter and twist
than silk thread from contemporary Safavid silk cloth.[23] By
the seventeenth century, Bengal had become the major source
of Indian mulberry silk exported to Europe through the East
India Company, while the nineteenth century saw the rise
of Karnataka as an entirely new centre of Indian mulberry
silk production.[24] Today, although muga, eri and tasar silk
continue to be produced in relatively small quantities, India is
second only to China as the world's largest source of mulberry
silk, centred in the present-day states of Karnataka, Andhra
Pradesh, West Bengal, Tamil Nadu, and Jammu and Kashmir.

METAL-WRAPPED SILK THREAD

The vast majority of Indian silk has always been woven without
woven metal-thread enhancement, a feature usually generically
referred to as *zari* (from Farsi and Urdu *zar*, meaning 'gold').
The official Mughal workshop (*karkhana*) at Ahmedabad is
known to have produced metal-enhanced silk velvets and waist
sashes (*patka*) in the seventeenth century. However, it was
really only after the rise of Varanasi as a weaving centre in the
late eighteenth century and especially during the nineteenth
that Indian silks woven in complicated weave structures
using metal-wrapped silk thread (the yarn specifically termed
kalabattun) became widely available (pl.10).[25] The gold-plated
and silver-plated metal that is loom-woven in India is rarely a
pure metal thread. Such a material would be almost impossible
to weave because it lacks the necessary strength and flexibility
for use as warps or wefts on most types of loom (pl.11). In China
the tradition was to gild sheets of paper, which were cut into
narrow strips that could then be used as wefts. In medieval
Spain, and in Central Asia after the Mongol conquest, animal
membrane was gilded and cut into thin strips for weaving
(sometimes wrapped around a cotton rather than a silk core),
but in India, Iran, the Middle East and in much of Europe the
tradition was to draw metal into extremely long, fine wires
by heating and successively pulling it through a series of ever

smaller holes in an iron plate. When sufficiently thin, the wire was flattened while simultaneously wrapped around a silk core, usually a yellow or orange thread if the wire was gold and a white silk thread if silver.[26] Such metal-wrapped thread was strong and supple enough to be woven on a loom to make sumptuous cloth (pl.10) or decorative motifs in a plain silk ground fabric (see pl.140), and also to make woven ribbon (*gota*) which was stitched onto cloth. It could also be used as an embroidery thread (pl.13). Metal-wrapped thread and metal strips are also often seen laid on the surface of a textile with couching stitches (pl.15) rather than piercing the fabric as embroidery thread.

It is believed, though supported by very little evidence, that such metal-wrapped thread was not used in India extensively, if at all, before contact with the Islamic world.[27] Through Arab merchants carrying exotic goods eastwards, seeking direct sea

trade with China, the practice might have spread from Iran and the Middle East to the ports of the Persian Gulf, across the Indian Ocean to western India and onwards across the Bay of Bengal to Southeast Asia and Japan. The production in India of loom-woven silks enhanced with metal-wrapped thread was fairly widespread, but as no example from earlier than the seventeenth century has survived, one must rely entirely on contemporary accounts for any understanding of its extent or variety. Even if the use of metal-wrapped thread was not South Asian in origin, it eventually became so widely used that minor differences between the craft practices of India and Iran developed. North Indian examples tend to have the metal thread wrapped around the silk core in a 'Z' (anticlockwise) direction, while almost all Iranian examples are wrapped in the 'S' (clockwise) direction.[28] There are exceptions, however: some Deccani and south Indian metal-wrapped threads contradict that general rule and may instead

11
Group of metallic embellishments
Left-hand group: silver-gilt
Left top:
Flattened and crimped strip, Hyderabad, Andhra Pradesh/Telangana, c.1855
Presented by the Nizam of Hyderabad
V&A: 05954:2 (IS)

Left bottom:
Fine flattened wire, Ahmedabad, Gujarat, c.1855
V&A: 6293 (IS)

Centre top:
Flattened strip, probably Gujarat, c.1855–79
V&A: 6346 (IS)

Centre bottom:
Flattened and crimped strip on spool, Hyderabad, c.1855
Presented by the Nizam of Hyderabad
V&A: 05954:3 (IS)

Right:
Skein of metal-wrapped silk thread, probably

Ahmedabad or Hyderabad, c.1855–79
V&A: 6354 (IS)

Right-hand group: silver
Left top:
Flattened strip, Hyderabad, c.1855
V&A: 05939:1 (IS)

Left bottom:
Skein of silver-wrapped silk thread, probably Hyderabad, c.1855
V&A: 6345 (IS)

Right top:
Fine flattened wire, Hyderabad, c.1855
V&A: 05939:2 (IS)

Right bottom:
Flattened and crimped strip, Hyderabad, c.1855
Presented by the Nizam of Hyderabad
V&A: 05959:1 (IS)

Clockwise from top left:

13
Panel (detail)
Triplicane, Chennai, c.1855.
Woven silk ground with
couched silver-gilt wire,
silver-gilt-wrapped thread,
seed pearls, coloured metal
foil and sequins
69 x 48 cm
V&A: 6502 (IS)

15
Head-cover (detail)
Hyderabad, Andhra
Pradesh, c.1880
Woven silver-gilt strip
and silk thread with tinsel
and coloured metal foil
217 x 82.5 cm
V&A: IS.2125–1883

14
**Length of woven silk and
silver-wrapped silk thread**
(detail)
Murshidabad, West Bengal,
c.1855–79
258 x 85 cm
V&A: 0708 (IS)

12
**Length of woven silver-
gilt strips and silk thread**
(detail)
Hyderabad, Andhra
Pradesh, c.1855
61.7 x 66 cm
V&A: 0695 (IS)

be 'S'-wrapped.[29] In centres such as Surat in Gujarat in the seventeenth century, and much later in Hyderabad and Varanasi, the production of metal-wrapped thread reached an extremely high level of technical perfection. Even today, when almost no pure gilt-silver wrapped silk thread is produced in India, Surat continues to manufacture a modern thread made of imitation gold wrapped around a synthetic core.

WOOL, PASHMINA AND TUS

Sheep's wool has always played an important role in the clothing of north Indians, for use as winter shawls and blankets (*kambals*) and for the manufacture of knotted-pile carpets, as well as felt in parts of Pakistan and in Rajasthan, especially in Tonk. Though the quality of local sheep's wool has, historically, been relatively poor when compared with that produced by selectively bred sheep from neighbouring Afghanistan, Iran, Nepal and Tibet, one breed from Rajasthan, the Chokla, was probably the source for the best-quality wool-pile carpets during the Mughal period, as well as for local weavings. Local sheep and yak hair was used in Ladakh to make sturdy shawls and the traditional coats and tie-dyed dresses worn by women (pl.16).

Known in Kashmir as 'pashmina', the lightweight fibre spun from the fine under-hair of a domesticated goat (*Capra aegagrus hircus*) originates neither in Kashmir nor anywhere within India's historic boundaries. And yet, from at least the early first millennium AD until the mid-nineteenth century, the weaving of pashmina into one of the world's lightest, softest and warmest cloths remained an almost exclusively Kashmiri monopoly (pl.18, and see pls 114–16, 183, 208–9).[30] The animals providing the pashmina only survive at very high altitudes on the dry Tibetan plain, the Changthang plateau adjacent to Ladakh and high desert regions of Central Asia, western China and Mongolia. But strangely neither the Tibetans nor the Ladakhis wove their local pashmina into fine textiles; this transformation required the unequalled skill of the Kashmiris

to take full advantage of the raw material. They painstakingly separated by hand the fine under-hair from the thicker hairs of the outer coat, sorting it into its different natural colours and then spinning the pashmina into incredibly fine, even threads, ready to be placed on the loom as warps or dyed the various weft colours if and when required. The level of skill achieved by the Kashmiris necessary to process raw pashmina into fine thread remained unmatched anywhere else in the world. While mostly used for weaving shawls, pashmina yarn was also used to produce high-quality gloves and socks, which were made using a form of the 'Afghan' or 'Tunisian' crochet technique rather than knitting.[31] The use of this crochet stitch belongs to a Middle Eastern and Central Asian tradition, in contrast to knitting, which was probably indigenous in some northern areas (using sheep's wool) but introduced by the British and Dutch into other regions such as Pulicat in south India.

The trade in pashmina beyond Tibet, Ladakh and the Kashmir Valley must have been an early development if the textile fibres discovered at Antinoë in Egypt and Palmyra in Syria – dated to around the third to sixth centuries AD and identified as 'cashmere' – originated in Kashmir.[32] Pashmina

16 (left)
Woman's dress
Ladakh, early 20th century
Wool, tie-dyed
Length: 145 cm
Karun Thakar Collection,
London

17 (above)
***Muhammad Riza Kashmiri
wearing a plain Kashmir
shawl***
Mughal, by Bichitr, *c.*1615–20
Page from the Minto Album
16.3 x 9.25 cm
Chester Beatty Library,
Dublin, In 07A.9

was significant enough to the local economy to have been commented on by both Xuanzang (Hsuan-tsang) and Yijing (I-tsing), two Chinese Buddhist monks who separately visited Kashmir in the seventh century.[33] It also seems probable that the reported gifts of *suf* (fine woollen cloth) dispatched in the fifteenth century by the Kashmiri Sultan Zain-ul-Abidin to the last Timurid ruler of Herat were pashmina, as the region had long been famous for its goat-hair textiles, having first been mentioned under the name *ranku* in early texts such as the Sanskrit thesaurus *Amarakosha* in around the fifth to seventh centuries.[34] However, such reports should be treated with some scepticism. It is also frequently reported that the Delhi Sultan Muhammad bin Tughluq (r.1324–51) sent his envoy, Ibn Battuta, with gifts of Kashmir shawls intended for the emperor of China. But in fact the original Arabic text does not mention Kashmir or even any word for 'shawl'; it simply uses *mar'iz,* a loanword of unidentified origin apparently meaning

some sort of goat hair.[35] Indian textile historiography is riddled with similar errors and ambiguities. However, as for so many other Indian textiles, Abu'l-Fazl's *A'in-i-Akbari* (completed around 1596) provides the first incontrovertible facts regarding pashmina shawl production in Srinagar. Shawls were evidently a favourite garment of the Emperor Akbar: Abu'l-Fazl claims that Akbar invented the custom of having them dyed and of wearing differently coloured shawls in pairs.[36] That information, as well as the evidence provided by contemporary miniature paintings (pl.17), allows us to be fairly certain that Kashmir shawls were first woven without the polychrome tapestry decoration now so closely associated with the later classic examples (see pls 114–16) and that, previously, they were left undyed, in the natural range of white, grey, brown and black goat hair.[37]

Much has been written about the loom used by Kashmiri shawl weavers. It has sometimes been claimed that this was a sophisticated introduction in the early fifteenth century from Samarkand when it was under Timurid rule,[38] but this is incorrect and cannot be substantiated by facts. The loom used to weave Kashmir shawls was actually a very simple horizontal treadle (frame) loom with just four sets of heddle harnesses (which separate the warp threads to allow for the insertion of the weft), four sets of pulleys and four treadles (see pl.58).[39] This had in fact been the standard loom for weaving woollen twill in much of the world since around AD 1000, so no Timurid influence would have been required by the Kashmiris. The weaving of shawls in plain 2 & 2 weft-faced twill (in which both warp and weft are interlaced over and under two threads) was done on looms that had been commonly used in the northern

18 (top)
Shawl (detail)
Kashmir, c.1850–1900
Goat hair (pashmina) in
herringbone twill weave
280 x 155 cm
Given by Christine Dodds in
memory of Helen Penelope
Roome, the original owner
V&A: IS.15–2010

(bottom left)
detail of pl.208

19 (bottom right)
**Shawl weaver inserting
coloured weft threads with
a *tojli* (spool)**
Srinagar, Kashmir, 2008

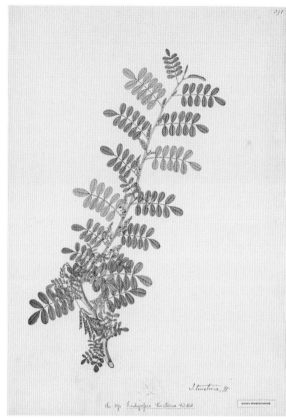

part of India and surrounding areas for centuries. Nor was the innovation of patterning in 2 & 2 weft-faced twill tapestry, which first began in Kashmir in the 1620s at the earliest, dependent on any advanced loom technology, since tapestry or *kani* weaving is done entirely by hand by inserting the separate colours by means of individual spools (*tojli*) (pl.19).

The overwhelming majority of Kashmir shawls have always been woven entirely of Himalayan goat hair (pashmina), although in the nineteenth century silk warps were substituted for pashmina warps in the narrow side borders (*zanjir*) of some shawls. However, a second source – whose fibres are even thinner, lighter and more valuable than goat-hair pashmina – is *shahtoosh*, the fine under-hair of *Capra pantholops hodgsonii* (Tibetan: *chiru*), a wild antelope. Though now an endangered species, the *chiru* once roamed the high Tibetan plains in herds of millions

but attempts in the late twentieth century to secure their precious under-hair (known also as *tus, tush, toosh* or *asli* [genuine] *tus*) have dramatically reduced their numbers.[40] Unlike domesticated pashmina goats whose under-hair is combed from the live animals by their goatherds, *tus* is combed from the antelopes after they have been killed. References to *tus* are as old as those to pashmina and trade records from the 1820s indicate that though *tus* was regularly sent to Srinagar, the amount was insignificant when compared to pashmina: 120,000 to 240,000 lbs of raw pashmina as compared with no more than 1,000 lbs of raw *tus* imported annually into Kashmir.[41] Strangely, no antique shawls woven entirely of *tus* are known in museum collections, though they must have existed in small numbers (or perhaps the *tus* was blended with pashmina to produce superior shawls). The only ones presently in published collections are relatively modern.

21
Indigofera tinctoria
Anonymous artist, India,
c.1789–1815
Watercolour on paper
52.3 x 37 cm
Roxburgh number 391
William Roxburgh
Collection, Royal Botanic
Gardens, Kew

20
An indigo dyer
Bagru, Rajasthan, 2012

DYES

So many textile dyes are native to India that the ancient Greco-Roman world, long before it had direct trading relations with India's inhabitants, closely associated India with dyes and considered Indian dyers to be the masters of the art of colouring. *Indikon*, the origin of the English word 'indigo', is simply the Greek name for the Indian subcontinent. Those living along the shores of the Mediterranean evidently associated the blue dye so closely with that faraway, mysterious land that this was also felt to be the most appropriate name for the colour.

INDIGO

For at least four thousand years, blue dyes have been prepared from many natural sources – plants diverse in appearance, habitat and distribution but all containing the same key molecule. However, the principal indigo variety native to India (*Indigofera tinctoria* – pl.21) has been found to contain some of the strongest concentrations of the active compound (indoxyl) when compared to the blue dye plants of other parts of the world, and also in comparison with *Marsdenia tinctoria* (locally called *sibu*) and *Strobilanthes cusia* (locally called *rum* – pl.23), the main blue dye-plants of Assam and other parts of India's northeast.[42] How the first Indian dyers in the third or second millennia BC managed to discover the secrets of transforming the unprepossessing shrubby indigo plant into a permanent, lightfast dye remains a mystery. Indigo plants require a complicated, controlled process of days or weeks of manipulation: the careful addition of other substances (lime, wood ash, sugars, carbonate of soda, etc.), and the maintenance of temperatures, levels of acidity and then alkalinity to

22
Group of indigo-dyed cottons (details)
(left to right)
Length of muslin
Srikakulam (formerly Chikacole), Andhra Pradesh, c.1855
1443 x 78 cm
V&A: 8910 (IS)

Piece of dyed cotton
Satara, Maharashtra, c.1855–79
198 x 85 cm
V&A: 8393 (IS)

Tie-dyed turban cloth
Delhi(?), c.1855
1191 x 21 cm
V&A: 7871 (IS)

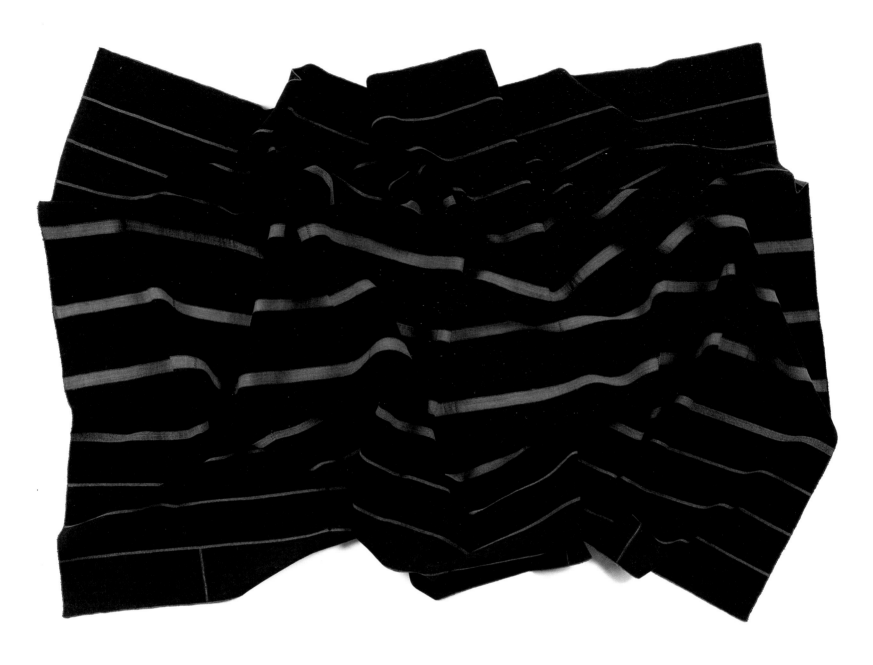

successfully convert the leaves into a dye that will permanently colour silk, cotton, linen or wool a lightfast, washable blue. Known as *nila* in Sanskrit, indigo was first mentioned in early Brahmanical texts: the Artharva Veda speaks of a particular dark blue shade, *asikni*, some time before the first millennium BC.

As one of the world's most commercially important natural dyes (before its replacement by synthetic indigo in the 1890s), indigo could either dye cloth directly using fresh indigo leaves fermented for a few days (but only producing relatively weak shades of blue) or it could be concentrated by being processed into dried cakes that were easily transportable and

able to survive long storage. Dried cakes of indigo would then be available for dyeing at any time of year, not just for a few days after the plant was harvested.

The *Periplus of the Erythraean Sea* (c. AD 40–70) specifically mentions indigo as one of the products shipped from 'Barbaricum', a now vanished city at the mouth of the Indus River, near present-day Karachi.[43] While indigo from India had been reaching the western world much earlier, the Arab invasion of western India and the final conquest of Sindh by AD 712 meant that direct exports of Indian indigo on Arab vessels to the Arabian Peninsula, Iran and the entire Middle

23
Lhota Naga man's cloth
Wokha, Nagaland, *c.*1940
Cotton, yarn dyed with
rum (Strobilanthes cusia),
embroidered with wool
186 x 105 cm
V&A: IS.115–1989

East rapidly expanded, becoming a major Indian commodity of great commercial importance. Medieval European cloth dyers (and artists) used Indian indigo, but because of its greater cost it was often mixed with cheaper European woad. Some Italian city states even banned the purchase of indigo in an attempt to support their local woad producers. During the Mughal period European traders were anxious to acquire Indian indigo, and there are many reports stating that the indigo produced in the towns of Sarkhej in Gujarat and Bayana in Rajasthan were the most costly as they were considered the finest in the world.

Following the British East India Company's annexation of Bengal after the Battle of Plassey in 1757, landowners were encouraged to grow indigo for export to Britain. Despite periodic rebellions by the workers because of slave-like conditions, Bengali indigo dominated the world market during the eighteenth and nineteenth centuries until its rapid replacement by a much cheaper synthetic equivalent. Though that invention was the final blow to the commercial use of

natural indigo, an earlier discovery made in Saxony in the 1740s had already signalled the beginning of the end. European chemists discovered that the complicated natural fermentation process could be circumvented if one dissolved indigo in sulphuric acid. The resulting dyestuff – Saxon Blue, and its variant Prussian Blue – could be applied directly to a cloth. Although it was not very lightfast, nor as resistant to water or as dark as natural indigo, if only small areas were to be dyed blue they could be painted with Saxon or Prussian Blue using a brush, without having to immerse the whole cloth in the indigo vat. A similar light blue surface application of indigo appears in small areas of several Indian textiles: the earliest example to come to light is a Gujarati block-print found in Egypt that has been radiocarbon-dated to the late thirteenth or fourteenth century.[44] The process is also visible on some seventeenth and eighteenth-century Indian chintzes (for example, see pl.132). These and many other examples make it clear that Indian dyers had in fact discovered a method of painting indigo onto the surface of a cloth long before its discovery by German chemists.

24
Woman's dress
Kohat, North West Frontier
Province, Pakistan,
c.1855–79
Indigo-dyed cotton
Length: 122 cm
V&A: 4815 (IS)

LAC

Another of the world's great dyes closely bound to the culture and history of India is lac (pl.26). This brilliant red colouring agent is extracted from the crushed bodies and eggs of tiny female sap-sucking scale insects (*Kerria lacca* or *Laccifer lacca*) that mass in large numbers (hence the name: 'lakh' means 100,000). They encase themselves on tree branches beneath a hard protective secretion that is the source of the clear varnish called 'shellac'.[45] Lac insects are native to large parts of India, particularly Assam. Worldwide there are many related scale insects that produce red dyes, perhaps most notably the

American cochineal (*Dactylopius coccus*) and dyers' kermes (*Kermes vermilio*) used in southern France and Spain. Each produces a slightly different shade of brilliant red, from bluish to more purple tones.[46] Lac can be used directly after it has been separated from the tree branches and shellac by crushing it into a fine powder, followed by repeated soakings and filtration. The resulting water-soluble concentrated dye has been used as a direct dye in Assam (pl.25), but when in the hands of more expert dyers the cloth is first soaked in a range of metallic salts called mordants (fixing agents most often derived from alum, tin or zinc) and only then are concentrated solutions of lac, kermes or cochineal dye applied to the prepared cloth to produce much more brilliant colours (see for example the red silk thread in pl.173). These are also more resistant to damage from acidic liquids or light, the great vulnerability of lac-dyed cloth.[47] These costly insect dyes are reserved for animal-based fabrics woven from silk, wool or pashmina as lac does not bond well with cellulose fibres such as cotton.

Lac has an ancient history in India. It was discussed at great length in the Artharva Veda (*c.*1500 BC) and by Panini in the fourth century BC, and the famous *lakshagraha* (house of lac) episode appears in the *Mahabharata*, where an unsuccessful attempt is made to destroy the Pandava clan by luring them into a beautiful but flammable palace made of lac and clarified butter (ghee). Later descriptions of how best to dye with lac have survived from the *Nayadhammakahao* (AD 454) and

25 (top)
(left) **Shawl** (detail)
Sibsagar, Assam, *c.*1855
Lac-dyed tasar silk
285 x 115 cm
V&A: 5091 (IS)

(right) **Waist cloth** (detail)
Assam, *c.*1855
Lac-dyed eri silk
264 x 90 cm
V&A: 5111 (IS)

26 (bottom)
Stick lac (*Kerria lacca*) on a twig
Odisha, 2000

a tenth-century work by the Kashmiri writer Ksemendra.[48] The colonization of Mexico by the Spanish conquistadors in the 1520s led to a Spanish monopoly of Mexican cochineal, which was exported all over North America, Europe and Asia. Many dyers preferred the bright scarlet hue of Mexican cochineal to the more purple-blue tones of Indian lac but, interestingly, some historic Ottoman Turkish, Safavid Persian and Mughal Indian textiles of the sixteenth and seventeenth centuries are now known (through dye analysis) to have been dyed with combinations of cochineal and lac. Dye analysis of Mughal knotted-pile carpets also indicates that some were dyed with mixtures of lac and Indian red dyes of the madder family.[49]

OTHER INDIAN RED DYES

Three plant groups have supplied most of the red dye that has coloured Indian textiles over the last four or five thousand years: *Rubia cordifolia* ('Indian madder', *manjeet/munjeet/manjistha*) and a subspecies *Rubia sikkimensis*; *Morinda citrifolia* ('Indian mulberry', *al*, also called *suranji*); and *Oldenlandia umbellata* (*chay*) (pl.29). A fourth dye plant, *Rubia tinctorum*, the common dyer's madder of Europe and the Middle East, was grown in Kashmir and Sindh but was probably not native and has not historically been a significant dye in India. The active red dye substances are concentrated in the roots and the bark, and *chay* is the plant with the highest concentration of dye-producing alizarin. In addition to these major red dye plants, there are

dozens of others known from Sanskrit lexicons and Vedic hymns, which have minor regional importance, but none of these has been used as widely or over such a long time as these three red-producing dyes.

All of these red dyes require mordants to fix the active colouring agents to the cloth fibres, whether cotton, silk or wool. The mordants – metallic salts found either in plants high in aluminium such as the ash of the Lodh tree (*Symplocos racemosa*) or the refined mineral *tuvari* (alum) – are either added at the initial stage of boiling up the roots or the cloth is mordanted separately before being dyed. Many formulas add additional red dye plants such as sappan wood (*Caesalpinia sappan*; *patanga*) to change the tint of red or intensify the

27 (top)
Wrapped garment (detail)
Ganjam, Odisha, c.1855
Cotton, dyed with *al*
1081 x 66.5 cm
V&A: 05556 (IS)

28 (middle)
Part of a chintz hanging
(detail)
Coromandel Coast,
c.1700–25
Cotton, mordant-dyed with
chay root and resist-dyed
82 x 70.5 cm
Given by J.B. Fowler
V&A: IS.2B–1967

29 (bottom)
**Bundle of *chay* roots
(*Oldenlandia umbellata*)**
Madurai, Tamil Nadu
30 x 15 cm (approx.)
Royal Botanic Gardens,
Kew, no.53776

colour; any number of other materials such as wood ash, lye, castor oil, or cowdung may be added to act as mordants, to aid absorption, or to change the acidity or alkalinity of the dye bath.

Manjistha was probably the dye used to colour the aforementioned tiny fragment of cotton found at Mohenjo-daro dating from around the third to second millennia BC, and it has remained popular in north and northeast India. It is one of the red dyes used in early block-printed textiles exported to Southeast Asia (see pl.157).[50] *Al* has been used in Gujarat and eastern India (pl.27) and, like *manjistha*, has been identified in the cotton textiles of the early first millennium AD exported west to the Roman world, and found buried in the dry sands of Egypt and along the shores of the Red Sea.[51] *Chay* is the brilliant strong red dye most closely associated with the superb chintzes of the Coromandel Coast (pl.28, and see pls 164, 176).

Despite their proven skills, Indian dyers also offered their clients a number of *kachha* (literally 'raw, uncooked') dyes, knowing they were not lightfast or that they would run if washed. Such dyes were used because they were readily available, they were cheap to acquire and the process was speedy. Kusumba or safflower (*Carthamus tinctorius*) is

probably the best-known example.[52] The safflower plant was widely cultivated in India for its dye and could be used without a mordant if the flowers were boiled in an alkaline solution. Though kusumba is mentioned as a dye as early as the Vedic period, it produced poor results because despite starting out a brilliant red, exposure to light quickly fades it to orange, then yellow and eventually all colour is lost. Furthermore, cloth dyed with safflower can never be washed because the dye remains water soluble. However, because at first it was such a brilliant red or pink colour, and it was cheap in India (though not in Europe), it was considered acceptable as a temporary (*kachha*) dye for customers less concerned about colour-fastness.

YELLOW DYES

Strangely, although thousands of plants around the world contain yellow dyes, no natural permanent, lightfast, water-insoluble yellow dye has ever been discovered. Kusumba, just discussed as a fugitive but brilliant red dye, could also be used as an impermanent yellow dye. Pomegranate rind is another easily sourced yellow dye[53] but the most popular Indian yellow dyestuff is turmeric (*Curcuma longa*), called *haldi* in Hindi (pl.30). It has always been used in India as both a spice and

30
Sari (*patolu*) (detail)
Gujarat, probably Patan, c.1900
Silk, the field dyed yellow with turmeric, double-ikat side and end borders,
cotton warps at outermost borders, gilt-metal thread wefts at ends
370 x 127 cm
V&A: IS.89-1963

a *kachha* dye. It is neither lightfast nor water insoluble, but as it is so commonly available and easy to use it became the standard Indian yellow dye. It is a direct dye – the turmeric rhizome is boiled in water and then wool, cotton or silk is introduced to the dye pot. If the dyed material is additionally rinsed in acidulated water, the colour becomes more fixed. Nevertheless, the shades of yellow dyed with turmeric are, like all natural yellow dyes, quite fugitive, though beautiful at first. Kes, kesuda or palas (*Butea frondosa*) is another source of yellow dye, though again it too is quite fugitive. Yellow larkspur (*Delphinium semibarbatum* or *Isparak*) is a yellow dye found mainly in Iran and Central Asia but used also in northern India (pl.31).[54]

The list of Indian dyestuffs producing a temporary yellow colouring is too large to even summarize here. However, one further example must be mentioned, even though it never had any commercial importance as a cloth dye: saffron (*Crocus sativa*; Sanskrit: *kunkuma*; Hindi: *kesar*). Because almost every dye book of the last two thousand years contains a recipe for dyeing silk with the dried stigmas of the saffron flower, it has been assumed that someone somewhere must have followed those recipes. But that is almost entirely untrue. While it would have been an easy process, it was commercially impractical

because of the high cost of saffron and because the dye, like all yellow dyestuffs, produces only a fugitive colour. As exactly the same result could be obtained using any other much cheaper dye such as turmeric, saffron was never used as a commercial dye and there are almost no examples of historic textiles dyed with saffron. Of the few rare examples that have been discovered (none of which is Indian), most were probably dyed with saffron more for its scent than its colour, and as an ostentatious display of wealth.[55]

BLACK

The traditional dyestuffs used in India to produce permanent blacks and browns tend to be quite destructive, in the long term, to the cloth to which they have been applied: many historical examples exhibit partial or even total degradation in the areas dyed black or brown. The exception is a repeated series of overdyeing with indigo, which approximates black. Most recipes for black dye include strong tannin-bearing plants, such as myrobalan (*Terminalia chebula* and *Terminalia bellirica*), pomegranate rind, tamarisk berries, galls and acacia bark, which react with iron mordants such as sulphate of iron or iron acetate to fix the dye.[56] The iron mordant is traditionally

31
Man's waist cloth
(***pitambar*** dhoti) (detail)
Varanasi, Uttar Pradesh,
c.1850
Silk, dyed yellow with
Delphinium semibarbatum,
and silver-gilt-wrapped thread
500 × 160 cm
V&A: 771–1852

32
Sari (*patolu*) (detail)
Gujarat, probably Patan,
late 19th or early
20th century   Direction of warp ⟷
Silk, double ikat, gilt metal   425 × 150 cm
thread wefts at one end   V&A: IS.189–1960

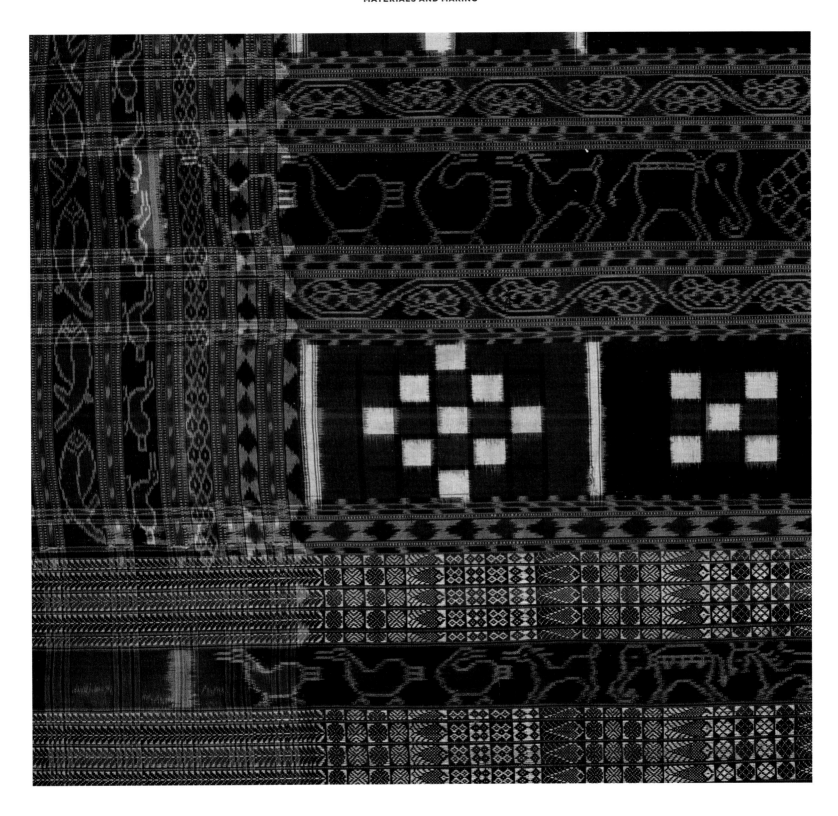

33
Sari (detail)
Odisha, probably from
Bargarh or Sonepur, c.1910   Direction of warp ←→
Cotton, warp and weft ikat,   380 x 91 cm
supplementary warp design   Given by Mr J.W.F. Morton
in borders   V&A: IS.60–1966

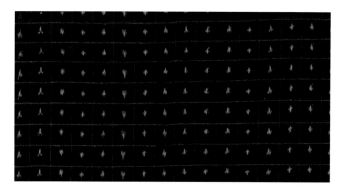

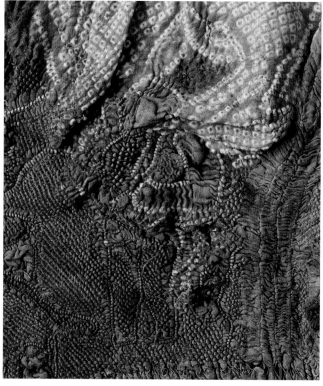

produced by placing iron filings or scraps of old metal in a pot of vinegar, country liquor or molasses for several weeks until the iron has dissolved in the acid.

COMBINATIONS OF DYES

Once the basic colours of blue, red, yellow and black are mastered, all other colours become possible by combining them. Blue overdyed with yellow produces the full range of greens, a colour that cannot normally be derived from any single natural dye.[57] However, as has been stated, yellow dyes are fugitive, so that in historic examples details that were once a distinct yellow have faded and green (indigo overdyed with turmeric or safflower) has often reverted back to shades of blue as the yellow has faded or washed out. Orange can be obtained from combining red and yellow; blue overdyed with red results in gradations of browns, purples, violets and so on, depending on how dark or light the original shades of blue and red were to begin with. The possibilities are almost unlimited.

TECHNIQUES USING DYES

A wide range of decorative techniques involves dyeing in various forms, either before or after weaving the cloth. Simply dyeing the warp and weft in contrasting colours results in cloth with a 'shot' effect. Laying out regularly alternating blocks of colour in the warp, the weft or in both directions produces vertical stripes, horizontal bands or checks respectively. Resist dyeing, in which areas of yarn or cloth are shielded from the dye by tying or by the application of a resist such as wax or gum, is used in a remarkable number of ways in India. One of the most important resist-dyeing techniques is ikat, in which

sections of a warp or weft (or both) are selectively protected according to a desired pattern, by tightly tying string, plant fibres or, nowadays, rubber strips around bundles of threads, and then dyeing the tied bundles.[58] When the string or rubber strip is removed, only the portions not covered by the string have been dyed while the rest remains undyed. This can be done several times, tying, dyeing and untying with a succession of different dyes. Then, in the final stage of this process, when those warps or wefts (or both) are finally placed on the loom to be woven into cloth, it creates a design made up entirely of the dyed and undyed parts fully integrated into the woven cloth, a process usually recognized by motifs that are slightly blurred at their margins where dye has seeped in at the junction between the tied and untied parts of the warp or weft (pls 32–4). Ikat, originally a Malay word but now an internationally recognized term for this technique, is known as *bandhani* (tied) in north and east India or *chitike* (spotted) in Andhra Pradesh.

34
Part of a sari (detail)
Chitradurga, Karnataka,
c.1866–7
Cotton field with warp ikat,
silk borders, silk wefts and
supplementary wefts in the *pallu*
165 x 100 cm
V&A: 4447 (IS)

35
**Woman's head-cover
(odhni)** (detail)
Gujarat, c.1871–2
Cotton, tie-dyed, still partly
tied after final dyeing
65 x 47 cm
V&A: 9109 (IS)

36
Sari (detail)
Probably Jamnagar or
Porbandar, Gujarat, late
19th or early 20th century
Silk, tie-dyed
396 x 122 cm
V&A: IS.205-1960

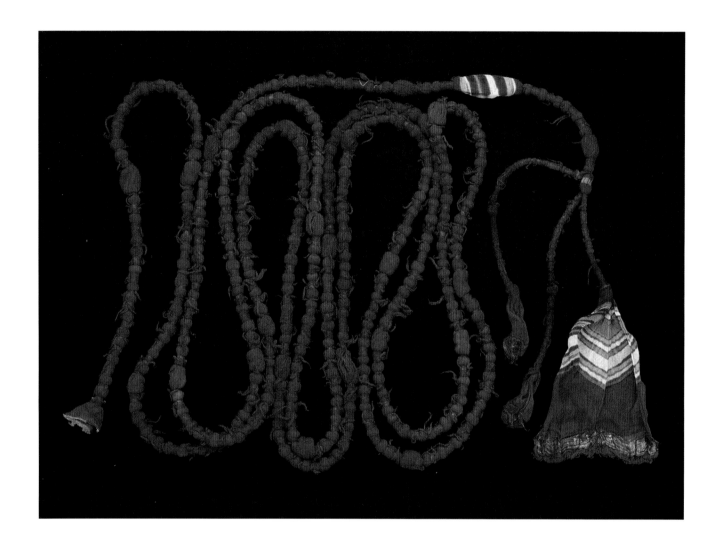

37
**Three turban cloths,
still tied after dyeing**
Rajasthan (probably Jaipur),
early 20th century
Cotton, wrap-resist dyed
(*lahariya*)
55 x 25 cm
Given by Mrs M. Hamill
V&A: IS.63B-1959

38 (opposite)
Turban cloth (detail)
Jaipur, Rajasthan, *c.*1860
Cotton, wrap-resist dyed
(*lahariya*)
700 x 20 cm
V&A: 5735 (IS)

Clockwise from top left:

39
Skirt cloth (detail)
Bagh, Madhya Pradesh,
c.1881–2
Cotton, block-printed,
resist-dyed and
mordant-dyed
1008 × 58 cm
V&A: IS.1698–1883

40
Skirt cloth (detail)
Kangra, Himachal Pradesh,
c.1855
Cotton, block-printed with
gum overlaid with gold and
silver powder; red cotton
waistband (not shown)
98 × 276 cm
V&A: 05562 (IS)

41
**Half of a woman's head-
cover (odhni) or sari**
(detail)
Gujarat, c.1920–40
Silk, resist-printed
203 × 114 cm
Given by Ann French
and Lynda Hillyer
V&A: IS.5–2014

42
Half of an *ajrakh* shawl
(detail)
Sindh, c.1855–79
Cotton, block-printed,
resist-dyed and
mordant-dyed
146 × 75.6 cm
V&A: 5473A (IS)

Ikat can be simple or sophisticated, depending on the skill of the designer and those tying the resists. The decorative effects range from tiny irregular white blips on an otherwise plain-dyed surface (pl.34), through relatively simple weft-ikat floral and fish designs used especially in Odisha (pls 7, 33), to the astonishing *patola* saris of Gujarat – warp and weft-resisted silk textiles so perfectly planned and executed that plants, animals, checks and wavy borders are all created through the alignment of horizontally and vertically resisted design elements (pl.32).

Lahariya and *chunari* are two more 'tie and dye' resist techniques but these are carried out on cloth after it has been woven. *Lahariya* (literally, 'wavy') (pls 37, 38) involves folding and tying part of a cloth so that when placed in a dye bath or mordant only those areas not tightly covered by the folds or ties will be penetrated by the dye or mordant. After successive immersions in dyes and mordants and tying and untying, rainbow effects such as parallel diagonal or wavy lines of multiple colours can be achieved; these are especially effective on turbans and scarves. *Chunari* (also called *bandhani*) uses the same technique as *lahariya* except that areas of a woven textile are bunched together rather than pleated before being tied with string. They can then remain as white undyed circles or rectangles if the rest of the cloth is dyed or they can be untied after the first dyeing, partly dipped in another dye, retied and dyed additional colours. The possible variations are almost unlimited but colourful circles and rectangles, sometimes minutely small and arranged into patterns are most characteristic of *chunari* (pls 22, 35, 36, and see pl.218).[59]

Another more common technique of selectively colouring cloth after it has been woven and removed from the loom is block-printing. The simplest block-printing involves direct application of dye to the cloth with one or two blocks; other types require the printing of a mordant onto the cloth before dyeing it red (pls 39, 46); and the most complex, for example the *ajrakh* prints of Kutch and Sindh (pls 42, 43, 48), involves block-printing a resist in order to achieve white designs alongside red and indigo blue. In many *ajrakh* designs, the finely detailed design and the combination of dyes, mordants and white resist mean that a large number of different blocks is required. A simple wax resist is also used for the printed silk saris and head-covers of Gujarat (pl.41). Prints such as the 'tinsel' and *roghan* work of north and western India use a printed oil-based adhesive that may be mixed with

colourants to form the design or can be covered with metallic foil or ground mica (pls 40, 44, 45).

In the production of chintz (pl.28, and see pls 102, 132, 174), the same sequences of mordanting, resisting and dyeing can also be carried out entirely by hand, without the use of any wooden blocks – or else outlines may be marked out in a fugitive colourant using block-printing while the rest of the process relies entirely on drawing by hand. The many stages of preparing chintz textiles on the Coromandel Coast have been extensively documented and are acknowledged to be among the finest of India's textile creations.[60] These processes may be summarized as follows (pl.49). The cotton (chintz is always a cotton textile) is washed and then boiled in a fatty substance such as buffalo milk with tannin (usually in the form of myrabolan) to make sure the mordants are absorbed but do not spread. The cloth is dried and the basic design is drawn with a fugitive material such as charcoal or red earth (*geru*), which later can easily be washed away. The areas to be dyed black are drawn with an iron mordant while those areas to become red are drawn or painted with an alum mordant. The whole cloth is then soaked in the red dye – usually *chay* if on the Coromandel Coast – which reacts to both mordants, producing permanent red and black areas on the cloth. It is then rinsed, and bleached in a dung bath to remove all the tannins, mordants and unfixed dye. Wax is now applied to all the areas that are not to appear as blue in the finished design. This includes fine white lines that are to be seen against blue or red backgrounds: these are drawn with the *kalam* (literally 'reed' or 'pen').

A block-printer at work on *ajrakh* fabric
Ajrakhpur, Kutch, 2005

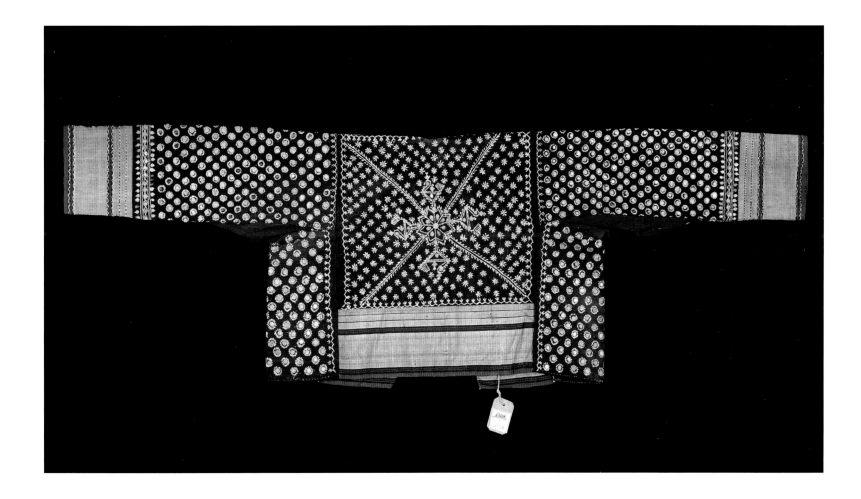

Bodice (choli)
Satara, Maharashtra,
c.1855–79
Cotton with silk borders,
block-printed with
gum overlaid with ground
mica and applied mirror-
glass pieces
Length: 28 cm
V&A: 6558 (IS)

44 (opposite)
Head-cover (odhni) (detail)
Jaipur, Rajasthan,
19th century
Cotton, printed with gum
overlaid with gold leaf
510 x 127 cm
V&A: IS.9–1983

46
Wrapped garment (detail)
Sanganer, Rajasthan,
c.1855–79
Cotton, block-printed
and mordant-dyed
271 x 105 cm
V&A: 4497 (IS)

47
**An unidentified man,
possibly the photographer
Mohanlal, wearing a printed
cotton wrapped garment**
Udaipur, Rajasthan, c.1875
Albumen print photograph
9.8 x 5.8 cm
Udaipur City Palace
Museum, CPMU
2008.01.0104

48 (opposite)
**Set of samples showing
the stages of *ajrakh*
production**
From the workshop of
Ismail Mohammad Khatri,
Ajrakhpur, Kutch, Gujarat,
2006
Cotton, block-printed,
resist-dyed and
mordant-dyed
96.5 x 17.4 cm (each sample)
V&A: IS.7–2007

49
**Samples showing
the stages of the
chintz process**
49.5 x 42 cm (each sample)
Given by W.S. Hadaway
V&A: T.1A–G–1920

A The outline is lightly
stencilled or drawn onto the
cotton cloth and outlined
with an iron mordant using a
kalam (bamboo pen).

D A second dye-bath with
alum and *chay* produces
deeper shades of red.

B The completed outline
is drawn with iron mordant
for black and alum mordant
for red.

E After rinsing, the cloth
is covered in wax except
for the areas to be dyed
blue.

C After dyeing with
red dye (*chay*): the alum
mordant has reacted with
the dye to produce red
areas and outlines.

F After dyeing with blue
(indigo) the wax is removed
by boiling.

G Yellow areas are created
by applying yellow dye onto
undyed surfaces; green areas
are created by applying
yellow dye onto blue surfaces.

G

The whole cloth is dyed blue in an indigo vat; the wax is removed by boiling; the cloth is rinsed and bleached again, leaving finished designs in red, blue and black, with white designs against the colours. Further colours, especially dark reds and purples, are added by additional use of mordants and dyes. The cloth is bleached and rinsed again to lighten the white ground. Yellow is painted over areas of blue to make green, and the decoration of the cloth is complete except for glazing with rice starch or beetling (flattening with wooden mallets) and folding.

The *kalamkari* of south India (see pl.151) is sometimes a combination of block-printing with hand-drawing and especially the application by hand of white resist patterns, although this feature became increasingly rare after the nineteenth century and has now entirely disappeared. The word *kalamkari* literally means 'pen work', but the same term is now indiscriminately used whether the piece is completely block-printed or hand-painted.

WEAVING AND LOOMS

The first looms used in India to weave the cotton cloth of the third to seventh millennia BC were simple ground looms, in which the warp was stretched out in front of the weaver in a figure of eight, and had one fixed heddle-rod. This was a simple piece of wood with loops of string (leashes) tied to alternate warp threads, which could be raised to create a space (the shed) through which weft threads would pass to form the woven cloth. As populations increased, there was a corresponding demand

for more woven material produced quickly, and labour-saving devices were added to the basic ground loom to raise and lower the warps more easily. The number of heddles was also increased, a feature necessary for the introduction of twill weaves.

The loom that became the most widespread across the entire Indian subcontinent (and remains the most common type of handloom used today) was the pit loom, which was probably already in use in India by 1000 BC (pl.50).[61] This was basically a ground loom stretched over a shallow pit dug under the warp. But now the weaver, sitting on the edge of the pit, could raise and lower the heddle shafts using long pedals in the pit once a crossbar had been fixed over the warp to support the heddle shafts. All basic weaves that involved a single warp and single weft – such as twill, plain weave and satin – could now be produced on the pit loom: additionally, with hand manipulation, the weaver could create discontinuous weft techniques such as brocading, as in *jamdani* and other brocaded weaves (pls 52, 56), and tapestry weaving (pls 53, 54). Double weaves such as *khes* were also produced on the pit loom (pl.51), as were most of the other textile types woven in India until the twentieth century (pls 55, 57), with few exceptions, such as the backstrap weaving of the far northeast (pls 59, 60). Ground looms, pit looms and backstrap looms all require the warps to be stretched out at tension in front of the weaver and therefore take up a lot of space, meaning they were usually set up outdoors. The upright frame loom pivoted much of the horizontal part of the warp into a vertical position and thus enabled weaving to take place

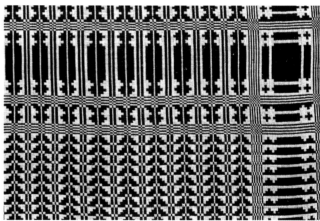

50
Silk Weaving
J.L. Kipling, Agra, 1870
Ink drawing on paper,
showing a weaver using a
pit loom
26.5 × 36.4 cm
V&A: 0929:40 (IS)

51
**Piece of double-weave
cotton fabric (*khes*)** (detail)
Sindh, c.1855–79
264 × 74 cm
V&A: 5142 (IS)

Clockwise from top left:

52
Part of a sari (detail)
Dhaka, Bangladesh,
mid-19th century
Cotton with extra-weft
brocading (*jamdani*)
255 x 105 cm
V&A: 9632 (IS)

53
Sari (detail)
Thanjavur, Tamil Nadu,
*c.*1855
Cotton warps and silk wefts,
metal-wrapped silk thread;
plain-woven field with
tapestry woven design in
the *pallu*
836 x 106 cm
V&A: 016 (IS)

54
Shawl (detail)
Manipur, *c.* late 18th
or early 19th century
Tapestry-woven silk
251 x 157 cm
V&A: 376–1905

55
Man's waist cloth (lungi)
(detail)
Gurdaspur, Punjab,
*c.*1855–79
Plain-woven silk and gold-
wrapped thread
228 x 76.5 cm
V&A: 7109 (IS)

56
Sari
Tamil Nadu, probably
Madurai or Thanjavur, c.1855
Silk warps and cotton wefts
with brocaded motifs in
metal-wrapped silk thread
692 x 89 cm
V&A: 6026 (IS)

57 (opposite)
Sari (detail)
Bengaluru, Karnataka,
c.1867
Silk and metal-
wrapped thread
790 x 109 cm
V&A: 6107 (IS)

in smaller, enclosed spaces. This loom is most often found in northern areas such as Kashmir, where the weather is less likely to be suitable for outdoor or semi-outdoor weaving (pl.58).

By the early years of the first millennium AD, weavers in Iran and China had independently invented a new type of loom that allowed them to more efficiently repeat patterns and to weave textiles with more than single warp and single weft structures: the drawloom. The Iranian drawloom (from which the Indian model is derived) was a modified pit loom invented to weave wool in weft-faced structures. On the other hand, the Chinese drawloom (from which the European type is derived) was a modified integral frame loom (itself evolving from earlier backstrap looms) invented to weave silk in warp-faced structures. Despite their differing origins, both looms needed to solve a common problem: how to integrate a ground weave with a repeating figurative pattern woven in a different weave structure. The solution in both cases was to use an existing loom system to weave the ground and to add a completely separate set of leashes to control the figurative elements, somehow integrating both weaves into a single textile.[62]

The Persian and Indian drawloom was a type of raised pit loom, with a weaver sitting operating the pedals that raised and lowered the warps of the ground weave while an assistant (the drawboy) sat above the warps on a raised platform and selected individual leashes to create the figurative patterns. This was the loom used to weave the earliest surviving Indian complex woven silks, the samite weaves with their two-warp systems (pls 61, 62).[63] A drawloom was also necessary to weave lampas, a weave even more complicated than samite. Lampas weaves need two sets of warps and two sets of wefts to form two visually distinct structures, the ground and the figured pattern. Some of the most elaborate and sophisticated of all Indian weavings are done in this technique (pl.63, and see pls 103, 104). But by the beginning of the nineteenth century the French had invented the jacquard loom, a semi-automated system that replaced the need for a drawboy. Rather than a person successively raising and lowering the warps for the figured part of a complex weave, the same action was imitated by a set of cards punched with holes, strung in the same order as the sets of draw-cords the drawboy had pulled after every weft pass. Spring-loaded metal pins went through these holes, directing the same warps to raise and then lower after each weft pass. Most Indian drawlooms were gradually replaced by semi-mechanical jacquard looms, except among a small number of hand-weavers in Gujarat and Varanasi. Even in Varanasi most drawlooms had already been modified with jacquard mechanisms in the twentieth century to weave the more complicated side and end panels of a sari, so that by the end of the twentieth century the commercial use of entirely hand-operated drawlooms in India had ceased.

58
A shawl-weaver at a vertical frame loom
Srinagar, Kashmir, 2008

59
A weaver using a modified back-strap loom
Arunachal Pradesh, 2011

60
Shawl (detail)
Nagaland or Assam,
c.1855–79
Cotton with
embroidered wool
158 x 93 cm
V&A: 4807 (IS)

61 (top)
**Fragment of
samite-woven silk**
Probably Gujarat, *c.* late 15th
or early 16th century
Direction of warp ⟷
55.9 x 57.2 cm
The Fine Arts Museums
of San Francisco, Gift of
George and Marie Hecksher,
2000.186.1

62 (bottom)
**Three fragments
of samite-woven silk**
Probably Gujarat,
c. 15th century
Direction of warp ⟷
17.8 x 29.3 cm
Given by Michael Franses
Metropolitan Museum of
Art, New York, 1993.2a–c

63
**Part of a hanging
or canopy**
Probably Gujarat,
c. 16th century
Silk, lampas weave
153 x 64 cm
Nasser D. Khalili Collection
of Islamic Art, TXT 003

KIMKHAB ZARBAFT JALDAR GANGAJAMNI GULNAR.

كلكار كبرى كيكسى پيپن سروكرى نزور سرد بر دوسرت سرن سرمرن دمر اسبى كاس كابا ايمها اسب

nscribed in both Persian script and Latin lettering with thick metal-wrapped thread, these words give credit where credit is due. Originally a single piece, this fine *kamkhwab* (often anglicized to 'kincob': patterned silk densely woven with metal-wrapped thread) was displayed in the Indian section of the Great Exhibition of 1851 in London. Of the thousands of textiles submitted from India, it was chosen as one of fewer than 70 textiles purchased directly from the exhibition by the South Kensington Museum (later the V&A) to serve as an example of exemplary design.[1]

Also purchased was a sister object to this piece: a second *kamkhwab* made for Mu'in Lal, but inscribed as the work of Budhu, a resident of the Rasulpur district of Banaras, modern Varanasi (V&A: 744–1852). The unusual inscriptions on the two works suggest they were ordered especially for display at the Great Exhibition. It is likely Mu'in Lal was a trader who commissioned the work of a variety of *karigars* (meaning 'craftsmen', a title reserved for Banaras *kamkhwab*-weavers)[2] from different districts of the city for submission to the local exhibition committee.

The contributions of India to the Great Exhibition were heavily mediated by an ascending scale of traders, donors and committees, and the resulting administrative confusion caused only a fraction to arrive in London with any information about their makers.[3] Instead, aside from a select group of artisans and donors who submitted work directly under their own names, the Indian contributions were identified only by the general locations of their manufacture. Despite their labelling efforts, the names of Baks Miyan, Budhu and Mu'in Lal do not appear in exhibition catalogues. Their contributions are listed only as 'productions of the native manufacturers of the City of Benares'.[4]

The representation of Indian artisans at nineteenth-century international exhibitions in the West became increasingly problematic, as romanticized visions of Indian labour largely erased individual Indian artisan identities. In 1880 the V&A became the final inheritor of a significant quantity of Indian textiles from these exhibitions, the vast majority of which had no corresponding maker identification. Examples such as this *kamkhwab* are therefore all the more valuable, as without its golden signature the weaver of this beautiful fabric would have been unknown for ever. **AF**

1   Great Exhibition 1852.
2   Agrawal 2003, p.135.
3   Great Exhibition 1851, vol.2, pp.857–9.
4   Dowleans 1851, p.54.

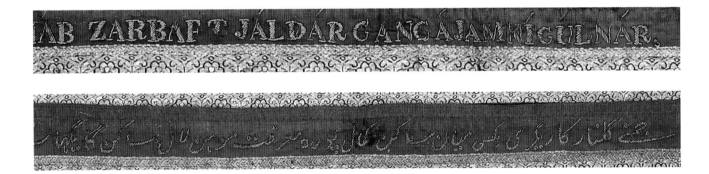

64 (opposite and details above)

Two lengths of woven silk with silver-gilt-wrapped and silver-wrapped thread
Varanasi, Uttar Pradesh, c.1850
228.8 x 79.7 cm and 135.5 x 79.2 cm
V&A: 752A&B–1852

Embroidered inscription in Persian script on 752A–1852:
Kamkhwab-i zarbaft jaldar ganga jumna gulnar. Karigari Baks Miyan sakin-i Kamalpura ma'rifet Mu'in Lal sakin-i Gaighat

(Gold-woven *kamkhwab*, trellis pattern in gold and silver with flowers. The craftsmanship of Baks Miyan, resident of Kalampura [district of Banaras], for Mu'in Lal, resident of Gaighat)

Embroidered inscription in Latin script on 752B–1852:
Kimkhab zarbaft jaldar gangajamni gulnar
(Gold-woven *kamkhwab*, trellis pattern in gold and silver with flowers)

However, in the early twenty-first century attempts to revive their use for specialized weaves such as *asavali*, samite, lampas and velvet continue (pl.68).

Gujarat is thought to have been the region in which many of the early advanced weaving techniques were developed, and indeed most silk-weavers throughout India trace their origins back to Gujarat, often retaining occupational names and even linguistic traces from that area.[64] This Gujarati diaspora of weavers occurred over centuries, and for a variety of reasons: one was certainly necessity (to escape famines such as the disastrous one of 1631–2, for example) but another reason was the invitation by rulers of other areas to set up workshops to produce luxury cloth. The famous stone inscription of AD 436 at Mandasor (Mandsaur) records one such invitation.[65] The migration of weavers from Gujarat at some time in the distant past might explain the presence of lampas, damask and other weave structures requiring drawlooms in Assam, in India's far northeast (pl.65). However, knowledge of this technology could also have been transmitted from the borders of China and Southeast Asia with the Tai-Kadai-speaking Ahom people who arrived and conquered much of Assam in the thirteenth century. Whatever the origin of drawloom technology in Assam, Gujarati technology was certainly responsible for the famous Baluchar saris of Bengal, and some other Bengali weaves, which are also clearly derivative of Gujarati weaves (pl.66).

The most complicated, difficult to weave and expensive of all the traditional Indian weave structures woven on a drawloom is velvet, a technique that was probably introduced from Iran (pl.69).[66] Often incorporating a background of metal-wrapped thread, velvet is made on an adapted drawloom that requires an additional pile warp that is not attached to the warp beam but hung with individual weights (pl.68). The rows of loops created during weaving have to be cut by hand to create the pile – an exacting and time-consuming process. But the main reason for the high price of Mughal velvet, apart from the complexity of the weaving and loom set-up, was the use of costly silk and metal-wrapped thread, as well as expensive dyes such as lac, which made it available to only the wealthiest patrons such as the Mughal emperors and their courtiers.

65
**Hanging with scenes
from the life of Krishna
(Vrindavani vastra)**
Barpeta, Assam, c.1560–70
Silk, lampas weave
226 x 79.9 cm
Los Angeles County
Museum of Art, AC.1995.94.1

66 (opposite)
Baluchar sari (detail)
Bahadurpur, West Bengal,
c.1855–79
Silk, with continuous
and discontinuous
supplementary wefts
479 x 110 cm
V&A: 6102 (IS)

VELVET PANEL WITH FIGURES

ozens of luxurious silk velvet textiles, some enhanced with metal-wrapped thread, have survived from the early seventeenth to the early nineteenth centuries, and we now feel confident enough to attribute them to Mughal northern India. These include floral and geometrically decorated floor coverings (see pl.110), tent panels, cushions and canopies. However, with the exception of a single *qanat* panel in Copenhagen depicting a woman standing beneath a cusped arch,[1] this fabric (along with three associated fragments in Baltimore and London[2]) is the only Indian velvet presently known that depicts human figures. A far greater number of visually similar lengths of figurative velvet have survived from Safavid Iran, most of them contemporary with this piece (pl.67). For that reason it was previously assumed that all the 'Persian-style' figurative velvets were the products of Iranian looms. However, a technical study published in 2011 compared the weave structures of classical Safavid, Mughal and Ottoman velvets and on the basis of those new observations we are now able, for the first time, to distinguish each group on a strictly objective basis rather than through supposed stylistic comparisons.[3]

In terms of weave structure, Mughal velvets such as this example differ from Safavid pieces in several important respects, including the direction of twist of the metal-wrapped threads ('Z' direction rather than 'S'), the number of colours per warp channel (two or three at most, as opposed to up to four in Safavid examples), and the absence of an extra weft ('vertical vice') on the

front. This kind of specific information allows us to assign this rare survival of luxurious, metal-enhanced, figurative silk-pile velvet to seventeenth-century Mughal India. When purchased in 1971, the curators at the Los Angeles County Museum of Art believed their velvet to be Indian simply on the basis of its colouring and design, although they lacked any structural proof.[4] That intuitive opinion has now been scientifically validated. **SC**

1   David Collection, Copenhagen, 37/1995; Cohen 2014 and ill.2.
2   Walters Art Museum, Baltimore, 83.630 (40.3 x 58.5 cm);
    Nasser D. Khalili Collection of Islamic Art, TXT 130 (35 x 57.1 cm)
    and Keir Collection (144 x 55 cm) (see Spuhler 1978, no. 119).
3   Jain 2011b.
4   Los Angeles 1974, fig.14

67 (top)
Panel with figures (detail)
Safavid Iran, 17th century
Silk velvet with metal-
wrapped thread
198 x 57.5 cm
Keir Collection – Ranros
Universal, SA, BVI

68 (bottom)
**Drawloom for patterned
silk velvet in the workshop
of Rahul Jain**
Varanasi, 2013

69 (opposite)
Panel with figures
Mughal India, 17th century
Silk velvet with metal-
wrapped thread
183 x 58.5 cm
Los Angeles County
Museum of Art, M.71.13

Clockwise from top left:

70

Child's dress
Sindh, c.1900
Silk, embroidered
with floss silk
Length: 59.4 cm
V&A: 49–1908

71

Boy's jacket
Rabari community, Kutch
or Sindh, 20th century
Cotton, embroidered
with silk and mirror-
glass fragments
Length: 48.5 cm
V&A: IS.7–2008

72

Child's dress (*angarkha*)
Sindh, c.1900
Silk, embroidered with silk,
lined with printed cotton
Length: 59 cm
Given by Lady Ratan Tata
V&A: IM.280–1920

73

Bodice (choli)
Bansali community, Kutch,
late 19th or early 20th
century
Cotton, embroidered
with silk and mirror-
glass fragments
Length: 45.7 cm
Given by Mrs A.R. Ditmas
V&A: IS.55–1957

EMBROIDERY

The fame of Indian embroidery is almost as well established as the antiquity and quality of Indian dyeing and weaving skills. Already mentioned in early Pali Buddhist texts of the first centuries BC,[67] very specific regional styles – markedly different from one another and immediately recognizable – developed in western India, northeastern India and the Deccan as well as in most regional courts, while at the same time vast parts of the subcontinent (notably south and Central India) are almost entirely devoid of known embroidery traditions.[68]

Western India – formerly including Gujarat, Rajasthan and Punjab in India and Sindh, Baluchistan and the former North West Frontier Province in Pakistan – is undoubtedly the area most closely associated with spectacular embroidery skills. The variety of stitches and materials found in the desert regions of Kutch, Baluchistan, Sindh and western Rajasthan are unequalled: silk, cotton and metal-wrapped thread embroidery are found in chain (pls 72, 74), Sindhi (pl.70), buttonhole, herringbone (pl.71), interlacing and running stitches, sometimes incorporating mirrors (pl.73), beads, sequins and appliqué (pl.75). Professional embroiderers of Cambay and other Gujarati urban centres had attracted the attention of European travellers from the early sixteenth century onwards with the skill of their fine polychrome silk chain-stitch embroidery on cotton (see pl.173).[69] Embroidery

74
Skirt cloth (detail)
Mochi community, Kutch,
Gujarat, c.1850
Satin-woven silk,
embroidered with
silk thread
74 x 194 cm
V&A: 791A–1852

75
Room hanging (*bithiya*)
Kathi community,
Saurashtra, Gujarat,
early 20th century
Cotton with cotton
and silk appliqué
1680 x 248 cm
Given by Mr and Mrs J. Burns
V&A: IS.24–1994

76
Coverlet (*kantha*)
Probably Faridpur,
Bangladesh,
early 20th century
Cotton, quilted
and embroidered
55.6 x 57.2 cm
Private collection

of this kind proved so popular with both the western export market and India's rulers that Gujarati silk chain stitch became synonymous with the highest level of embroidery commissioned for the Mughal and Rajput courts (see pl.111).

A continuous area extending from eastern Punjab and Haryana up to the valleys of Indus Kohistan and Swat uses a floss silk surface-darning stitch (called *phulkari* in Punjab) to decorate coarsely woven cotton head-covers, skirts and other items of clothing, sometimes completely hiding the ground cloth (imitating more expensive woven silk) while at other times incorporating the unembroidered ground as part of the design (pl.80). Double darning stitch, in which the thread is also visible on the reverse of the fabric, was used for the fine, courtly embroideries (generically called *rumal* or coverlets) of Chamba

and other hill states (see pl.137) as well as more rustic pieces made in the area.[70]

Bengal, in the northeast, is another region with its own very distinct embroidery traditions, using materials such as local cotton for the quilted *kanthas* (pl.76) and tasar silk to embroider the world-famous sixteenth and seventeenth-century quilts of Satgaon (near present-day Kolkata) in chain stitch and back stitch (see pl.166). Lucknow and adjacent villages in modern-day Uttar Pradesh were and still are known for their unrivalled white cotton *chikan* embroidery on semi-transparent fine cotton grounds (pls 202, 203). Some Kashmir shawls were almost certainly embroidered in the Mughal period, a practice that increased rapidly from the early nineteenth century, resulting in some spectacular designs that are quite independent of woven shawl patterns (pl.79).[71]

Central India, southeastern and south India are notably almost entirely without an embroidery tradition, an absence perhaps explained by a very strong and diverse tradition of woven textiles based on unstitched, loom-woven, wrapped garments. However, in the nineteenth century Muslim courts such as that at Hyderabad did use lavishly embroidered bolsters, *masnads* (dais covers) and canopies, as well as tailored garments encrusted with metal-thread embroidery.[72] Also, the silk-thread and metal-thread embroidered cotton floor-spreads exported to the West in the eighteenth century (see pl.134) clearly drew on influences from other Islamic traditions as well as Europe itself.

There are exceptions to the absence of embroidery in south India: *kasuti* embroidery carried out today in Mysore may be derived from a type found in a few pieces from Dharwar (also in Karnataka, pl.78), and the Toda people of the Nilgiri Hills embroider their cotton (formerly 'Nilgiri nettle') shawls (*puthkuli*) with a counted thread darning stitch (pl.81); Hindu deities were appliquéd and embroidered on woollen temple hangings in Tamil Nadu;[73] and a large South Indian temple hanging (pl.87) combining appliqué and embroidery, while possibly unique, might indicate the existence of one more area of traditional embroidery in the South which has yet to be identified.

78
Bodice (choli)
Dharwar, Karnataka,
c.1870–4
Cotton with silk borders,
embroidered with floss silk
Length: 31 cm
V&A: 8249 (IS)

This bird's-eye view of the city of Srinagar is bisected by the Jhelum River, while the irregularly shaped Dal Lake dominates the upper half. The map is oriented with east at the top of the shawl, so that the Mughal pleasure gardens of Nishat Bagh and Shalimar Bagh, shown with multicoloured rocks and landscape, run along the upper part. The pale blue waters of the lake are crowded with *shikaras*, the agile local boats that are the main mode of transport on the lake, and even their distinctive, heart-shaped paddles are visible. Landmarks such as the Friday Mosque (Masjid-i Jami') – shown as a cross-shaped building near the centre of the map (see detail on p.73, top) – and the city's bridges are all shown, as are houses and gardens, temples, mosques and the parade ground. All of these landmarks are named in minutely embroidered Persian script, even down to individual gardens (*bagh*) and plane trees (*chinar*) scattered throughout the city.

Around the edge of the map is a border with meandering rivers and landscapes which are labelled in diagonal compartments, also in Persian script. Each of these inscriptions gives the name of one of the small districts (*parganas*) or towns (*qasaba*) in the region surrounding Srinagar, indicating where each ends by the phrase '... *taiyar shud*' (was completed). Several recognizable Kashmiri place names are visible: Vernag and Shupiyan in the right-hand border, Baramula and Sopur in the left, and Martand and Anantnag in the top border.

This shawl is one of a very small number of known embroideries showing the city of Srinagar and surrounding beauty spots. Other examples are in the National Gallery of Australia (the Godfrey shawl), the British Royal Collection (on loan to the V&A) and the Sri Pratap Singh Museum in Srinagar. A further newly discovered example is now in the Josefowitz Collection, and a smaller but related stole or sash is in the TAPI Collection in Surat. None of the large 'shawls' was meant to be worn: they were made as presentation pieces. The Royal Collection example (the only one to have inscriptions in English rather than Persian) was probably sent as a gift to Queen Victoria by one of the rulers of Kashmir, while the one in the Sri Pratap Singh Museum was intended to be presented by its maker to Maharaja Ranjit Singh, although Ranjit Singh died in 1839, before its completion. The Godfrey shawl is recorded

as being one of two embroidered maps made on the orders of Maharaja Ranbir Singh of Kashmir for presentation to the Prince of Wales (later King Edward VII) during his tour of India in 1875–6. It is possible that the V&A's piece, which sadly has no provenance history, is the other embroidered map of Srinagar made at this time, and that Ranbir Singh is the haloed figure seen boating near the Shalimar Garden at the top left of the shawl (overleaf). **RC**

See further:
Gole 1989, cats 49, 56, 57; Crill 1993; Brand 1995, p.70; Crill 2012, cat.120; Ames, forthcoming

79 (opposite, details above and overleaf)
Map shawl
Srinagar, Jammu and Kashmir, c1875
Woollen embroidery on twill-woven goat-hair (pashmina)
228.6 x 198 cm
Given by Mrs Estelle Fuller through the Art Fund
V&A: IS.31–1970

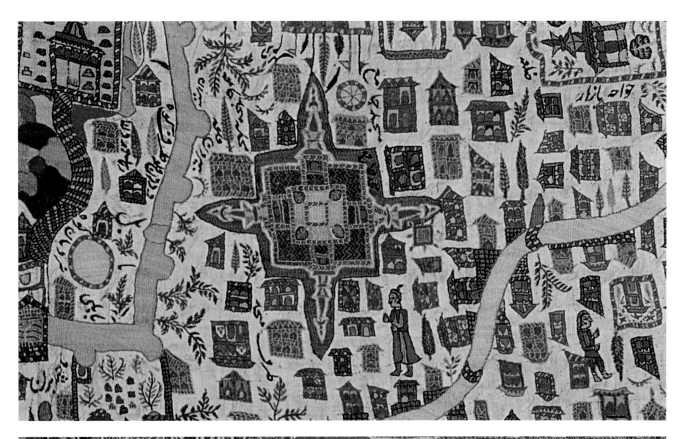

(opposite and above)
Details of pl.79

80
**Wedding shawl
(bagh)** (detail)
Hazara, Pakistan,
late 19th century
Cotton, embroidered
with floss silk
241 x 135 cm

Given by Karun Thakar
in memory of his brother
Dinesh Thakar
V&A: IS.1–2014

81 (opposite)
**Toda woman's
shawl (puthkuli)**
Udagamandalam
(Ootacamund), Tamil Nadu,
c.1900–20
Embroidered cotton
and 'Nilgiri nettle'
(Girardinia diversifolia)
232 x 128 cm

Given by
Miss A.W. Dickinson
V&A: IM.34–1925

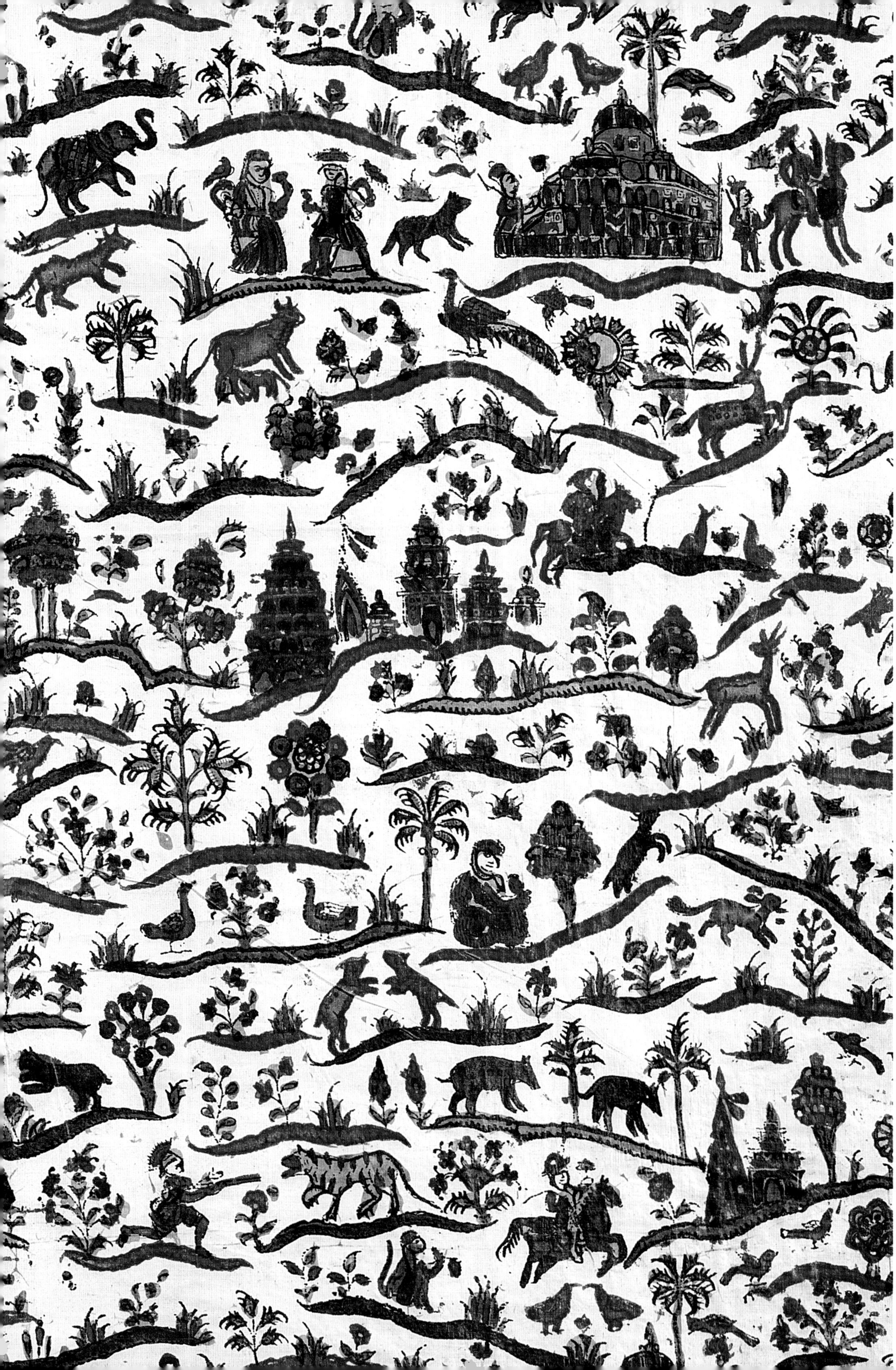

2

LOCAL AND GLOBAL: PATRONAGE AND USE

'WHERE PROCURABLE: Bazaar'. These succinct words frequently appear on the labels attached to textiles acquired by the India Museum from the Paris International Exhibition of 1855 (pl.82). Over a thousand of these everyday textiles had been sent from Madras (Chennai) to represent the manufactures of what was then the Madras Presidency.[1] While they were sent primarily to demonstrate 'how great and varied be the capabilities of India to minister to the wants of the Western world',[2] the printed list of the selected pieces notes that they were all purchased 'in the market' and would thus have been part of a wide range of goods available to ordinary local buyers.

These pieces, like the vast majority of textiles made and sold in India, were fabrics sold in the bazaar to be used as household furnishings and dress. In many cases the same rectangular length of cloth could serve as a shawl, bedcover, turban, baby-carrier, lungi, canopy, cradle, facecloth, container to carry one's belongings – in short, anything that it could be required to do. Unstitched lengths of fabric are especially versatile in the subcontinent, as draped or wrapped garments have always been a staple element of India's wardrobe. From the turban, shawl and shoulder-cloth to the dhoti, lungi and sari, these are garments that can be used immediately and without modification, exactly as they are when taken from the loom. In practice they would often be subjected to a range of different treatments – such as beetling (producing a surface shine by beating the fibres flat with wooden mallets), burnishing with a conch shell, starching and folding – before being offered for sale in the bazaar. Unstitched and uncut pieces were considered ritually pure by Hindus as they had undergone a minimum of potentially polluting human touch. Garments requiring cutting and sewing were traditionally more favoured by Muslim society as they could be made to cover the body more fully. These would be cut and stitched by local tailors (*darzi*) who often worked in the midst of the bazaar itself, although well-off

families of any religion would maintain a dedicated tailor in their households.

The fabrics available in local bazaars varied from place to place, with locally available textiles predominating. In this way, until relatively recently a cloth market in Odisha would be full of ikat saris and bedcovers, a *hat* (local market) in Bastar would offer the local thick cotton saris and shawls with simple *al*-dyed designs, a Rajasthani bazaar would provide tie-dyed lengths (unopened) for turbans and *odhnis* (head-covers) as well as local block-printed cottons, a south Indian market would be full of checked cotton lungis, and so on. While vestiges of these local variations remain in some parts of India, the majority of urban bazaars today offer a much more uniform range of factory-made textiles, with a tiny proportion, if any, of the goods on sale being locally handmade.

In addition to local textile specialities, the bazaar would provide plainer locally made cloth for utilitarian purposes. Usually these would be of cotton, but if the most readily available material was silk – in Assam and other parts of northeast India, for example – or wool in northern areas, these would naturally be more in evidence. While these everyday fabrics are usually undecorated in terms of print, dye or embroidery, they would not necessarily be plain-woven: the V&A's collection of nineteenth-century cotton fabrics, which were inexpensive and clearly made for everyday use, show a remarkable variety of weaves. Many of these pieces are described on their original labels or accession registers as 'towels' or 'napkins', and a textured weave would be an advantage for absorbency (pl.5). Others described as 'dusters' have a soft open-textured cotton in twill or plain weave.[3]

The handmade textiles found in the markets of the past were made by professional, usually male, weavers, dyers, printers and embroiderers, in small-scale workshops or in single-family units. In most parts of India the occupations of weaving and spinning (a process usually done by women[4]) were seasonal, and would be combined with agricultural work, although this normally applied to the production of coarser types of cloth: the

82 (opposite)
Group of textiles with exhibition labels (from top)
Length of uncut checked handkerchiefs
Chennai, *c*.1855
Cotton
700 x 90 cm
V&A: 4849 (IS)

Length of striped silk
Thanjavur, *c*.1855
Silk with metal strip
70 x 46 cm
V&A: 8194 (IS)

Length of dress fabric
Machilipatnam (Masulipatam), *c*.1855–79
Block-printed and resist-dyed cotton
175 x 96 cm
V&A: 5364 (IS)

ENG. NAME. *Checked Handkerchief*
SYN. *8 in a Piece*
TAMIL. *Goodday*
PRODUCE OR MANUFACTURE. *Madras*
PRICE PER *Piece 2 Rupees 12 Annas*
WHERE PROCURABLE. *Bazar*
USE.
REMARKS.

Fast Color

ENG. NAME. *Womens Jacket 1 Nº*
SYN.
TAMIL. *Ravooky*
PRODUCE OR MANUFACTURE. *Tanjore*
PRICE PER *14 Annas*
WHERE PROCURABLE. *Bazaar*
USE.
REMARKS.

R.4.

MADRAS TARIFF.

ENG. NAME. *Glazed Chintz*
SYN.
TAMIL. *Cheetee*
PRODUCE OR MANUFACTURE. *Masulipatam*
PRICE PER *Piece 4½ Rs.*
WHERE PROCURABLE. *Bazar*
USE.
REMARKS. *Box 12*

weaving of the finest Dhaka and Santipur muslin, for example, was a full-time occupation.[5] Some kinds of fabric demanded seasonal bouts of activity for practical reasons: silk-rearing, for example, had phases of activity depending on the life cycles of the different silk moths, and in Gujarat the finer *nekanees* (a kind of striped cotton cloth) were produced before the dry winds of November started to blow, whereas blue and red-striped *chelloes* were woven during the rainy season, after their yarns were dyed in April.[6] The weavers of fine Bengali muslins took advantage of the year-round moist climate of that area, which facilitated spinning the fine thread and stopped the warp threads from breaking, while the makers of Coromandel Coast chintzes needed to wait for local rivers to clear of silt after the rainy season before they could be used for rinsing the dyed cloth. All of these arrangements were of course dependent on favourable weather conditions: a sudden cold spell could kill precious silkworms, while drought could easily ruin a crop of cotton or the dye plants needed to colour it, or could make it impossible to carry out the repeated washes and rinses needed to finish off dyed cloth.

Original documentation tells us that a number of the utilitarian fabrics represented in the India Museum's collection were woven in India's prisons, notably those of Agra, Lahore and Mysore, as revenue-earning schemes (for the jail rather than the inmates).[7] Other jails, such as Yeraoda in Pune, specialized in flat-woven durries and wool-pile rugs, and the south Indian Chingleput jail achieved an Honourable Mention at the Madras Exhibition of 1857 for its 'Blue dyed Trowser cloth'.[8] Some textiles, however – those made by women in their homes, for their families' use – were never seen for sale in the bazaar. These were generally embroideries: garment pieces, coverlets or hangings that would be worked on in a small space with minimal equipment and picked up and set down as intervals in the working day presented themselves. The *kantha* embroideries of Bengal (see pl.76) and the many different types of domestic embroidery in Gujarat, Rajasthan and modern-day Pakistan (see pls 70–3) are cases in point. It is noticeable that the V&A's holdings of domestic embroideries from these areas derive from individual collectors, often women, who had access to these pieces and built up personal collections, rather than from male collectors. The India Museum's emissary Caspar Purdon Clarke, who in 1881–2 trawled the bazaars for objects for the collection (or had pieces brought to him by

runners), brought back around 700 textiles, but did not acquire any Bengali *kanthas* or western Indian domestic embroidery, which would have remained unseen by him in village houses. The same applied to the international exhibitions from which much of the Museum's collection was acquired: the pieces sent for display were made by professional male weavers, printers and embroiderers, some of whom are named in the exhibition catalogues, on labels or, in some cases, on the pieces themselves (see pl.64). The names of female makers rarely appear on textiles except for occasional embroideries, notably Bengali *kanthas*.[9]

TEXTILES AND RELIGION

The use of cloth permeates the religious practice of all faiths in India, from its basic form as unwoven thread, through simple cloths and saris offered to local deities, to the most elaborate decorated hangings for display in major temples. The sacred thread worn across their chests by Brahmins (pl.83); the coloured yarn wrapped around the wrists of worshippers, the trunks of venerated trees or the grilles of revered tombs and shrines (pl.84); and the tied cord of a married woman's *mangalsutra* marriage necklace all illustrate the symbolic power of the unwoven thread, especially when knotted, to protect against spiritual pollution and to consolidate vows. Textiles with designs created by tying, using *bandhani* and ikat techniques, are in certain regions especially favoured for cloth

83
**A group of Brahmins
with sacred thread**
Chennai, 2005

seen as auspicious, particularly as gifts to family members or temples. Saris and other cloths are traditionally donated to temples, either to drape around images of deities or simply as offerings, which may be returned, after being blessed, to the owner or resold in aid of the temple. These cloth donations may range from the simplest cotton square to the most elaborate *zari*-embellished hanging or sari, depending on the level of patronage involved. Outside the Jagannath temple at Puri, Odisha, for example, simple cotton cloths of three different colours are on sale for a few rupees each, each colour to be presented to a different member of the Jagannath triad.

Textiles made for use within religious institutions often perform more specific functions than these donations by individual devotees. Islam, Jainism and Christianity all use textiles for religious purposes to some extent, but Hinduism, India's dominant religion, provides us with the widest range of textiles for sacred or ritual use.

Perhaps the most immediately striking of these textiles, because of the large scale of the pieces involved as well as their very public display, are those used for narrative storytelling. While many of these cloths tell the *Ramayana* story,[10] other local myths also appear. The huge Gangamma cloths of Andhra Pradesh, for example (pl.86), tell the story of the local hero Katamaraju and his clan. Interspersed with this specifically

located story are well-known episodes from broader Hindu myth, such as the Churning of the Milky Ocean, while at the centre looms the imposing figure of the clan's tutelary deity Gangamma, in whose honour the saga is recited. Textiles like this are hand-drawn in the *kalamkari* process, allowing the artist freedom – within the constraints of the narrative and its traditional iconography – to create an individual and unique work. The creation of these hangings is considered a devotional act, and the finished textiles are treated with reverence equivalent to that shown to three-dimensional images of deities. Their format, in registers of episodes from the appropriate myth, is clearly linked to wall paintings in south Indian temples (pl.85). They were hung on walls that did not have such paintings, or were used as screens on the wooden *ratha* (chariots) that carried the temple images on their periodic processions through temple towns.[11] An exceptional embroidered and appliquéd hanging (pl.87) confirms that these large hangings were also on occasion made in techniques other than *kalamkari*.

Episodes in the life of the Hindu god Krishna, the eighth incarnation or *avatara* of Vishnu, provide a huge store of imagery for use in textiles, as also in painting. *Pichhwais*, the hangings that are placed behind images of Krishna (the name means 'placed behind'), usually depict one event or period in the deity's life as a human incarnation, most often from his

84
Cotton thread and plastic strips tied to the grille of a Hindu shrine
Orchha, Madhya Pradesh, 2013

youth in Vrindavan, in which he worked as a cowherd and
caused all the female cowherds (*gopis*) to fall in love with him.
These *gopis* often appear on either side of Krishna, or flanking
a tree symbolizing his presence (pl.88). Some *pichhwais*
allude to specific festivals associated with Krishna, such as
the Gopashtami, when he became a fully-fledged cowherd
(pl.89), or seasons, such as those with cooling lotus-pond
images, to be displayed at the height of summer.[12] Traditionally,
pichhwais would be changed according to the season or festival,
with generic summer or winter cloths being installed during
intervals between specific festivals. The majority of *pichhwais*
are pigment-painted on cotton, but some special commissions
from the Deccan are dyed using resist and mordant techniques
(pl.88). Gujarati examples may be embroidered in fine chain
stitch on silk (pl.89) and others, also from Gujarat, loom-woven
in silk and metal-wrapped thread with images of Krishna, the
gopis and their cows (pl.90).

85
**Narrative wall painting in
the Narumpunatha temple**
Tiruppudaimarudur, Tamil
Nadu, probably 17th century

86
**Temple hanging of the
goddess Gangamma**
Machilipatnam, Andhra
Pradesh, ascribed to
Koppala Subbarayudu of

Irapalli, 1881–2
Cotton, mordant-dyed
(*kalamkari*)
373 × 195.5 cm
V&A: IS.1759–1883

EMBROIDERED TEMPLE HANGING

This immense and magnificent temple hanging portrays scenes from the *Ramayana*, highlighting the deeds of Hanuman, the greatest devotee of Rama, the seventh incarnation of Vishnu.[1] The selection of episodes is based on the *Kishkinda* and *Sunder khanda* (Books 4 and 5) of the *Ramayana*. The central field has seven panels, and two long continuous border panels run along the top and bottom. These are all indigo-dyed, appliquéd and embroidered in cotton thread with figurative designs, and they are divided by red panels (now faded to brown), with floral, geometric designs, appliqué work and fish motifs.[2] The hanging is embroidered with a remarkable variety of stitches including running, stem, satin, herringbone, filling, couching, cross, Sindhi, long-short, chain, French knot and feather stitch.

The largest panel, in the centre, depicts the *Ramapattaabhishek*, in which Rama assumes the kingship of Ayodhya (detail A). The crowned and bejewelled Rama and his wife Sita sit on a lotus throne, under the canopy of the Naga king Sheshanaga; Hanuman sits below Rama's right foot. On either side of the couple are saints performing the *jalabhisheka* (coronation with [holy] water), attendants holding *chauris* (fly whisks) and umbrellas; the monkey king Sugriva and other courtiers are also present. In the adjacent panel, on the left, the three-headed, four-armed god Brahma holds a *kamandalu* (spouted vessel) and rosary in two of his hands (B). Next to him is a two-armed human chieftain, embroidered with a red face, holding a sword. The last panel at the left shows the two-armed figure of Jaya, one of the two mythical gatekeepers (*dvarapala*) of Vishnu's heavenly abode, Vaikuntha. The other gatekeeper, Vijaya, is shown on the opposite side of the hanging. Both Jaya and Vijaya are shown with one foot raised over a snake and holding a *gada* (mace). To the right of the central panel the four-armed god Indra holds a *vajra* (thunderbolt) and trident(?); his upper body shows the eyes that appeared on his body due to the curse of the *apsara* Tilottama after he had looked at her disrespectfully. The chieftain and Vijaya figures, next to him, are similar to their counterparts on the opposite side.

The upper and lower border panels illustrate eleven episodes from the *Ramayana*. The depiction starts and ends with a four-armed, seated Yoga Narasimha.[3] The upper border panel narration mainly concerns the story of the monkey chiefs Bali and Sugriva and starts (from left to right) with Sugriva's home; the first meeting of Hanuman with Rama and Lakshman (C); the friendship between Rama and Sugriva; Rama killing the buffalo demon Dodunbhi and his demonstration of shooting through seven trees (*sapta-tal-vriksha*); the discussion between Rama and Bali; the fight between Bali and Sugriva; the death of Bali; the anguish of Bali's wife Tara, and finally Sugriva's coronation. The lower border narrative starts with Rama advising Sugriva, then shows Hanuman's journey; his meetings with the bear Jambhavanta, a Muni (saint), the eagle Sampati the brother of Jatayu, the winged under-sea mountain Mainakam and Sursa the mother of snakes (D); Hanuman's fight with Lankani (the female guardian of Lanka, Ravana's

capital); Hanuman searching for Sita in the palaces of Lanka; his meeting with Sita in *ashok vatika* (the garden where Sita was kept); Hanuman destroying *ashok vatika*; his fight with Megnath; Hanuman at Ravana's court; his meeting with Sita; and ending with Hanuman giving news of Sita to Rama. Hanuman's appearance[4] in such detail in most of the scenes suggests that the patron was a great devotee of Hanuman.[5]

The line work of the centre panels resembles the temple stone sculptures of the Vijaynagar and Nayaka periods (sixteenth to eighteenth centuries) and wall paintings of that region.[6] The composition shows many classical features of Tamil Nadu paintings and folk features of the *Yaksha-Gana* performance of the Karnataka region. The piece's great size, the selection of episodes and its creative execution suggests that this temple hanging was a commission by a ruler or chieftain of the Nayaka period, perhaps to decorate a Vaishnava temple. **AP**

87

Temple hanging depicting scenes from the *Ramayana*
Karnataka or Tamil Nadu,
Nayaka period, last quarter
of the 18th century
Cotton, embroidered
with cotton thread and
appliqué decoration
205 x 1040 cm
National Museum of India,
New Delhi, 62.538

1 Published in Welch 1985, p.41; Mittal 2004, p.31 (dated by Jagdish Mittal to c.1700, and attributed to the Tamil Nadu–Andhra Pradesh border).
2 134 small fish motifs are embroidered in indigo thread with white outlines. The fish shape is similar to the fish that appeared on many coins issued by the Madurai Nayaka rulers. The National Museum of India also has a square copper Nayaka coin, which depicts a similar style of fish motif.
3 Many Yoga Narasimha sculptures are in the temples of Hampi, Vijaynagar. One giant monolithic granite image of Yoga Narasimha, carved out of a single boulder, was commissioned by Krishnadeva in AD 1528. See Sen Gupta 2010, p.195.

4 Hanuman is shown with a particular kind of hair bun, which is knotted from the middle with the pointed end portion turned upwards. Interestingly this represents the typical hairstyle of Brahmans of Tamil Nadu and Andhra Pradesh, where it is known as kudumi.
5 Portraying royalty, nobles, chieftains or patrons in artworks was a popular trend among the Vijaynagar and Nayaka rulers. See Sharma 1992, p.286, pl.206.
6 Mahalingam 2012, pp.138–9; Sivaramamurti 1985, pp.52–4; Vyas and Daljeet 1988.

A Central panel depicting Ramapattaabhishek, the coronation of Rama when he returned to Ayodhya after 14 years of exile after defeating Ravana, king of Lanka.

B Brahma with four arms and three heads stands under an arch on the right side of Ramapattaabhishek panel. He holds a rosary and water vessel in two hands while the other two hands are folded, and stands facing Rama.

C (top) A scene from
the upper portion of the
hanging depicts Hanuman
as a Brahmin standing
in front of Rama and
Lakshman. He is identified
by his distinctive hair bun
(*kudumi*).

D (bottom) A scene from
the lower border of the
hanging depicts Hanuman's
meeting with the winged
Mountain Mainakam, who
is depicted partly in human
form.

88
**Hanging (*pichhwai*)
for a Krishna shrine**
Deccan, 18th century
Cotton, mordant-dyed,
resist-dyed and gilded
73 x 81 cm
Chhatrapati Shivaji Maharaj
Vastu Sangrahalaya,
Mumbai, 63.34

Pichhwais are particularly associated with Rajasthan (especially the Shrinathji shrine at Nathadwara) and Gujarat, as well as some areas of the Deccan settled by Gujarati traders who follow the *Pushtimarg* (Path of Grace) founded by Vallabhacharya. In Assam the worship of Krishna inspired very different types of textile, most notably a group of remarkable woven silks depicting scenes from Krishna's life, images of other *avataras* of Vishnu and individual episodes from the *Ramayana* (see pl.65). The ordering and making of the original silk fabric, often called the *Vrindavani vastra* (Cloth of Vrindavan), is known from Assamese texts that tell of Prince Chilarai commissioning the piece from the Assamese saint and reformer Shankaradeva in about 1565.[13] The tradition of weaving silk hangings depicting aspects of the Krishna story persisted in Assam until the nineteenth century, but the imagery and weaving became progressively cruder over time. However, a small number of pieces survive that are of such high quality that they may be remnants of Shankaradeva's original weaving (see pl.65).[14] It is not known precisely how these cloths would have been used in Assamese Vaishnavite ritual, but present-day *sattras* (Assamese monasteries with congregational halls) use textiles to wrap images and to drape

over sacred stands for the holy text of the *Bhagavad Gita*, and it is likely that the *Vrindavani vastra* would also have been used in such a way. Today the textiles used in the *sattras* are the simpler but distinctive Assamese woven red and white cotton *gamusa* (cotton cloth), but it is likely that these could have been of silk, and more elaborately decorated, at an earlier period.

The *avataras* of Vishnu appear in another rare textile from northeast India: a tapestry-woven silk shawl from Manipur that would probably have been used by a Hindu priest (pl.91). This technique, relatively uncommon in India, is thought to have originated in Manipur (see pl.54) but is now more associated with neighbouring Burma, where it is used especially in the *acheik* or *luntaya* technique used for silk sarongs. The Manipuri shawls are associated with the Vaishnavite Hindu Meitei community, so it is appropriate that their ritual shawls should be decorated with the incarnations of Vishnu and the names *Hare Krishna*.

The use of the names of deities as decoration on ritual textiles is widespread in India but especially so in eastern and northeast India. Bengali cotton shawls called *namabali* (row of names), printed with the names of Radha and Krishna, and Baluchari saris with woven inscriptions of the same names are

89
**Part of a hanging
(*pichhwai*) for
a Krishna shrine**
Saurashtra, Gujarat,
late 19th century
Cotton, embroidered
with silk
158 x 151 cm
V&A: IS.40-1977

90
**Panel from a hanging
(*pichhwai*)**
Ahmedabad or Surat,
Gujarat, 19th century
Silk and metal-wrapped
thread
25.5 x 25.5 cm
Dehejia Collection
of Krishna Art

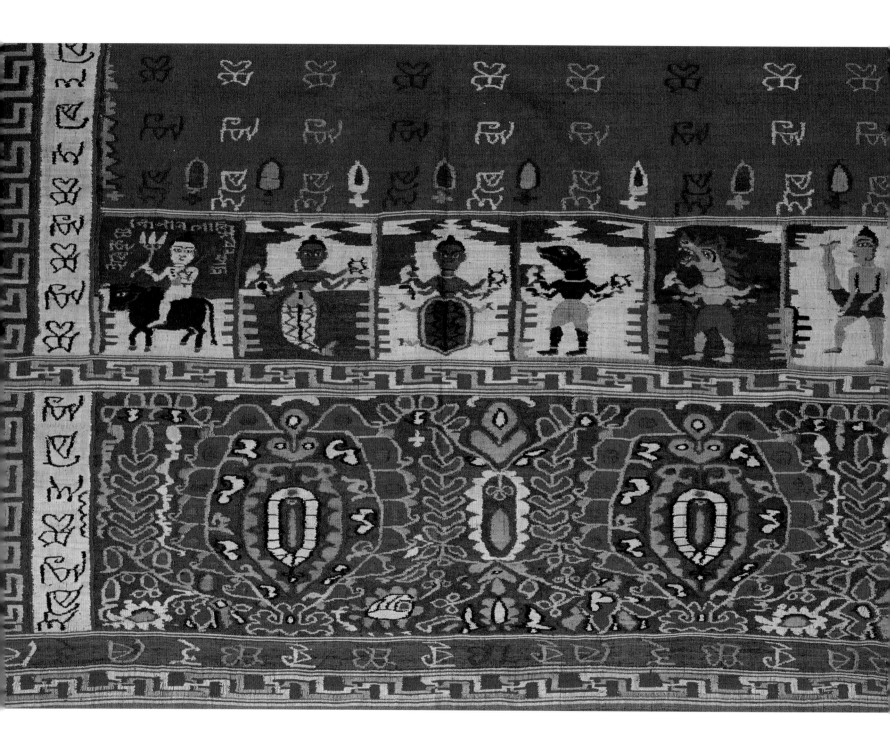

91
**Shawl with avatars
of Vishnu** (detail)
Manipur, 19th century
Silk, tapestry-woven
280.4 x 74.9 cm
Philadelphia Museum of Art,
1991-37-1

cases in point (pl.92). A rather small number of Kashmir shawls also occur with ritual names woven into them: one in Bengali script with the 10 names of the goddess Kali, and several with Devanagari inscriptions praising the Vishvanath temple in Varanasi.[15] The *gamusas* of the Assamese *sattras* have the name of Rama woven into them, and the ikat *Gita Govinda* cloths of Odisha go even further, as they include whole verses of the sacred text in shawls to be worn by priests at the Jagannath temple in Puri.[16] A similar use of woven text occurs in some examples of the Assamese *Vrindavani vastra* mentioned above: while the majority of these pieces have simple woven names identifying the figures, an exceptionally large hanging in the British Museum has whole verses by Shankaradeva woven into the panels.[17]

Other religious textiles, such as the printed *Mata ni pachedi* or *chandarvo* of the Vagri community in Gujarat, are part of the worship of specific local deities (pl.93).[18] Large hangings like these, with their episodic layout arranged in registers around a central figure, parallel similar imagery painted on temple walls. They presumably developed using local textile techniques of hand-drawing with the *kalam* (reed pen) and dyeing (and block-printing in the case of the *Mata ni pachedi*), as portable equivalents of such wall paintings, adapted for use at festivals and ceremonies in rural locations or in locations without built temples. These portable shrines would be carried from place to place as required or when a ritual had been commissioned, and they blur the boundary between textiles and painting, as do the painted cloths (*phad*) dedicated to the Rajasthani heroes Pabuji and Devnarayan.[19] Comparable but smaller-scale painted narratives on paper scrolls have traditionally been used in many parts of India in ritual practice, with West Bengal historically being one of the richest areas for this kind of material.[20]

Among India's other religious traditions, Buddhism is the only one to have flourished outside its country of origin rather than within it. Buddhism was essentially obliterated in India by the twelfth century AD, as a result of a combination of factors that included the rise of Hindu Brahmanism and a succession of invasions by Huns and, most importantly, Muslims, who conquered the last remaining Buddhist dynasty, that of the Pala-Senas, in the twelfth century. Buddhism flourished, however, in Tibet and Nepal along with Indian trade to those areas, and textiles were sent over the Himalayas for use in

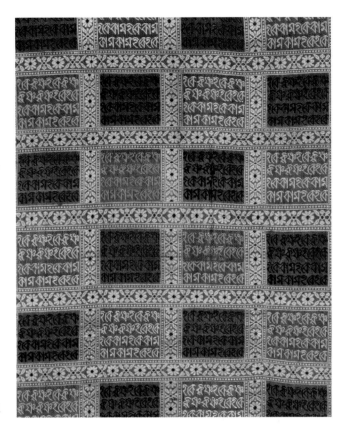

temples and monasteries. While some of these were clearly designed to appeal to Buddhist cultures – by using the lotus roundel (see pl.63), for example – other rather surprising choices such as the overtly Hindu *Vrindavani vastra* (see pl.65) were also used in Tibetan and Bhutanese temples, as canopies, screens and backings for *tangkas* (Tibetan Buddhist religious paintings). This seemingly indiscriminate use of a textile clearly associated with Hinduism in a Buddhist context may seem odd, but imported rarities such as Indian woven silks were highly prized and were seen as appropriate objects for high-status usage such as temple hangings, whatever their visual imagery. Almost all of these early silks were found in Tibet (pl.104, and see pls 61–3), as were most of the other early silks, and the lotus piece (see pl.63) was almost certainly woven with Buddhist patronage in mind, either as a canopy or a wall hanging. Fabric panels attached to the ceiling in Himalayan Buddhist temples

92

***Namabali* (row of names) shawl with woven inscription:** *Hare Krishna Hare Krishna/Krishna Krishna Hare Hare/Hare Rama Hare Rama/Rama Rama/Hare Hare*

Murshidabad district, West Bengal, 19th century
Woven silk
251.8 x 123.2 cm
TAPI Collection, India, 00.76

93
**Temple cloth (*Mata
ni pachedi* or *mata
ni chandarvo*)**
Ahmedabad, c.1967
Printed and dyed cotton
138 x 275 cm
V&A: IS.6–1967

such as those at Tabo and Alchi are painted with designs clearly imitating elaborate silk textiles of this kind.[21] Other early woven silks with lotus roundels have also been discovered in Tibet and are now in museum collections.[22] Textiles made for the Tibetan and wider Himalayan market (including Tibetan communities in India) continue to be made in Varanasi today. Called *gyasar*, a term probably derived from the Tibetan for 'Indian gold fabric', these are heavy woven silks with metal-wrapped thread in designs based on Tibetan and Chinese auspicious motifs and religious figures, although some modern *gyasar* seem to show the rather surprising influence of Italian Renaissance woven silks.[23]

Jainism is a religion that developed around the same time as Buddhism in about the third century BC and shares several of its key doctrines, especially an adherence to non-violence. The austerity that marks out Jain practice is reflected in the relative scarcity of decorated objects in a Jain shrine or home, and the extreme simplicity, or even complete absence, of the clothing of religious figures. One of the earliest surviving pieces of Indian embroidery is a narrow band decorated with compartments in which are seated eight goddesses (*vidyadevis* or goddesses of learning) (pl.95). It is thought that this embroidered strip and its companion pieces in the Calico Museum of Textiles in Ahmedabad and the Jagdish and Kamla Mittal Museum, Hyderabad,[24] were given to a Jain nun or nuns on their initiation, perhaps to wrap around manuscripts or the brush that they always carry to sweep small insects out of their path, or perhaps to hang behind the platform where Jain religious leaders held discussions.[25] The style of drawing of the goddess figures is clearly that of fifteenth- and sixteenth-century Gujarat, with their pointed noses and use of the 'projecting eye' (see pl.162). Other decorative textiles are few in Jain ritual – later embroidered book covers are minor examples[26] and elaborate hangings (called *puthiya*: 'backdrop') decorated with metal-thread embroidery used as backdrops for monks delivering sermons are more recent expressions of patronage from well-off merchant donors (pl.96).[27]

Textiles play a prominent role in Islamic tradition. Islam has been practised in South Asia at least since the conquest of Sindh by Arab forces in AD 712, and Muslim culture has had a huge and pervasive influence across the subcontinent. The ritual use of textiles is seen across the

SHRINE FLAG

A figure lies bleeding in the centre of a packed scene. Surrounded by chaos, a lone mourner weeps over the body (right). Spectacularly rendered in cotton appliqué on a huge double-sided flag, the figures depict a scene from the story of Sayyid Salar Mas'ud, or Ghazi Miyan, an eleventh-century Muslim warrior saint. The legend of his martyrdom varies widely in its details, but it is generally believed that the 19-year-old Ghazi ('holy warrior') died in battle on the eve of his marriage, in around 1033–4. He is venerated by both Muslims and Hindus as a miracle worker, credited with posthumously curing ailments ranging from blindness to leprosy. At his annual *mela* (fair) thousands of Muslim and Hindu pilgrims visit the Ghazi's *dargah* (shrine) in Bahraich, Uttar Pradesh. It is a long tradition: records of this pilgrimage go back as far as the fourteenth century.[1]

Some carry multicoloured flags on their journey as devotional offerings in exchange for the Ghazi's intercession. At the close of each festival the flags of those pilgrims whose prayers are answered are auctioned, the proceeds used to fund the operations of the *dargah*.[2] This flag was acquired sometime after 1896 by A.W. Richardson of the North-Western Provinces Indian Police, whose cantonment had adopted Ghazi as their patron saint.[3] It was donated to the V&A in 1912.

Complete with attached pole cover, the flag is remarkable for the strong effect of its appliqué portraying the Ghazi's final battle and death. On one side of the flag the body of the Ghazi is centrally depicted as bleeding from the head and body, while all around him both sides of the flag are crammed with soldiers, cow-herders, water-carriers, animals, blooming trees and shrine structures. An early-twentieth-century observer described a similar but even larger flag, 40 feet long by 15 feet wide, as 'a wonder of small figures of ridiculous conception ... carried on a bamboo, erect, the whole 38 miles and back again, by admiring devotees'.[4]

Often referred to as *kanduri* cloths (from the Persian for 'tablecloth'), appliquéd Ghazi Miyan banners have usually been associated with *kanduri* food rituals.[5]

Though the term *kanduri* can refer generally to a saint's festival, evidence suggests that more appropriate terms for these cloths would be *'alam* or *nishan,* meaning 'standard' or 'banner'.[6] Though there are many surviving twentieth-century examples of such Ghazi Miyan appliqués, the V&A's is especially impressive for its scale, double-sided construction and age. **AF**

1 Suvorova 2004, pp.158–60.
2 Schwerin 1984, pp.149–51.
3 Temple 1884, vol.1, p.98.
4 Rockey 1913, p.253, as quoted in Schwerin 1984, p.150.
5 Finn 2014, pp.192–9.
6 Mahmood 1989, p.35.

94 (opposite)
Shrine flag ('alam or nishan)
Uttar Pradesh, c.1896–1910
Cotton appliqué
404 x 347 cm (body)
Given by Alexander
William Richardson
V&A: IM.32-1912

Above: Detail showing the death of Ghazi Miyan and his grieving general.
Right: The other side of the flag.

Muslim world: its focal point, the Kaaba in Mecca, is itself traditionally draped in embroidered hangings, and Muslim tombs are covered with silk cloths, which are also often suspended above them as canopies. Flags, standards and banners have been carried to glorify the faith since the early caliphates of the Middle East, and this usage has continued in South Asia: flags are frequently carried in religious processions, sometimes being planted in front of their destination. Banners placed outside both Hindu and Muslim shrines are a common sight across the region, although few are as large as the V&A's appliquéd example from the shrine of Salar Mas'ud in Bahraich (pl.94).

Prayer in Islam involves kneeling and touching the forehead to the floor, and prayer mats and carpets are used to provide a clean surface for worshippers wherever they might be performing *namaz* (prayer). At home or when travelling, Muslims use their own personal prayer mat or carpet. In mosques the floor itself or the floor covers laid over it are often divided into sections indicating the space for one person to kneel in (pl.98). The joined strips used in congregational mosques throughout the Islamic world are known by the Arabic word *saf* (row). A great many were produced in Machilipatnam in southeast India (pl.99), probably for use in Iran rather than in India itself, as the floral design is of the type used there for furnishings and dress.

The written word, especially that of the Quran, is hugely important in Islam, and calligraphy is revered in the Muslim world as one of the highest art forms. Images of living things have traditionally been avoided in Muslim religious contexts such as on mosques and tombs or in religious texts,

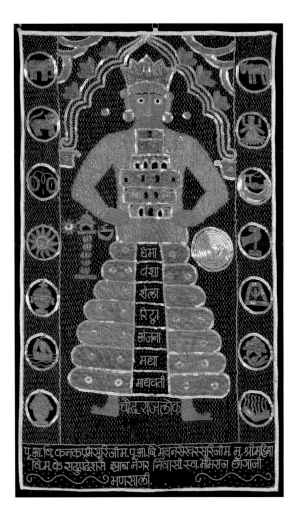

95
Embroidered panel
(and detail opposite)
Gujarat, *c.* 16th century
Cotton with silk embroidery
and couched *kusha* grass
126 x 15 cm
Musée national des arts
asiatiques – Guimet, from
the Riboud Collection,
MA 5684

96
**Hanging (*puthiya*)
for a Jain temple**
Gujarat, 20th century
Velvet with metal-wrapped
thread embroidery
142 x 83 cm
V&A: IS.2-2015

although human and animal forms are freely used in secular art and decoration. Verses (*suras*) of the Quran are used on a monumental scale as an integral part of the decoration of mosques and tombs (the Taj Mahal is perhaps the most famous example), and are also written in smaller scale on objects used in mosques such as lamps, woven into carpet borders, and inscribed on banners and protective garments. An adaptation of manuscript illumination of the pre-Mughal Sultanate period was used for the calligraphy and decoration of protective or talismanic garments (pl.97). These simple tunics, imbued with the power of the Quranic text, would be worn under battle dress for protection. Variations of the type are known from other parts of the Islamic world, especially Ottoman Turkey, but the style of decoration of this piece, as well as the Bihari script used in the border inscriptions, can be specifically linked to Indian Quran manuscripts of the fifteenth and early sixteenth centuries.[28]

Manuscripts also provided the source material for the iconography of hangings made on the Coromandel Coast of southeast India for use by Armenian Christians, both in India and at their settlement in New Julfa, outside Isfahan in Iran (pls 100, 102). Armenian merchants had been active in Indian trade since at least the sixteenth century, and became more prominent in the subcontinent with the foundation of New Julfa in 1605.[29] As well as trading from Bengal and Gujarat, Armenians were significant in the south Indian textile trade, operating mainly from the port town of Machilipatnam. They

dealt primarily in printed and dyed cotton textiles for export to Iran (pl.99, and see pl.151), but they would also have been aware of the elaborate hand-drawn and resist-dyed and mordant-dyed chintzes that were being made along the coast for local use and for export to Europe. The hand-drawn outlines and expert dyeing used in the chintz technique allow naturalistic and complex designs to be created (as opposed to the repeat designs used in block-printing), and it is therefore well suited to the hanging (pl.102) and the priest's vestment called a *p'orurar*

97 (left)
Talismanic shirt
India, late 15th or early 16th century
Cotton, inscribed and painted in ink and red and gold paint
Length: 64 cm
Given by Col. F.G.G. Bailey
V&A: T.59–1935

98 (above)
Interior of Shah Jahan's mosque showing prayer mats in use
Located within the Dargah Sharif complex, Ajmer, Rajasthan

99
**Length of joined
prayer mats**
Machilipatnam, Andhra
Pradesh, c.1881–2
Cotton, resist-dyed,
mordant-dyed and block-
printed
91.4 x 452 cm
V&A: IS.1761–1883

in Armenian (pl.100). Christ's Crucifixion is depicted on the hanging, and the Descent from the Cross and Entombment on the smaller vestment. A considerable number of other chintz hangings made in India for Armenian churches survive, both in Iran and in Armenia itself, as well as in Jerusalem (pl.101), although these may have been brought at a later date from Iran or India. Several of these are impressively large altar curtains, some of which bear dedicatory inscriptions, and date from the second half of the eighteenth century.[30] Textiles made for other Christian communities in India, such as the Catholics in Goa, the Syrian Christians in Kerala, or the more recently converted Protestant Christians of the northeast, have tended to follow the forms and decorative techniques of their originating Christian Church, such as the predominantly Portuguese-style vestments historically used in Goa.[31] They incorporate few, if any, elements of their adopted Indian culture, unlike the Armenian market pieces that draw on the chintz technique of southeast India and combine it with Armenian imagery.

South Indian *kalamkari* artists have in recent years started to incorporate Christian imagery into their repertoire of hangings, following the format of traditional Hindu narrative temple cloths, but these are purely decorative rather than for use in Christian churches.[32]

100 (left)
Stole (*p'orurar*) for an Armenian church
Coromandel Coast, late 18th century
Cotton, mordant-dyed and resist-dyed (chintz)
145 x 57 cm
V&A IS.2-1953

101 (above)
An Indian chintz choir curtain, dated 1789, in use on the altar of the Armenian church of Saint Toros in the Monastery of St James in Jerusalem

102 (opposite)
Hanging for an Armenian church
Coromandel Coast, c.1760–80
Cotton, mordant-dyed and resist-dyed (chintz)
139 x 101 cm
V&A: IS.3-1953

TEXTILES FOR THE COURTS

Many textiles made for everyday use or for presentation to
religious institutions were skilfully and often beautifully
made, but the creation of the most remarkable pieces required
patronage at the highest level. Historically this was provided
mainly by rulers and their chief courtiers. Laborious, time-
consuming techniques combined with costly materials and dyes
are evident in the finest textiles made for use in Indian courts,
especially those of the Mughals, but also to a lesser extent
those of the Deccani sultanates, north Indian Rajputs and the
Marathas of Central and south India.

We can gain an impression of the immense scale and
superb quality of the textiles made for the various courts
from the accounts of visitors, both foreign and local, from the
pre-Mughal Sultanate period to the nineteenth century. We
know, for example, that in the royal *karkhanas* (workshops) of
Muhammad bin Tughluq (r.1325–51) in Delhi there were '4,000
silk workers who weave and embroider different kinds of cloth
for robes of honour and garments', even though no textiles of
the period survive.[33] A small number of complex-weave silks
from a little later in the pre-Mughal period survive (pls 103, 104,
and see pls 61–3), giving an idea of the richness of materials and
technical skill available to Sultanate-period patrons.

The French doctor François Bernier, who was
attached to the Mughal court from 1658 to 1669, described
the 'consumption of fine cloths of gold and brocades, silks,
embroideries' in the Mughal harem as 'greater than can be
conceived'.[34] Mughal textiles survive in greater number than
those of the Sultanate period, but much of our knowledge of
the contexts in which they were made and used comes from
travellers' accounts such as Bernier's, written records by local
historians and the minutely detailed paintings done by Mughal
court artists between about 1590 and 1800.

The *A'in-i-Akbari* (Institutes of Akbar) is an account
of the organization of every department of Emperor Akbar's
court. Completed in the mid-1590s by the emperor's minister
and confidant Abu'l-Fazl 'Allami, it is exceptionally rich in
information about textiles at the court. The 32nd *A'in* is called
the *A'in-i shal* (shawl cloth) but its remit is far wider than shawls,
as it lists all the types of cloth in the royal storerooms, divided
into such headings as 'gold stuffs', silks, cotton and woollen cloths.
These lists include fabrics made in *karkhanas*, those purchased

103 (opposite)
Hanging
Probably Gujarat, *c.* 16th
century
Silk, lampas weave
172 × 111 cm
Metropolitan Museum of
Art, New York, 1991.347.1

104
Part of a hanging
Probably Gujarat, *c.* 16th
century
Silk, lampas weave
202 × 63 cm
Nasser D. Khalili Collection of
Islamic Art, TXT 013

TENT HANGING

This is one of only three known Indian lampas-woven *qanat* (tent panels) featuring near life-size human figures.[1] The first to come to light, now in the Los Angeles County Museum of Art, displays the image of a young male courtier holding a wine cup, drafted in a late sixteenth-century Safavid Iranian style (pl.105). The present example features a female doorkeeper or guard wearing late Akbar-period dress, holding a staff in one hand and a short whip in the other (pl.107). The most recently discovered of the group, now in the David Collection in Copenhagen, depicts a dhoti-clad man playing cymbals (pl.106). All three panels have been woven in the same complex lampas weave; the spandrel decoration in the cusped arch above each woven figure is the same, and their function as individual parts of a *qanat* – a decorative cloth screen – is also identical.

Lampas weaves are so technically complex that they can only be woven on a drawloom (see p.54). Drawlooms were invented to repeat identical patterns, but the larger the size of each pattern unit, the more time and skill it takes the pattern-maker (*naqshband*) to create. This panel and its two companions were made using some of the largest single pattern units in the history of lampas-weaving and could only have been created through patronage at the highest level.

Qanats were formed by joining several individual panels together, creating long horizontal screens of any length. We can assume that these luxurious silk panels were originally accompanied by even more components – either identical mirror images or panels displaying different large figures. The subject matter, style and dress shown in these three pieces suggest that they were designed at different times, ranging from the late sixteenth century to the first few decades of the seventeenth. They therefore appear to be remnants of three different *qanat* sets originally consisting of more individual panels. Whether all the others were figurative or were alternated with floral or even plain panels we do not know. However, surviving Mughal-period lampas-woven, velvet, embroidered and chintz *qanats*, in addition to those depicted in miniature paintings, prove that all of these arrangements are possible. **SC**

1   Cohen 2014, pp.170–99; Jain 2013, pp.26–30; Jain 2011a, pp.64–7.

105
Tent hanging
Mughal India, probably
Gujarat, c. late 16th century
Silk, lampas weave
195.5 x 121.28 cm
Los Angeles County
Museum of Art, M73.5.702

106
Tent hanging
Mughal India, probably
Gujarat, c.1600–20
Silk, lampas weave
201.8 x 95.8 cm
David Collection,
Copenhagen, 19/2011

107 (opposite)
Tent hanging
Mughal India, probably
Gujarat, c.1575–1600
Silk, lampas weave
151 x 77 cm
Nasser D. Khalili Collection of
Islamic Art, TXT 017

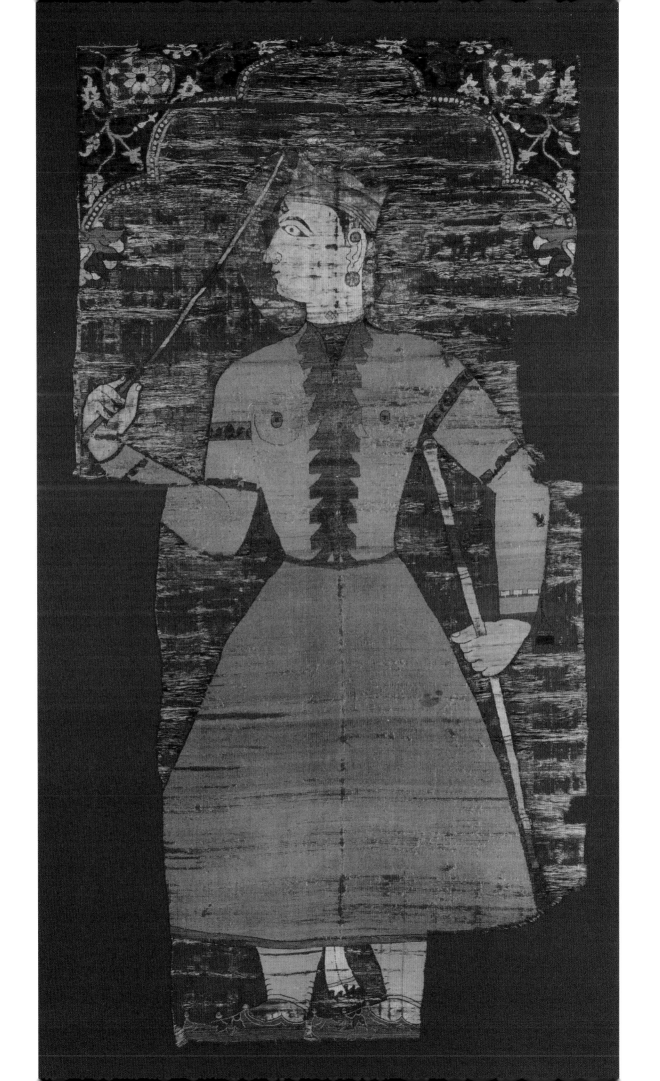

or given as gifts from other parts of Akbar's lands in India, and textiles from Iran, Turkey, Europe and China. The same chapter describes the hierarchy of colours by which pieces were stored, from 'ruby-coloured' to the more dusky greys and lilacs, while *A'in* 31 recounts how the emperor liked to invent new styles of dress, new terminology and new ways of wearing existing garments.[35]

The illustrations to the *Akbarnama*, the historical narrative of Akbar's reign, give a sense of the lavish use of textiles at the court, especially the tents and cloth screens (*qanats* or *saraparda*: see pl.117). Moreover, paintings done for Akbar's successors Jahangir (r.1605–27) and Shah Jahan (r.1627–55) provide us with remarkably detailed visual references for all kinds of dress and furnishings at the seventeenth-century Mughal court (pls 112, 120).[36] The main item of court dress for men was a long robe (*jama*) with a diagonal tied fastening, a style that came originally from Central Asia (pl.108). Akbar had decreed that the

jama should fasten on the right side for Muslims and the left for Hindus, a directive that seems to have been observed with surprising frequency, and has become a helpful aid to distinguishing between Muslim and Hindu courtiers depicted in paintings. Woven or embroidered patterned silk and printed cotton textiles were used for both upper garments (pls 109, 111) and the trousers worn with them, and decorative sashes (*patka*), often of lavish silk and gold, were tied around the waist (pls 121, 122). Fine Kashmir goat-hair shawls were used as upper garments by both men and women (pls 114–6, and see pl.17). Female courtiers are rarely shown in Mughal paintings (women who do appear are usually servants or dancers rather than members of the royal household), but from generic images of women included in Mughal albums we know that female dress at the Mughal court also consisted of trousers under a diaphanous robe, usually open at the front (pls 124, 125), with a large head-cover falling down the back for Muslim women.

108
Man's robe (*jama*), waist-sash and shoulder-cloth
Mughal, mid-18th century; worn by Captain John Foote, c.1761
Cotton, embroidered
with floss silk and metal-wrapped thread
Robe length: 153 cm; sash: 559 × 41 cm; shoulder-cloth: 256 × 51 cm
York Art Gallery, 2003.4

109 (top)

Length of dress fabric
(detail)
Rajasthan, probably early
18th century, but with a later
ink inscription dated 1772
Cotton, block-printed
896 x 65 cm
V&A: IS.64-1978

110 (bottom)

**Velvet border from a
floor-spread** (detail)
Mughal India, probably
Gujarat, c.1650
Silk velvet with silver-
wrapped thread
35.5 x 265 cm
V&A: 320-1898

MAN'S RIDING COAT

Mughal dress for both men and women was often highly patterned, and this embroidered jacket is one of the most densely decorated Mughal garments to have survived. It is worked on white silk satin fabric in twisted silk thread using chain stitch, the signature stitch of the professional male embroiderers of the Mochi community from Kutch in Gujarat. Originally shoemakers, they adapted their expert use of the embroidery hook from leather to cloth and provided superb pieces for the Mughal court and for export to Europe from the seventeenth century onwards (see pl.173). They also continued to produce high-quality embroideries for their own community in their home in Kutch (see pl.74). The extremely high quality of this coat suggests that it was made in an imperial workshop (*karkhana*), either attached to the court itself or perhaps in Ahmedabad in Gujarat, where skilled weavers and embroiderers provided textiles for use at the Mughal court.

The design is made up of a repeating pattern that includes a pair of reclining lions, a lion hunting gazelle, naturalistic flowers and trees, a scene of ducks on a pond and a peacock in flight (detail, right). The lions, animal combats and flowering trees are mainly derived from Iranian manuscript painting, which had already assimilated Chinese elements such as the flowering plum blossom and cranes. However, the large single flowering plants – including recognizable poppies, daffodils, tulips, primroses and irises – are based on European prints that were brought to the Mughal court by the Jesuits, who sent missions to Akbar's court from 1580 onwards.

Shah Jahan (r.1627–55) is the Mughal ruler most associated with the floral motif, especially in inlaid stone decoration on buildings such as the Taj Mahal in Agra. But his father Jahangir (r.1605–27) was also very interested in the natural world: floral decoration was carved on Akbar's cenotaph in around 1612, and recent research has shown that Jahangir's court artist Mansur was already copying European floral imagery by 1616. The Europeanized floral motifs on this coat clearly reflect a familiarity with western botanical illustration.

The decoration on the coat combines the use of landscape as seen in manuscript borders of Jahangir's reign (pl.113) with the single naturalistic flowering plants that became ubiquitous under Shah Jahan. Had it been made during Shah Jahan's reign, it would surely have been decorated exclusively with these naturalistic

flower motifs, with no suggestion of a landscaped background (pls 110, 127). This coat was made at the moment when Mughal decoration was changing from the poetic, Iranian style of the Jahangir period to the more measured 'classic' style of Shah Jahan.

In his memoirs, Jahangir writes of a jacket he introduced into the Mughal court, which was already known in Iran as *kurdi* (Kurdish) but which he renamed *nadiri* (rarity) and bestowed on favoured courtiers as a robe of honour (*khilat*). He describes it as sleeveless and thigh-length – as is this piece – so this may be a unique survival of one such 'rarity'. **RC**

See further:
London 1982, cat.252; Stronge 2002, pp.172–3; Stronge 2008

111 (opposite and detail above)
Riding coat
Mughal, c.1620–5
Satin-woven silk embroidered with silk thread
Length: 100 cm
V&A: IS.18-1947

عمل منصور

112 (opposite)
***Prince Khurram
(later Shah Jahan) riding
with companions***
Mughal, by Manohar,
c.1618–20, with faces over-
painted c.1630 by Murar
Page from the Minto Album
23.6 x 16.8 cm (image)
V&A: IM.12-1925

113
**Album page with
landscape border** (details)
Mughal, Jahangir period
(1605–27)
Page from the Wantage
Album
Gold paint on blue paper
38.9 x 26.4 cm
Bequeathed by Lady
Wantage
V&A: IM.112A-1921

114 (opposite)
Shawl (detail)
Kashmir, c.1750–1800
Goat hair (pashmina),
twill tapestry weave
320 x 132 cm
TAPI Collection, India, 04.41

115 (top)
Shawl
Kashmir, late 17th century
Goat hair (pashmina),
twill tapestry weave
241 x 126 cm
Museum of Fine Arts,
Boston, 45.540

116 (bottom)
Shawl
Kashmir, c.1720,
Goat hair (pashmina),
twill tapestry weave
310.5 x 130.6 cm
TAPI Collection, India,
99.1767

117 (opposite)
***Akbar hunting within
a qamargah (enclosure)***
Mughal, by Miskina and
Sarwan, c.1586–9
Page from an *Akbarnama*
manuscript
32.1 x 18.6 cm
V&A: IS.2:55–1896

118
Hanging
Probably Ahmedabad,
Gujarat, c.1650
Silk, lampas weave
212 x 97 cm
Museum für Indische Kunst,
Berlin, I.364

119
Hanging
Mughal, made by Gujarati
embroiderers, c.1640–50.
Cotton embroidered
with silk
117 x 81.25 cm
Given by Miss F.J. Lefroy
V&A: IS.168–1950

120

Khan Dawran wearing a floral sash (patka)
Mughal, by Hashim, c.1650
Page from the Late Shah Jahan Album
21.5 x 13.7 cm (image)
Chester Beatty Library, Dublin, In 07B.36

121 (top)

Man's sash (*patka*) (detail)
Mughal, probably Gujarat,
c.1700
Silk, cotton and metal-
wrapped silk thread;
complex weave,

taqueté(?) ends and
side borders with twill
damask ground
330 x 52 cm
Museum of Fine Arts,
Boston, 66.863

122 (bottom)

Man's sash (*patka*) (detail)
Mughal, probably Gujarat,
c.1700
Silk, cotton and metal-
wrapped silk thread; samite
and taqueté with brocading
in ends and side borders;

damask, twill and plain
weave with brocading
in the field
Width: 50.5 cm
Musée national des arts
asiatiques – Guimet, from
the Riboud Collection, 5709

123
***A Hindu lady with
two peacocks***
(depiction of the musical
mode *kakubha ragini*)
Mughal, late 17th century
Page from the Small
Clive Album
32.5 x 23.5 cm (page)
Given by John Goelet
V&A: IS.48:17/B–1956

124

***A Muslim lady holding
a flower***

Mughal, late 17th century
Page from the Small
Clive Album
35.5 x 23.5 cm (page)
Given by John Goelet
V&A: IS.48:24/A–1956

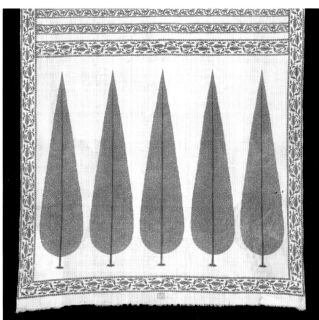

Hindu women often favoured the skirt, bodice and head-cover combination that is traditional in Rajasthan and Gujarat today (pl.123).

In the absence of most types of freestanding furniture, and also of framed paintings on the walls, textiles took on a very significant role in interiors, with hangings, floor covers, cushions and awnings providing comfort, colour, warmth and often privacy in the palace interiors. The very palaces themselves could also be made of cloth when the court was on the move – lavish tents were made for the ruler and his nobles when they went on campaign or when visiting other cities (pl.131). The royal tent usually had a plain red outer wall, while the inside would be beautifully decorated with woven, embroidered or printed floor coverings and hangings (pls 118, 119, 127, 132, and see pls 105–7). The classic Mughal design of a standing flowering plant within a cusped arch lent itself especially well to rectangular tent panels: while this motif originated in Jahangir's reign and was elaborated for use in all media from architecture to manuscript borders, it continued to be popular throughout the eighteenth century, although by this time the plants had lost most of their naturalistic appearance.

125

Woman's dress (peshwaz)
North India, c.1800–50
Cotton, with coloured
metal foil, silver-gilt strips
and sequins
Length: 140 cm
V&A: 5842 (IS)

126

Man's sash (patka) (detail)
Mughal, probably
Burhanpur, c.1700
Cotton, block-printed
and dyed
533 x 71 cm
Bequeathed by Sir Michael
Sadler
V&A: IM.94–1948

127 (opposite)

Floor-spread
Mughal India, possibly
Burhanpur, Madhya
Pradesh, c.1650
Cotton, printed, mordant-
dyed and resist-dyed
967 x 392 cm
V&A: IM.77–1938

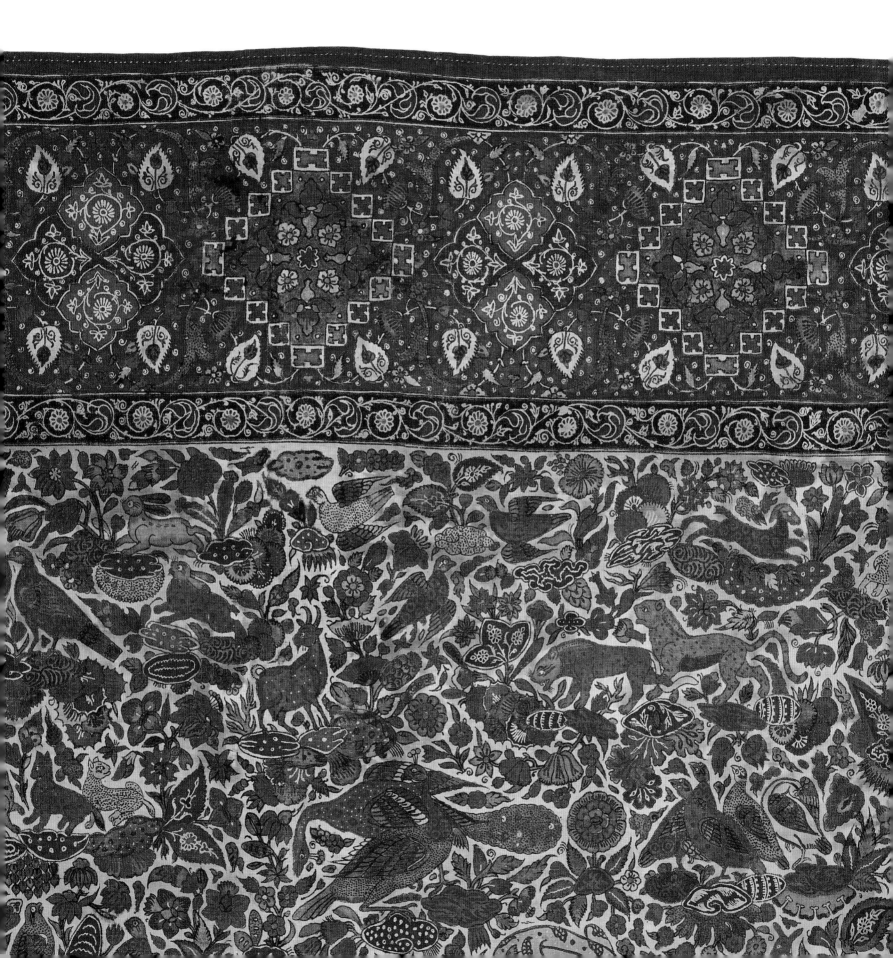

 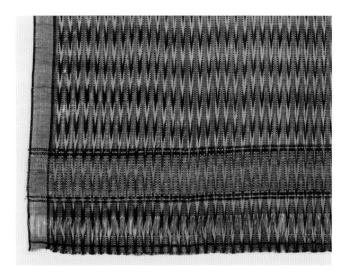

The courts of the Mughals' contemporaries in the Deccan sultanates shared many general characteristics of dress and furnishing, but textiles from this region differ in one important respect: the dominant use of resist-dyeing and mordant-dyeing on cotton as the preferred method of producing textiles for the court (pl.128). This was the complex technique perfected on the Coromandel Coast that came to be called 'chintz' when exported to Europe. While other centres such as Sironj and Burhanpur were also producing textiles in these techniques (pls 126, 127, 131), some of the finest pieces of this kind (pls 128, 129, 132) are thought to have been made for the Golconda court in the coastal area around the Krishna delta, which was under the rule of the Golconda sultans. Superb ikat textiles were also produced for the court at Hyderabad (pl.130) as well as in more vernacular forms on the southeastern coast (see pl.34).[37]

A distinctive and bold style of embroidery used on floor-spreads both for the local courts and for export to Europe was also made in the Deccan and perhaps further south (pl.134). These are in a style and technique distinctly different from Mughal embroidery, which is predominantly in fine chain stitch done with tightly twisted silk thread on a cotton ground (pl.119). The Deccani pieces by contrast favour satin stitch in floss silk, with areas of metal-wrapped thread or sometimes a background completely covered with metal-wrapped thread

embroidery. While the pieces made for export sometimes reflect contemporary floral chintz designs,[38] those made for local use are often in a format ultimately derived from Islamic book covers, with a central medallion and corner motifs (pl.134). Other examples, presumably for Hindu patrons, include elements such as planetary or zodiacal figures.[39]

Hindu courts such as those of the Rajputs and the Marathas also had their own cultures, which included the use of local styles of dress and local textile techniques in addition to those of the dominant Mughal court. The Rajputs of northwest India (today's Rajasthan) were conquered by the Mughals in the late sixteenth and early seventeenth centuries and their compulsory attendance at the Mughal court led to their emulation of Mughal palaces, interiors and dress. Local textile specialities such as fine block-printing and tie-dyeing (*bandhani* and *lahariya*) (see pls 37, 38) contributed, along with local styles of painting, decorative arts, literature and music, to keeping local culture alive in the often Mughal-dominated court environment. The wealthy court at Amber, home of the Kachhwaha Rajputs, the first Rajput group to ally themselves to Akbar, contained in its storerooms many great textiles from other parts of India, including the finest chintz floor-spreads (for example, pl.132), tent hangings (pl.133) and Mughal velvets.[40]

128 (opposite)
The Reynolds Coverlet
(probably a floor-spread)
(detail)
Coromandel Coast, possibly
for the Golconda court,
c.1625–50
Cotton, mordant-dyed and
resist-dyed
269.2 x 226 cm

Given by the Gloster
Heritage Society
Rhode Island School
of Design Museum,
Providence, 83.023

129
Coverlet (rumal)
Coromandel Coast, for the
Golconda court, c.1625–40
Cotton, mordant-dyed and
resist-dyed
74 x 89 cm
National Museum, New
Delhi, 48.7/103

130
Length of ikat fabric
(detail)
Probably Hyderabad,
Andhra Pradesh/Telangana,
probably early 19th century

Silk with gilt-silver strips,
warp ikat
249 x 108.5 cm
Gift of Praful and Shilpa Shah
V&A: IS.4-1999

TIPU SULTAN'S TENT

India's climate is well suited to outdoor living, especially for daytime leisure activities and while travelling. Canopies serving as sunshades have an immeasurably long history there, and were used as a symbol of a ruler's authority. The use of elaborate decorative tents is a practice that goes back to at least the Sultanate period in the thirteenth century and was further developed by the Mughal rulers, who saw the tent as part of their Central Asian heritage. Freestanding tents in Central Asian style, with folding trellis walls and domed roofs, are seen in illustrations to histories of the first Mughal emperors Babur (r.1526–30), Humayun (r.1530–56) and Akbar (r.1556–1605). During the latter's reign the range of tent forms was increased, with a greater use of tents with fabric walls and peaked roofs extended by guy ropes under tension – these are often shown in paintings of later Mughal and Rajput rulers. According to Akbar's chronicler Abu'l-Fazl, the Emperor considered the royal tent 'an excellent dwelling place, a shelter from heat and cold, a protector against the rain, as the ornament of royalty. He looks upon its efficiency as one of the insignia of a ruler, and therefore considers the care bestowed upon it as part of Divine worship.'

The suite of tents used by a ruler was as much his seat of power as a solid building would be, and, mirroring a palace complex, it would be surrounded by the tents and enclosures of lesser nobles. Rulers' tents would often be highly decorative, and floral designs in printed cotton were especially popular for interior walls, roofs and awnings from the later seventeenth century onwards; earlier references are to velvets and brocades for tents, with appliqué work also known. Printed fabrics like that of Tipu Sultan's tent were made in several places in India in the seventeenth and eighteenth centuries, and centres such as Burhanpur, along with Agra, Sironj, Multan and Masulipatam (modern Machilipatnam), were noted for fine products made for the Mughal court.

Tipu Sultan's tent is very much in the Mughal style, with its peaked roof of eight triangular panels (each in three facets) combining to form a pyramid, and a fabric wall stiffened by battens. Its stylized floral patterns date it to the first half of the eighteenth century – that is, before the reign of Tipu himself (1782–99) or that of his father Haidar 'Ali (1761–82). Later replacements incorporate chintz panels from south India that are more likely to date from Tipu's reign (including some that include a pair of tigers in the design). We do not know when the tent entered the Mysore royal household, but it was among the 'Tipu relics' that were removed from Seringapatam after Tipu's defeat by the British in 1799 and that entered the collection of the 2nd Lord Clive, now housed at Powis Castle in Wales. In a poignant aftermath to its royal use in India, it served as a marquee for garden parties at Powis for many years, before its inclusion in the Clive Museum there in 1987. **RC**

131
Tent of Tipu Sultan of Mysore
Mughal India, possibly Burhanpur, c.1725–50
Cotton, block-printed, mordant-dyed and resist-dyed
Approx. total height: 354 cm; approx. perimeter of canopy: 2508 cm; max. height of wall: 205 cm
The National Trust, Powis Castle

See further:
Archer, Rowell and Skelton 1987; Stronge 2009

132 (and detail opposite)
Floor-spread
Coromandel Coast,
probably for the Golconda
court, c.1630
Cotton, mordant-dyed and
resist-dyed
251.5 x 330 cm
V&A: IM.160–1929

133
Tent hanging
Coromandel Coast,
probably for the Golconda
court, c.1625–50
Cotton, mordant-dyed
and resist-dyed
207 x 295 cm

Given by Miss Lucy Aldrich
Rhode Island School
of Design Museum,
Providence, 37.010

134 (opposite)
Floor-spread
Deccan, 18th century
Cotton embroidered
with floss silk and
metal-wrapped thread,

312.4 x 238.8 cm
Purchase, The Robert A.
and Ruth W. Fisher Fund
Virginia Museum of Fine
Arts, Richmond, 95.79

135
Maharana Sangram
Singh II receiving
Maharaja Sawai Jai
Singh of Jaipur in camp
Mewar, attributed to Jai
Ram, c.1732

Opaque watercolour on
paper
40.5 x 45.5 cm
Felton Bequest
National Gallery of Victoria,
Melbourne, AS 100.1980

The Rajputs of the more northerly courts, in the hills of what is now Himachal Pradesh, were more distant from the Mughal court both physically and culturally than their Rajasthani counterparts, and as well as developing strong local traditions of painting they also cultivated a distinctive embroidery style, often based on local miniature painting styles, for coverlets and hangings (pl.137).

In central India, the Marathas, who split from the Deccani sultanate of Bijapur in the mid-seventeenth century, were in many ways indistinguishable in appearance and dress from their Mughal or Deccani contemporaries. Fabrics from neighbouring areas such as Gujarat were used (pl.140) but local specialities such as the 'Paithani' tapestry-woven saris and huge rectangular shawls (*shela*) (pl.138) and even distinctively shaped headwear (pl.139) contributed to the creation of a specific visual identity for the Maratha elite, a group sometimes seen as more militaristic than culturally aware.

The Hindu courts of south India retained a strong visual identity that owed little to the Islamic culture of more northern areas. Wall paintings in palaces such as the Ramalinga Vilasam in Ramnad (modern Ramanathapuram) in Tamil Nadu and temples such as those at Lepakshi in Andhra Pradesh provide some evidence for the appearance of dress and textiles at southern courts.[41] The Islamic scrolling floral motifs or the semi-naturalistic flowering plants that pervade so much of north Indian textile design are used sparingly, if at all. Instead, geometric forms, stripes, squares and circles dominate. The style of one such court (perhaps that of Thanjavur or Madurai) is illustrated to great effect in the Musée Guimet's superb *kalamkari* hanging, which depicts a seventeenth-century ruler and his court in various settings (pl.141). Here, all but one of the male figures wear dhotis instead of tailored robes and are bare-chested, while the women wear saris, wrapped in pleated south Indian style, with cholis (bodices), rather than the trousers and skirts of the north. Interiors are hung with floral garlands suspended from cusped arches. Later south Indian courtly as well as vernacular textiles maintain the preference for checked and geometric designs rather than floral ones, often with regionally popular ikat (pl.130) and gold-brocaded motifs providing distinctive decoration (pl.142).

136
Two parts of the border of an embroidered set of *gaddi* (throne) furnishings
Rajasthan, probably Jaipur, c.1780–800
Cotton embroidered with silk and metal-wrapped silk thread
(left) 28 x 54 cm;
(right) 28 x 44 cm
Musée national des arts asiatiques – Guimet, from the Riboud Collection, MA 5703 and 5704

137
Hanging depicting
the mythical battle of
Kurukshetra (detail)
Chamba, Himachal Pradesh,
c.1800
Cotton embroidered

with floss silk
76 x 945 cm
Given by Gopal Singh,
former Raja of Chamba
V&A: IS.1185–1883

Jacket
Woven in Gujarat, tailored
in Indore, Madhya Pradesh,
c.1855

138 (opposite)
'Paithani' shawl (detail)
Sent to the Great Exhibition
from Dholpur, Rajasthan
in 1851; probably made in
Aurangabad or Paithan,
Maharashtra, c.1851
Cotton, silk and gold-
wrapped silk thread in
tapestry weave
334 x 190 cm
Purchased from the Great
Exhibition of 1851
V&A: 765–1852

139 (top)
Hat
Pune, c.1865
Papier-mâché base covered
in metal-wrapped silk
thread with sequins
24 x 32 x 9 cm
V&A: 0363 (IS)

Silk with metal-
wrapped thread
Length: 78 cm
Presented by H.H. Maharaja
Tukojirao Holkar II of Indore
V&A: 05578 (IS)

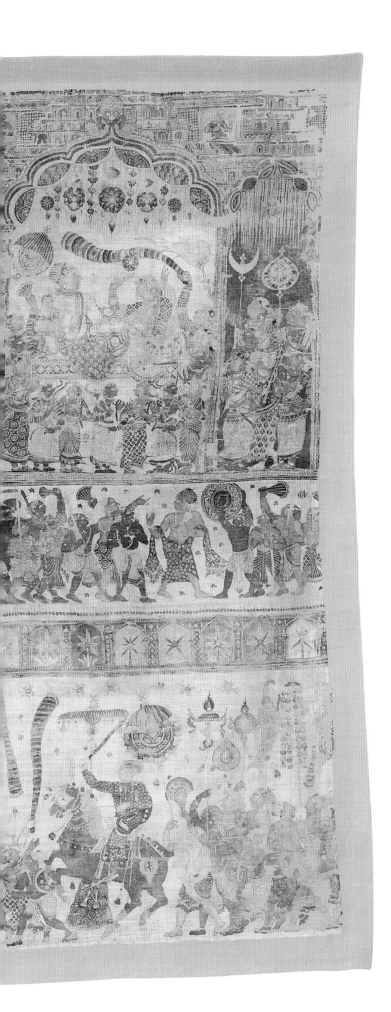

HANGING

This piece has often been hailed as the masterpiece of the Riboud Collection, and has been the subject of many essays.[1] It is a large mid-seventeenth-century *kalamkari* hanging, recently restored, depicting courtly scenes and processions. Its patron is not known, but the style of dress and architecture suggests that it was made for one of the Nayaka rulers of seventeenth-century Tamil Nadu, perhaps of Thanjavur or Madurai. A genre of Nayaka literature popular in both these centres describes the daily activities of the ruler, from his awakening, to listening to music, to travelling in procession through his capital. It has been suggested that this narrative hanging is a visual version of such a literary work.[2] The very high quality of the drawing, resists and dyeing indicates an origin somewhere on the Coromandel Coast rather than in interior Tamil Nadu, where such fine pieces were not made.

The piece is drawn in two main registers, divided by a horizontal strip that creates a sort of frieze. Architecture is omnipresent in the design, featuring thin columns with lobed arches surmounted by a pyramid-shaped structure made up of small shrines akin to the towers (*gopuram*) of south Indian temples and palaces. These architectural structures divide the field into several niches, each featuring individual scenes whose main character, undoubtedly a king or a princely figure, is always the same. These scenes alternate with niches containing female attendants. At the top left we see the ruler seated on a platform with his consort, who is playing a stringed instrument. The ruler holds his sceptre in his left hand, while female servants or courtiers wave fans and fly whisks. Below the throne a row of female musicians accompanies the consort. We see the ruler again in the middle of the piece but this time framed by soldiers and courtiers holding weapons. In the lower register he is shown wearing Mughal-style dress while riding in procession. A separate fragment, now detached, shows him carrying an *ankus* (goad), indicating that the piece also included an elephant procession and was once considerably larger than it is now. **AS**

1   Among the major studies are Gittinger 1982; Gittinger 1989; Varadarajan, Filliozat and Gittinger 1986; Lefèvre 2006.
2   Lefèvre 2006, p.134; Rao, Shulman and Subrahmanyam 1998, p.65.

141
Hanging
Coromandel Coast,
for a Nayaka court,
mid-17th century
Cotton, mordant-dyed
and resist-dyed
155 x 220 cm
Musée national des arts
asiatiques – Guimet, from
the Riboud Collection,
MA 5678

KARUPPUR SHAWL

The historic cotton and metal-thread textiles attributed to the village of Kodali Karuppur in Tamil Nadu, southeastern India, are among the most technically hybrid and subtly beautiful fabrics ever produced on the subcontinent. When casually observed, many resemble conventional red-ground south Indian printed saris, dhotis and turbans intended for the domestic Indian market. But on closer examination one discovers that the geometric, floral and, more rarely, animal designs created by a skilful application of white resists and red, black and yellow dyes overlay unexpected gold-wrapped threads. While the use of precious metal-wrapped thread is more commonly an embellishment of silk weaving – Karuppur cloths are cotton – that feature is not what makes them so unusual. Rather, it is the fact that dyeing techniques are not normally combined with metal-wrapped thread because the glittering gold or silver effect will always be reduced by the standard *kalamkari* processes of mordanting and dyeing. However, here we can see that enough metallic shine remains under the dyed surface to create a less ostentatious but still highly attractive cloth, which obviously appealed to the wealthy Maratha patrons who commissioned them. They would probably have been worn at the southern Maratha court at Thanjavur, but other examples have also been recorded at Satara, the Maratha's base further north in Maharashtra.

In addition to the small surviving body of dyed examples, undyed white cloths similarly patterned with gold-wrapped thread have survived in Sri Lanka (pl.143). Known as *kasav tupottiya*, they became the highest status garment of the Kandyan nobility in the eighteenth and nineteenth centuries (pl.144). All of the presumed Karuppur pieces made for export to Sri Lanka are undyed. This suggests that these examples might represent the original tradition and that treating these textiles to an additional dyeing process after their removal from the loom might indicate a later eighteenth-century innovation that was developed from existing local south Indian dyeing traditions by the Maratha nobility of Thanjavur. SC

See further:
Watt 1903, p.266; Hadaway 1917, pp.9–10, figs 6–10, 12–17

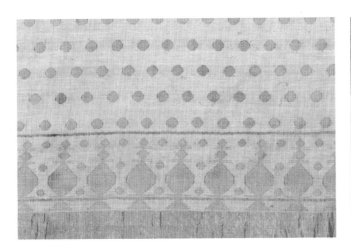

142 (opposite)
Shawl (detail)
Kodali Karuppur, Tamil Nadu, late 18th or 19th century
Cotton with brocaded metal-wrapped thread; mordant and resist-dyed
472.5 x 180 cm
Metropolitan Museum of Art, New York, 15.95.144

143
Kandyan nobleman's wrapped garment (detail)
Kodali Karuppur, for export to Sri Lanka, 19th century
Cotton, with brocaded metal-wrapped thread
457 x 86.6 cm
V&A: IS.156-1965

144
Chiefs of the Central Province, Sri Lanka, wearing formal dress
Kandy, Sri Lanka, c.1910–20

TEXTILES FOR EXPORT MARKETS

Providing textiles to suit the tastes of different export markets has been a strength of the Indian textile maker (and trader) for many centuries, and is a key reason for India's domination of textile supply across the globe up to the period of western industrialization. Different markets required very different products, and they rarely overlapped: an ikat *telia rumal* (head-cover) sent to the Persian Gulf would not be well received at the Thai court, which preferred finely drawn flaming patterns in deep-dyed chintz, and the monochrome tasar silk embroideries from Bengal that were traded at the hajj fairs would not find buyers in chinoiserie-obsessed Britain. India's domination of this global trade only waned with the invention of machinery in Europe that could, superficially, imitate the appearance of these trade goods, and that could be produced more cheaply. It was the influx of these machine-made textiles in the nineteenth century that overwhelmed India's trade in handmade cloth (see p.185).

The oldest Indian textiles have survived outside India, either in the dry climates of Egypt, Tibet and Central Asia or in the smoky rafters of Indonesian clan-houses. The Indian monsoon climate is not conducive to the preservation of cloth, and in any case there is very little tradition in India of honouring ancient pieces as heirlooms. Much of what we know about early Chinese, Central Asian and Middle Eastern textiles has been learnt through the study of burial sites and tombs (both Asian and European) in which textiles, often of the highest quality, were used as wrappings or clothing for the honoured dead. This tradition does not exist in India, so our knowledge of early Indian textiles must come from other sources.

The earliest surviving actual textile fragments from India date from the early centuries AD, and include the woollen fragment excavated by Marc Aurel Stein (pl.147) and cotton fragments excavated at the Roman port of Berenike on the Red Sea coast. The fact that these pieces were found in distant Central Asia and Egypt respectively confirms that the Indian textile trade was far-reaching even at such an early period. Fragments of resist-dyed block-printed cotton textiles excavated in the desert site of Keriya in Xinjiang, datable to about the third century AD, also may well be Indian.[42]

THE MEDITERRANEAN AND THE MIDDLE EAST

Archaeological evidence indicates that the Indian textile trade reaches back a lot further even than the Central Asian material suggests, at least in the Middle East: cotton yarns twisted in the 'Z' direction typical of Indian production (as opposed to the 'S'-twisted Middle Eastern yarns) at the fifth–fourth millennium BC site of Dhuweila in Jordan are very likely to have come from the Indus Valley, where cotton is known to have been spun and woven around that time, as was the case even earlier at Mehrgarh in Baluchistan.[43] The Greek and Babylonian words for cotton – *sindon* and *sindhu* – found in texts of around the seventh century BC are clearly linked to contemporary terms for 'India' and thus also imply an Indian origin for the fibre. The Hebrew Book of Esther, written between the fifth and third centuries BC, refers to 'cotton curtains', using a form of the Sanskrit word *karpas* for cotton.

By the early centuries of the Christian era the use of Indian cotton in the Mediterranean was clearly an escalating phenomenon: writing in the first century AD, Pliny complains that the purchase of Indian luxuries, including fine muslins (the famous *ventus textilis*, meaning 'woven wind'), is a drain on the Roman economy. In an evocative comment on the rise of international trade, he remarks that India has been 'brought

145
Fragment
Gujarat, Carbon-14-dated
to c. 8th century
Cotton, block-printed resist,
dyed with indigo
39.5 x 54 cm
Ashmolean Museum,
Oxford, 1990.259

near by gain'.[44] India was 'brought near' in more physical terms at that time by a wider understanding of the monsoon winds, which enabled ships to travel back and forth between India and the Middle East in the same year, a development that greatly increased trade in the Indian Ocean.

The *Periplus of the Erythraean Sea*, the well-known guide for traders by sea between Egypt and India written in about AD 40–70, describes a fully-fledged trade in a wide variety of goods emanating from the ports of south, west and eastern India. The anonymous author mentions several varieties of Indian silk and cotton textiles, from 'ordinary cloth' to silks and 'thin clothing of the finest weaves', which were available in Indian ports and markets.[45] While none of the fine muslins or desirable silks have survived from this early period, some humble but significant pieces of cotton fabric identified as sail cloth, woven from 'Z'-spun Indian cotton, dating from the first century AD, have been excavated at the port of Berenike on the west coast of the Red Sea.[46] These provide a tangible link to the written accounts – an especially close link as Berenike is the starting point of the itineraries described in the *Periplus*. Although the Greek and Roman ships that might have used the *Periplus* only travelled as far as Arikamedu on the southeast Indian coast, the list of goods mentioned in the text makes it clear that the Indian Ocean route was often just one segment in a larger global enterprise that also incorporated China and Southeast Asia. This trade was concerned with a wider range of goods than just textiles: spices, minerals and exotic goods such as pearls and tortoiseshell also played key roles.

Other Indian cotton textile fragments, this time with resist-dyed indigo blue designs, dating from the fourth to fifth centuries AD, have also been found at Berenike.[47] But it is from the eighth century onwards that we start to find the most substantial and numerous surviving pieces of actual textiles (pls 145, 146). The vast majority of the Indian block-printed cotton fragments that exist today in museum collections came to light in the Cairo souks in the early twentieth century.[48] A small number of closely related pieces were excavated at other sites, most notably the port of Quseir al-Qadim (near present-day Quseir on the Egyptian Red Sea coast), which was active (in its second phase of occupation) from the thirteenth to the fifteenth centuries.[49] The fragments bought in Cairo had reportedly been recovered at Fustat, which had been founded

as the new Egyptian capital in AD 641, and continued as such until 969 when the Fatimids moved the capital to adjacent Cairo. Fustat eventually became the rubbish disposal area for Cairo. The textile fragments had apparently been discarded on these heaps over time and were thus not excavated in a true archaeological context.[50] Since the appearance of these textiles, their dating has been attempted first by analysis of the designs and more recently by Carbon-14 dating.[51] This has yielded dates as early as the eighth century in one example (pl.145), and eleventh and twelfth centuries in others.[52] The majority, however, are now thought to date from the thirteenth century onwards.

The place of origin of these fragments has been convincingly attributed to Gujarat, for several reasons: first, the dyes and techniques used to decorate them are typical of that area historically and even today. Two red dyes have been found in the fragments: an Indian form of madder (*manjeet* in Hindi, *Rubia munjista* or *Rubia cordifolia* in Latin) and *al* (*Morinda citrifolia*), both used extensively in western India (see pp.33–4).[53] The blue is indigo, as would be expected from

146
Fragment
Gujarat, *c.* 14th century
Cotton, resist-dyed and
mordant-dyed
33 x 23 cm
Ashmolean Museum,
Oxford, 1990.1128

PART OF A RUG, BLANKET OR SHAWL

n 1906, 18 fragments of a thin, plain-woven, woollen textile with bands of colourful tapestry-woven decoration were excavated by Marc Aurel Stein at the oasis city of Niya in Central Asia. His published description was ambiguous: no provenance was proposed, the material (sheep's wool) was not mentioned, and even the number of fragments was unclear.[1] However, we know from associated objects that the house where the fragments were discovered had been abandoned towards the end of the third century, which provides this rug, blanket or shawl with its latest possible date of production. Stein remarked on the textile's strong visual resemblance to modern Indian cotton flat-woven rugs (durries) and, in terms of design as well as weave structure, there seems little reason to doubt that these fragments are of Indian origin. If this is so, this piece and its other fragments (together with fragments of cotton sail-cloth and sleeping mats excavated at Berenike[2]) are the world's oldest surviving Indian textiles. However, that assumption remains impossible to prove definitively as no other surviving Indian or even Central Asian textile from the first three centuries AD resembles it.

Niya was a prosperous trading post along the southern branch of the Silk Road linking China to the West, and in addition it was positioned along the route providing access to Central Asia from north India via Kashmir. Both culturally and linguistically, Indian influence dominated Niya until the fourth century,[3] so the textile could easily have been imported from north India or woven locally by Indian settlers using local wool. The only other logical possibility would be a Chinese origin, but this can be ruled out on structural, material and aesthetic grounds. As no other textile found at Niya or any other Central Asian site closely resembles these fragments, it is unlikely to have been produced locally. The fact that it was considered valuable enough to repair and reuse after becoming damaged

only reinforces the probability that it was a prized Indian import.

Though possibly a unique survival, this woollen textile is not the only fragment of Indian cloth discovered by Stein in Central Asia: there was also a tiny piece of tie-dyed pashmina (V&A: Stein 557a). Tie-dyed and resist-printed cotton and woollen fragments, all likely to be Indian, have since been excavated at Karadong in 1959 and most recently at Keriya, both once important stops along the Silk Road. The Keriya material has been dated to around the middle of the first millennium BC to the third–fourth century AD.[4] **SC**

1   Stein 1907, p.397 and col. pl.LXXV, no.N.vii.3. See also Cohen 1999.
2   Wild 2006, pp.176–81.
3   Wilson 1995, p.26.
4   Debaine-Francfort and Idriss 2001, p.80.

147 (opposite)
**Part of a rug, blanket
or shawl**
Probably north India,
c. 1st to 3rd centuries
Wool, plain-woven and
tapestry-woven
48.5 x 34 cm

Excavated at Niya,
Xinjiang, China
British Museum, London,
1907,1111.105

148
**Marc Aurel Stein's
excavations at Niya,
Xinjiang, 1906**

most parts of India except the far northeast. The red is mordant-dyed and a printed resist has been used to create white areas of design against the coloured grounds: both these techniques are also found elsewhere in India, but the use of block-printing for both the mordant and the resist (as opposed to drawing it by hand or painting it onto the cloth) is usually associated with northwestern India. These techniques are still used today in the *ajrakh* prints of Gujarat and Sindh (see pls 42, 48). In addition, the designs themselves show noticeable parallels with Gujarati architectural and manuscript decoration. In a few cases, fragments with strikingly similar designs have been found in both Egypt and Indonesia, testifying to the global reach of the trade in these pieces by the medieval period (pls 146, 157).[54] Pieces like this also provide tangible illustrations to observations like that of the Portuguese apothecary-turned-diplomat Tomé Pires, who wrote in about 1515 that 'Cambay', the main port of Gujarat at the time, 'chiefly stretches out two arms: with her right she reaches out towards Aden and with the other towards Malacca [Melaka, today in Malaysia] as the most important places to sail to.'[55]

The Arab presence in Sindh from AD 712 onwards provided the basis for the growth of a Muslim trading community in western India. Early Arab commentators on India included the historian and geographer al-Mas'udi (d. AD 956), whose book *The Meadows of Gold and Mines of Gems* includes a description of Cambay, which he visited in 915. He found it a great emporium and admired not only the locally produced textiles but also the fine Bengali muslins that were also being exported from Cambay.[56] By the time the Moroccan traveller Ibn Battuta visited India in 1333–46, Cambay had become so full of foreign merchants that they formed the majority of the population.[57] Aden in South Arabia (modern Yemen) in its turn had a thriving colony of Indian merchants, leading Ibn Battuta to call it 'the port of the Indians', with Indian ships docking from Cambay as well as Quilon and Calicut on the Malabar Coast.[58] But by the seventeenth century Cambay's port had started to silt up, and it gave way to the more accessible Surat as the area's major port.

Mecca, with its port at Jeddah, was also a major trading centre, attracting merchants from all over the Islamic world, not only to participate in the hajj but also to attend the huge

149

Pair of *telia rumals*
(one shown)
From the workshop of
Gunti Bhaskar Rao, Chirala,
Andhra Pradesh, 1994

Cotton, warp and weft ikat,
supplementary
weft in corners
107.5 x 230 cm
V&A: IS.9-1994

150
Scarf
Dhaka, Bangladesh, c.1855
Cotton and muga silk,
embroidered with
muga silk thread
116 x 117 cm
V&A: 6038 (IS)

annual fair there. In the eighteenth century this was described as 'perhaps the richest fair in the world [where] millions of items of merchandise from the Indies change hands',[59] and this had no doubt been the case for several centuries by the time this was written. Ibn Khurdadbih, in his *Book of Roads and Kingdoms* written in about AD 870, confirms that Jeddah was an important trading port at that time, with products of Sindh, Zanzibar and Persia on sale there.[60] Bengali cottons are frequently mentioned by later visitors such as Duarte Barbosa, who adds, in about 1516–21, that 'the Arabs and Persians make them into veils and kerchiefs in such quantity that entire shiploads of such stuffs are sent out'.[61]

The later Middle Eastern trade continued to demand certain types of Indian textiles in great quantities. Cotton cloth for turbans was sent to North Africa, Turkey and Iran as well as to the Arab lands of the Eastern Mediterranean.[62] Kashmir shawls were sent in large numbers (and reportedly of high quality) to Iran, Turkey, Egypt, Russia and the Gulf.[63] In these regions they were worn less as shawls around the shoulders than as turbans and waist sashes, the latter by both women and men. Some regions required specific items for their local

dress: Yemeni women, for example, favoured (and still wear) a block-printed cotton textile from Ahmedabad, called a *sitara* in Yemen, which is preferred over other imports in spite of its garish colours and consistently poor printing.[64] Ikat *telia rumals* from Chirala on the coast of Andhra Pradesh (pl.149) were until very recently exported to the Middle East, especially Aden and the Persian Gulf, for use as head-wraps.[65] Some generic items such as Bengali cotton and muga silk embroidered kerchiefs (pl.150) were traded throughout the Middle East, often being acquired by pilgrims on hajj; and seemingly endless variations on the coloured skullcaps incorporating pious inscriptions (pl.152) are to be found throughout the Indian Ocean world in different shapes and sizes.[66] Printed and hand-drawn *kalamkaris* were made for the Iranian market in huge quantities in the nineteenth century in the area around Masulipatam (modern Machilipatnam) (pl.151) and were imitated in Iran, especially in Isfahan. Men's wrapped garments across the Indian Ocean world – lungi in India, sarong in Southeast Asia and *futa* in the Middle East – were (and are) often made of south Indian checked fabric, and Indian ikat versions in imitation of Indonesian originals are popular even today.[67]

151

Length of dress fabric
(detail)
Machilipatnam, Andhra
Pradesh, for the Iranian
market, dated 1297 AH (AD
1879); printed with the name

Muhammad Mahdi
[of] Shiraz
Cotton, block-printed and
resist-dyed
96 x 330 cm
V&A: IS.1765–1883

152

Hat
India, c.1850–70
Folded silk pieces stitched
onto quilted cotton base
Height: 15.2 cm;
diameter: 9.2 cm
V&A: 5756 (IS)

AFRICA

The establishment of trade along the Swahili Coast of East Africa was for Gujarati seafarers a natural continuation of their relatively short voyages to the Gulf and the Horn of Africa. Material and literary evidence for Indian presence in the area is scarce, but oblique references by commentators such as al-Mas'udi, who visited East Africa in AD 916, suggest that trade, primarily in ivory, was already current between the two regions at that time.[68] The only early textile of any kind to have come to light from East Africa is a fragment excavated at Mtambwe Mkuu, an island close to Zanzibar in present-day Tanzania. It dates from the twelfth century and is indigo-dyed in 'Z'-spun cotton, factors that suggest an Indian place of manufacture.[69] Vasco da Gama visited the port of Malindi (in present-day Kenya) in 1502 on his second voyage and was presented with 'a white embroidered canopy for a bed, the most delicate piece of needlework', which he identified as having been 'made in Bengal'.[70] We read in Portuguese accounts that by 1505 'quantities of cotton cloth from Cambay' were to be found at Mombasa.[71] Lists of cloths found in Portuguese archives indicate that the types of textile sent to East Africa included

blue and white checked or striped cloth (*capotins*), coarse calico dyed blue or black (*canequins*), indigo-dyed *zuartes* (perhaps from the Dutch *zwart*, meaning 'black') and more expensive narrow white cloth called *samateres*.[72] While some of these textiles would have been intended for everyday use, at least by elite groups, they clearly had ceremonial and ritual functions, as well as being given as official gifts to both religious and lay figures.[73]

Gujarati merchant communities dominated the trade with East Africa during the eighteenth and nineteenth centuries, with Daman and Diu their main ports of departure. Ivory was a major trade commodity, but slaves were also sent, albeit in relatively small numbers, to western India, where they had been a feature of court life for centuries, appearing from time to time in local miniature paintings as attendants and grooms.[74] Known as Sidis, some became prominent members of society: Sidi Said, for example, who built the famous mosque that bears his name in Ahmedabad, was a slave of Sultan Mahmud III (r.1537–54).[75] The textiles sent to East Africa increasingly came from one main centre: the town of Jambusar in Saurashtra, whose weavers supplied cloth solely for the East African market.[76]

153
Length of four handkerchiefs (detail)
Mangalore, Karnataka,
c.1855; according to the
original label, woven
at the German Mission
industrial school
Cotton
344 x 88.7 cm
V&A: 4869 (IS)

154
Archival photograph of Jamaican woman with Madras check headtie
Jamaica, c.1900

Nowadays, however, the name of Jambusar is associated not with weaving but with a distinctive regional type of printed and painted mother-goddess hanging (*Mata ni pachedi*).[77]

The West Africa trade provides a different case history to that of East Africa in two main respects: it was under the control of western trading companies rather than Indian or Arab traders, and it included large numbers of textiles from southeast India and from Gujarat. Furthermore, all of the Indian textiles sent to West Africa were exported from India to London and then re-exported to Africa. The Portuguese had been exploring the commercial possibilities of the region since the late fifteenth century, and had established trade in gold, ivory and pepper. The English had also experimented with trade there since the mid-sixteenth century and established their first trading settlements in Gambia in 1618 and on the Gold Coast (today's Ghana) in 1631.[78] The English Royal African Company was founded in 1672. Although India was geographically much further away from West Africa than the eastern coast of the continent, Indian textiles became an essential part of the region's trade from the seventeenth century onwards, with checked cottons and indigo-dyed *zuartes* ('black cloth') or 'blue baftas' being particularly sought after. As in East Africa, in some regions these textiles entered African society as currency and were accumulated as wealth. Considerable quantities of English goods such as metal wares, guns and English woollen cloth were sent to Africa to pay for traded goods, but Indian textiles were a dominant part of the trade. In some areas Indian cowrie shells were also sought after as currency.

While gold, ivory, dyestuffs and gums were the original mainstays of European trade with Africa, this soon also came to include slaves. Several forms of slavery had existed within Africa for centuries before Europeans arrived, but the discovery of the New World and the need for labour to work in Spain's newly conquered territories stimulated the Atlantic slave trade. This trade widened its scope after the Dutch introduced sugar-cane cultivation into the Caribbean in the mid-seventeenth century (it had already been brought to South America by the Portuguese). British-held islands such as Barbados and Jamaica were soon producing sugar in huge quantities for use in Britain, and African slave labour quickly replaced local workers in the plantations. These slaves were bought in West Africa, using British goods and Indian textiles.

155
A group of Kalabari men in Madras check wrappers
Buguma, Nigeria, 1991

Indian textiles that were sent to West Africa are sometimes known generically as 'Guinea cloth', although that name also seems to apply specifically to a type of indigo-dyed cotton textile.[79] As with most of India's export textiles, certain categories of cloth were popular in specific areas. One of the most widespread types throughout West Africa was the checked cotton handkerchief or *rumal* (pl.153), imported from south India and often referred to as a 'Madras handkerchief' after the main port of export or 'Pulicat handkerchief' after the town and port of that name a few miles north of Madras, one of the primary centres of production. These handkerchiefs were also exported in quantity to Britain and the Netherlands (see p.165), but certain types of 'stout, even quality' were destined specifically for Africa. The Madras Dispatches of the East India Company refer to handkerchiefs of 'Ordinary cloth but the colour being bright is highly approved for Africa'.[80] These checked cotton squares were used primarily as headties by West African women, and this usage travelled with West African slaves to the plantations of the West Indies. Today in certain parts of the Caribbean such as Jamaica, the Madras headtie has become part of traditional dress (pl.154). In West Africa itself, certain communities, most notably the Kalabari of Nigeria, embraced the Madras check as a ritual and ceremonial object. The Kalabari accumulated Indian handkerchief lengths (known locally as *injiri*, from 'India') for use in life-cycle ceremonies from birth to funerals, as well as in masquerade festivals (pl.155).[81] They favoured red, blue and white checks, but other parts of West Africa preferred other colour combinations: yellow, for example, was popular in Sierra Leone.[82]

A variety of other Indian cloths were being sent to Africa in the eighteenth and nineteenth centuries. Many of the names found in Company records are the same as the more basic stuffs exported from India to Britain and North America: anglicized Indian names such as baftas, brawls, calicoes, pulicats or nicanees all denote everyday types of relatively cheap cotton cloth. One of the Madras Dispatches of the East India Company mentions, in a list of goods to be provided from Masulipatam, 'Allejars, Callawapores, ditto blue, Sastracundies: these 4 last articles have much increased in demand for the Africa trade'.[83] John Irwin has found descriptions of these cloths in earlier East India Company records: 'allejars' (in a variety of spellings, including 'alleja' and 'allegaes') are red and white or blue and white checked cottons; 'callawapores' (or 'Callaway poose') is a type of red-dyed cloth ('*chay* goods') from the Coromandel Coast, which seems also to come in an indigo-dyed variety; 'sastracundies' (or elsewhere 'sacergunties') are recorded in 1690 as being cotton cloths 'dyed in the thread before made', which Irwin suggests refers to the ikat technique.[84]

It is perhaps surprising to find that among these simply patterned checked, striped or plain cottons, flowered Indian chintz or pintados were also being sent to West Africa. From the 1670s onwards, British Treasury documents record textiles called by both the English/Dutch term 'chintz' and Portuguese 'pintado' going to Cape Coast Castle on the Gold Coast (today's Ghana); Whydah (Ouidah) and Offra in modern Benin; Sherbro, now in Sierra Leone; and for trading on the Gambia River.[85] A distinction is made between pintados and chintz, as some records list both; for example, from October 1680, 'a good cargo for the Gold Coast would include red ground pintados & chintz'.[86] White-ground chintzes with red flowers are mentioned frequently as being the most sought-after at Whydah and other places. An insight into the direct relationship between textiles and the purchase of slaves is provided by a document of 1707 from Whydah that states that 'Capt. Hamilton, a 10% man [private trader] brought a sort of Persian chint as he called them ... he said they cost about 7s6d each – they took well and traders liked them because they could give 9 or 10 for a slave.'[87] Also, in September 1709 at Cape Coast Castle, Mr Hicks of Whydah lists goods for purchasing 100 Negro men: 56 broad chintz, 'the ground white with red flowers with green ... 8 [men].'[88]

It might be supposed that British trade with West Africa would have ceased after the abolition of the Atlantic slave trade in 1807, but this was not the case: Britain still wanted other commodities from Africa. The Industrial Revolution in Britain, which had been brought about in such a large part by the British desire to imitate Indian textiles, generated huge numbers of new machines, all of which needed lubricating. The best material for this purpose was held to be African palm oil, and Indian textiles continued to maintain their key position in the trade for this and other materials, including dyewoods and gum arabic from Senegal. Like most aspects of the Indian textile economy, however, the African trade suffered serious damage from competition with British mill-made goods in the mid-nineteenth century.

156 (opposite)
Two south Indian checked cotton sarongs (details)
(left) For the Malay market (Singapore), c.1867
137 x 91.5 cm (sewn into a tube)
Given by the Temunggung (Sultan) of Johor
V&A: 5129 (IS)

(right) For export to Indonesia (Sulawesi), c.1855; labelled 'Bugis sarong'
423.5 x 67 cm
V&A: 5128 (IS)

157 (overleaf)
Ceremonial hanging (detail)
Gujarat, for export to Indonesia (used in Sulawesi), Carbon-14-dated to c.1300–80

Cotton, block-printed, mordant-dyed and resist-dyed
95 x 512 cm
Purchased with the assistance of the Art Fund
V&A: IS.96–1993

SOUTHEAST ASIA

Indian textiles had been traded to both insular and mainland Southeast Asia long before the arrival of Europeans on the subcontinent. While no actual pieces from this trade survive from before the fourteenth century (pl.157), scattered early references confirm its existence by the early centuries AD. A Chinese document of the fifth century mentions unidentified Indian textiles being taken to China as part of an Indonesian diplomatic mission.[89] Further references occur in Javanese tax records of the ninth and tenth centuries,[90] and a copperplate inscription of AD 876 specifically mentions *buat kling putih*: white cloths from Kalinga (Odisha or the greater east coast of India).[91] But in general the textile trade between India and mainland Southeast Asia, as well as the 'spice islands' of what is now Indonesia, only began to be recorded with the arrival of the Portuguese in the sixteenth century.

Portuguese observers such as Duarte Barbosa and Tomé Pires have left very useful records of what was traded to the spice islands and how cloth was used there. Much of the cloth was used to buy cloves, pepper, nutmeg and mace, and ships arrived in ports such as Malacca (modern Melaka, a Portuguese colony since 1511, where Pires was based) from both Cambay in Gujarat and the Coromandel Coast bearing many different types of cloth.

Most of these would have been pieces for ordinary use. While none have survived from this early period, they may perhaps have been simple checked cottons (pl.156). The more decorative cotton textiles were of two main types: block-printed pieces with repeating patterns (pl.157), and the even rarer

freely drawn pieces with human figures (pl.161). Some of the block-prints share designs with those sent to Egypt, but they certainly would have had different uses in the spice islands: while the so-called 'Fustat' pieces were clearly intended as furnishings and dress, the format of surviving textiles found in Indonesia – long, horizontal, banner-like rectangles (pl.157) – suggest a ceremonial function of some kind. The textiles with elaborate figurative designs would have been very time-consuming to produce: they are made by complex mordanting and resist-dyeing processes that are usually associated with the Coromandel Coast, but their strong visual connections to Gujarati manuscript painting points instead to a Gujarati origin (see pp.156–7).

Silk double-ikat *patola*, some in designs used exclusively for the Southeast Asian export trade, were especially highly prized in the islands of Eastern Indonesia and Sulawesi, as well as in Java, where even today they play a role as part of the ceremonial dress of the royal court.[92] Some *patola* for export to the islands were made in the format of shoulder-cloths (*slendang*) for ceremonial wear. These were usually in the abstract open circle or 'basket' design also made for domestic use in Gujarat, but with the distinction that the export pieces often have cotton rather than silk side borders.[93] Other *slendang*-sized pieces favoured a lattice design used only for Southeast Asian export.[94] Both of these abstract *patola* designs had a profound impact on the manufacture of local textiles, which often show an adaptation of similar patterns. The most highly prized *patola*, however, were made in banner-like lengths, with designs used exclusively for the island market.

158
Victory banner
(***jayatra yantra***) (detail)
Gujarat, dated 1447
Cotton, painted with
gouache, ink and gold
137 x 110 cm
V&A: IM.89-1936

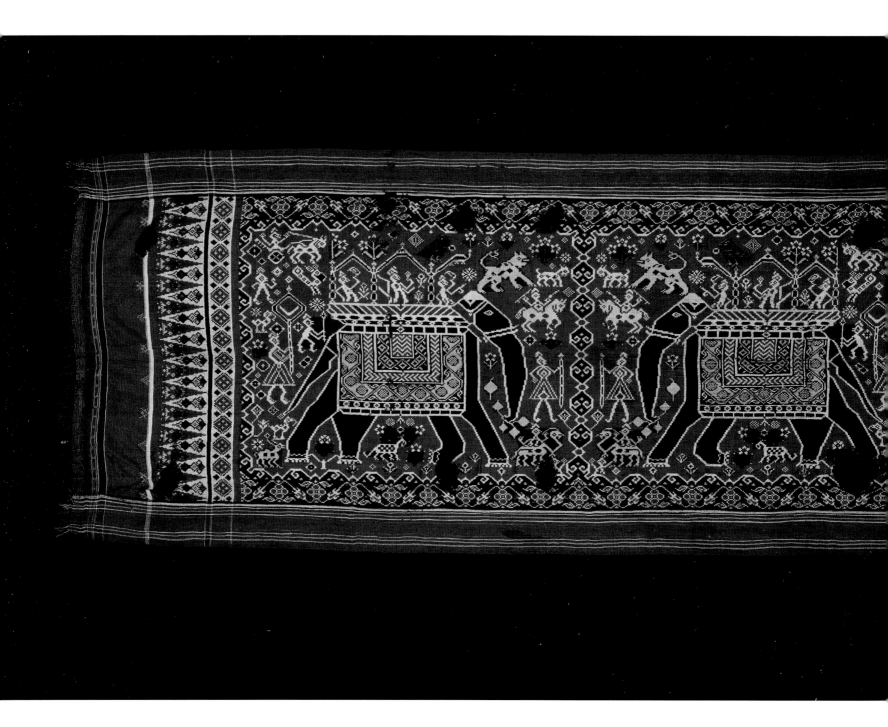

160
Ceremonial textile
(*patolu*)
Gujarat, probably Patan, for
export to Indonesia, *c.* mid-
19th century or earlier
Silk, double ikat, with cotton
warps in outer borders
100 x 480 cm
V&A: IS.74-1993

CEREMONIAL HANGING

This magnificent textile is one of a small group of pieces that were made in India specifically for use in what is now Indonesia. Their precise use in the region remains unclear, but they were clearly revered as ritual objects of high value. This particular piece poses an intriguing puzzle concerning the way in which it was made and what this implies about its place of origin. The outlines of the design are entirely hand-drawn, probably with a simple bamboo pen (*kalam*), rather than printed. The mordants needed for the red dye were also applied with a brush, and not printed. These may seem obscure and rather minor technical distinctions, but they overturn the usually accepted perception that hand-drawn and hand-mordanted cotton textiles were historically produced exclusively in coastal southeast India (the Coromandel Coast) and that textiles from Gujarat did not use these techniques but were block-printed.

Basing an attribution purely on technical grounds, this textile might be assumed to come from southeast India. But the style in which the figures are drawn points instead very strongly to a Gujarati origin. Although the artists of the Coromandel Coast were adept at creating textiles that appealed to a host of different markets, it is unlikely that they could have adopted so convincingly the distinctive western Indian style of drawing that we see in manuscript paintings of the fifteenth and sixteenth centuries from Gujarat (pl.162). Features this textile shares with manuscript paintings include the 'projecting eye' (see also pl.95) and the way in which the wrapped textiles are

161
Ceremonial hanging
Gujarat, for export
to Indonesia (used in
Sulawesi), Carbon-14-dated
to c.1450–1500
Cotton, mordant-dyed and
resist-dyed
102 x 550 cm
TAPI Collection, India, 01.51

drawn – coming stiffly to points standing away from the wearer's body – as well as decorative elements such as the large, circular earrings, long plaits of hair, pointed headdresses, and the use of flowers and animals as infill decoration between the figures.

Very few textiles of this type survive: the TAPI Collection owns a second example with dancing ladies (without the central male figure of this piece) and another hand-drawn piece with trees;[1] another example with female musicians is in the National Gallery of Australia in Canberra[2] and another is now in the Asian Civilisations Museum in Singapore.[3] Apart from these grand, ceremonial textiles, a crucial piece of evidence that hand-drawing of outlines and resist material and hand mordant-painting were carried out in Gujarat is provided by

pieces recovered from Egypt that are more utilitarian, bearing vegetal designs (including pl.146). These are also clearly of Gujarati origin and yet there is no evidence of block-printing on them.[4] None of these textiles dates from later than the sixteenth century, so it appears likely that in Gujarat the practice of hand-drawing and hand-application of resists and mordants died out after that date, to be replaced by the faster and cheaper process of block-printing. **RC**

1   Barnes, Cohen and Crill 2002, cats 14 and 3.
2   Guy 1998, ill.147.
3   Unpublished.
4   Barnes 1997, vol.I, p.60; cats 1116, 1121.

162
Victory banner (*jayatra yantra*) (detail)
Gujarat, dated 1447
Cotton, painted with gouache, ink and gold
137 x 110 cm
V&A: IM.89–1936

(opposite)
detail of pl.161

Expert *patola* designs were based on animals and human figures, in hunting scenes or with alternating squares containing tigers and elephants. The most magnificent were the long cloths that featured just four monumental elephants interspersed with smaller figures of human attendants and tigers (pl.160). These precious textiles, both silk *patola* and figural cottons, clearly transcended mere trade goods and made a transition to ceremonial use. Many became revered as sacred heirlooms, especially in eastern Indonesia. They were displayed only on ceremonial occasions. It is this tradition of reverence and preservation that has ensured their survival, as they were often stored in the rafters of village clan-houses, out of the reach of vermin and insects and additionally preserved by domestic smoke fumes.

A different range of textiles was sent to the Southeast Asian mainland. Here they did not acquire ritual status, although in Thailand the finest types of Indian cloth were reserved for royal use.[95] 'Kling [Indian] cloths in the manner of Siam' were mentioned by Pires as early as 1512–15,[96] but we only have surviving examples from the eighteenth and nineteenth centuries to give an idea of what these may have been like. Designs for the Thai market are distinctively elaborate, and relate to the 'flaming' outlines of Thai architectural and manuscript decoration. These textiles were produced in several techniques and materials, and at several levels of patronage. The finest are in the same chintz technique as pieces made for export to Europe, and show similar levels of incredible skill at

163
**Ceremonial cloth
(*pha yok*)** (detail)
Gujarat, probably
Ahmedabad, for export
to Thailand, 19th century
Silk and metal-wrapped
thread
266 x 82 cm
V&A: IS.35-1987

164
Skirt panel (*pha nung*)
(detail)
Coromandel Coast,
for export to Thailand,
c. 18th century
Cotton, mordant-dyed and
resist-dyed, painted (chintz)
130 x 101.5 cm
V&A: IS.40-1991

both drawing – especially the fine lines of white resist – and dyeing the rich colours required by the Thai court (pl.164). More luxurious in materials, but less time-consuming to produce, are Gujarati silks woven with gold-wrapped thread (pl.163), which also reference the flaming outlines of the Thai courtly aesthetic. These too were clearly already being traded in the sixteenth century, as Pires mentions 'brocades from Cambay' in his account of the trade from Melaka to Thailand.[97] Also from Gujarat, simple cotton block-prints for a less wealthy Thai market (pl.159) emulate in a much cruder form the refined hand-drawn and dyed chintzes.

Simple block-prints and less refined chintzes were also destined for other parts of the Malay Peninsula: a sombre-coloured piece from Kumbakonam in Tamil Nadu was collected by Caspar Purdon Clarke on his buying trip to India in 1881–2 and was described as being 'for the Singapore market' (pl.165). Repeat-pattern glazed chintzes from the Coromandel region were also labelled as being 'for Malay women to cover their heads with'.[98] Like the rest of India's textile production, the trade to Southeast Asia suffered serious setbacks by the mid-nineteenth century as a result of the introduction of British printed cottons, and the trade came to an end with the disruption caused by the Second World War.

EUROPE

The arrival of Europeans (pl.171) – first the Portuguese, then the Dutch, British, French and Danes – as part of the Asian trading community provided the impetus for the spread of the Indian textile trade into Europe, a development that had resounding implications for all sides of the partnerships concerned. The initial lure of Indian textiles, for all the foreign traders and trading companies, was their desirability as exchange goods in the hugely lucrative spice trade: the recognition of their appeal to European consumers followed soon after.

The Portuguese were the first Europeans to settle in India and to engage in trade. After Vasco da Gama's first sea voyage to India in 1498, they were quick to position themselves on India's west coast, establishing their major settlement at Goa in 1510. As early as 1508, Lisbon church records mention vestments made of patterned fabrics from Calicut and Cambay, and

165
Scarf or wrap (detail)
Kumbakonam, Tamil Nadu,
for export to Southeast
Asia, c.1881–2
Cotton, block-printed,
mordant-dyed
and resist-dyed
235 x 107 cm
V&A: IS.2307–1883

Portuguese pedlars sold Indian cloth throughout the Iberian Peninsula and beyond.[99] We learn of Portuguese traders selling 'Callicowte Cloth' in the English port city of Southampton by 1541, and several English merchants in the same city listed calico sheets and 'pillowbears' (pillowcases) in their inventories from 1555 to 1571.[100] These are likely to have come from Portuguese traders, or perhaps to have been acquired by British seamen in Lisbon, which at that time was the world's major centre for the sale of Indian cloth and spices.

While Portuguese traders were importing huge amounts of Indian woven cotton and silk cloth by the early seventeenth century,[101] they were also developing a taste for Indian embroideries, albeit on a much smaller scale. They had established a trading post at Satgaon, near modern Kolkata, in 1536, and started to have large bedcovers made, often drawing on local traditions of *kantha* embroidery. The earliest of these combine large geometric designs in the centre with animal and human figures in the borders, showing western men hunting,

reclining in palanquins or playing chess. Only two of these early examples have so far come to light, one in Lisbon and the other in Hardwick Hall in England.[102] Far more survive of a slightly later type, dating from the end of the sixteenth century or beginning of the seventeenth century. These bedcovers are elaborately embroidered with biblical and mythological scenes, along with the coats of arms of Portuguese families who had commissioned them (pl.166). Local tasar silk is used, although figures are sometimes outlined in blue or red silk, and the tasar's natural yellow colour is often enhanced with turmeric dye.[103] Several of these quilts found their way to England as well as Portugal: a record of a sale in London in 1618 described 'a Bengalla quilt ... embroidered all over with pictures of men and crafts in yellow silk' which sold for the high price of £20.[104] Another type of embroidered bedcover, also from Bengal, uses silk chain stitch often on a dark blue silk ground (pl.167). These frequently copy Portuguese designs, with the five senses a favourite theme.

167
**Coverlet, with images of
the Five Senses**
Bengal, c.1650
Silk, backed with cotton,
embroidered with silk
thread
284 x 218 cm

Given by the Friends
of the Philadelphia
Museum of Art, 1988
Philadelphia Museum
of Art, 1998-7-4

COLONEL T.H.HENDLEY, C.I.E., I.M.S., INSPECTOR-GENERAL OF CIVIL HOSPITALS, BENGAL.

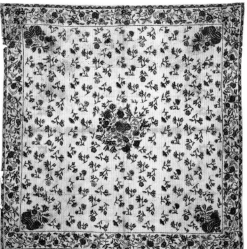

168 (above)
**Group of Bengali
handkerchiefs** (details)
(left to right)
Length of tie-dyed silk
handkerchiefs
Baharampur (Berhampur),
West Bengal, c.1880
479 x 82.5 cm
V&A: IS.678–1883

Cotton and silk handkerchief
with the name and titles of
Col. T.H. Hendley
Santipur, West Bengal,
c.1898–1903
51 x 49.5 cm
V&A: IS.218–1992

Printed silk handkerchief
West Bengal, c.1820–50
89.5 x 75 cm
V&A: IS.17–2008

169 (right)
Handkerchief
Southeast India, for export
to Europe, 18th century
Cotton, hand-drawn
outlines, mordanted and
resist-dyed ('chintz')
87 x 88 cm
Given by G.P. Baker
V&A: IS 166–1950

GROUP OF HANDKERCHIEFS

Now aged and fragile, these nineteenth-century handkerchiefs do not inspire grand visions of fashion or industry, yet they are rare survivors of a once booming trade that saw handmade Indian cloth infiltrate the everyday lives of individuals around the world. Between the early eighteenth and early nineteenth centuries alone, millions of Indian handkerchiefs were exported internationally.[1] India was once the world's leading supplier, and it is perhaps its handkerchiefs that best illustrate its ability to meet diverse market demands.

Fundamentally, all Indian handkerchiefs were cut from a *than*: a full warp length of one pattern repeated up to 12 separate times. Beyond this basic structure, however, each export market required different and quite specific designs.

Bengal specialized in handkerchiefs for the European and American markets, turning *kora* (plain undyed silk) into spotted 'bandannoes' (from Hindi *bandhana*, meaning 'to tie') and flowery 'choppas' (from Hindi *chhapna*, meaning 'to print'). Despite a prohibition on their sale in Britain between 1701 and 1826, huge quantities of Bengal handkerchiefs were smuggled through to eager British buyers every year.[2] Rampantly popular, they are frequently found in images from the period, tied around the necks of sailors, preserving the modesty of women in low-cut gowns (pl.170) and casually held by refined gentlemen sitting for portraits. By the early 1800s, America was ordering many times the quantity of its whole population, the demand for Bengali handkerchiefs expanding with the country.[3] The all-American bandannas we now associate with everything from the Wild West to inner-city gang violence are the direct successors to these imports.

'Real Madras Handkerchiefs' – or RMHK as they came to be known ('Madras' referring largely to southeast India) – were a crucial currency of the eighteenth and nineteenth-century Atlantic 'triangular trade'. These South Indian *rumals* (from Persian, meaning literally 'face wipe') were among the goods both traded in exchange for slaves and used to clothe slaves from West Africa.[4] In the West Indies, market preferences were recorded, even down to the number of individual threads dividing a pattern's checks.[5] RMHK became vital to cultures on both sides of the Atlantic – whether ritualized in Kalabari rites of passage (pl.155)[6] or symbolically tying the descendants of slaves to their shared histories.[7]

Meanwhile double-ikat *telia rumals* (pl.149) from Andhra Pradesh were so popular in the Middle East, East Africa and Southeast Asia that the handkerchiefs became known locally as *Asia rumal*.[8] *Telia rumals* were carried even as far as Japan, where the Dutch may have imported them as early as the seventeenth century.[9] There they belonged to the category of *sarasa* ('textiles from other lands')[10] and would become valued as diplomatic gifts, to wrap precious tea ceremony equipment, and be made into beautiful under-robes (pls 179, 180).

By the time Colonel T.H. Hendley, then stationed in India, commissioned (or was given) his personalized plain white cotton-silk-mix handkerchief sometime between 1898 and 1903, the Indian export handkerchief industry had been supplanted by western industrial imitations. From luxury goods of the late seventeenth century to daily necessities of the late nineteenth, the Indian handkerchief had reached nearly every corner of the world, creating a demand that mill-made versions would eventually overwhelm. Although India is no longer the world's supplier, the cultural legacies left by its handkerchiefs will likely last for many centuries to come. **AF**

1   Murphy and Crill 1991, p.186
2   Ibid., pp.160–9
3   Bean 2006, p.223
4   Tulloch 1999, p.71
5   EIC Correspondence 1802, p.825
6   Eicher 2006
7   Tulloch 1999, pp.71–2
8   Crill 1998, p.93
9   Ibid., p.98
10 Fukuoka 2014, p.13

170

An English woman wearing a tie-dyed handkerchief
Detail from George Stubbs, *Reapers*, 1785
Oil paint on wood
90 × 137 cm

Purchased with assistance from the Friends of the Tate Gallery, the Art Fund, the Pilgrim Trust and subscribers 1977
Tate Britain, London, T02257

From Goa, which remained under Portuguese rule until 1961, colourful metal-thread and silk embroideries made in the Deccan were exported to Portugal in the seventeenth and eighteenth centuries, although these were of a type also used in India itself (see pl.134). Their bright floss silks (especially the use of vivid yellows and greens) and use of metal-thread embroidery recall European embroideries of the early eighteenth century, and the Indian pieces may have acquired their distinctive colour palette in response to European examples.[105]

Like the Portuguese, the British were drawn to India primarily as an entry point to the lucrative spice trade, though they also hoped to find a market there for British woollen broadcloth and other goods such as iron and tin.[106] Indian cloth had to be purchased as barter for spices in Indonesia, and the East India Company, set up in 1600, planned to generate the income with which to buy the cloth through sales of English goods. It established its first base in Surat in 1608 to this end, but sales were disappointing and the Company turned to the re-export trade to raise funds: Indian cotton textiles were shipped to London, and then sent on to North Africa and the Middle East, which had a huge hunger for Indian muslin turbans and sashes, as well as to West Africa (see pp.145–7).

The possibility that Indian fabrics, specifically dyed cottons or pintados, might 'vent well' in England occurred to perceptive agents such as William Finch, the Company agent in Surat, as early as 1609, and by 1613 Company records show that they were on sale in London, albeit in small quantities. By the 1670s the Company's focus had completely swung away from trading for spices in Southeast Asia to supplying textiles to the home market, especially cotton textiles from Bengal. The story of the introduction of Indian cotton textiles into Britain from the seventeenth century onwards, and the profound impact they had on British furnishings, dress and design, is a well-known and complex one that has been recounted by many authors.[107] By far the bulk of the trade was in plain, striped or checked fabric, each with its own trade name, usually an anglicized version of a local term. Only a few of these names are still known today – gingham, calico, chintz, dungarees, tussar and seersucker, for example – while dozens of others have fallen from use and are identifiable only in the broadest sense (pl.172). The humble handkerchief, checked, printed or spotted by tie-dyeing (*bandhna:* the origin of the term 'bandanna'), was a major

category of textile imported from India, and was an accessory that people of almost all levels of society could afford (pl.168).

A much smaller component of the trade was in richly patterned and dyed chintzes and embroideries. Superbly embroidered bed hangings and, later, dress fabrics were made in silk chain stitch by Gujarati embroiderers (pl.173). These were developed to suit western taste, with designs or 'musters' being sent out for the craftsmen to copy. The designs were initially based on English crewel-work embroideries, which could also be copied in chintz,[108] but like all the export textiles they evolved into hybrid creations that combined western, Indian and later East Asian components.

171 (opposite)
Hanging
Coromandel Coast,
c.1640–50 (the borders
early 18th century)
Cotton, mordant-dyed
and resist-dyed (chintz)
259 x 152 cm
V&A: 687–1898

172
Bill of sale of East India
Company goods
24 February 1734
British Library, London

173 (and detail opposite)
Bed or wall hanging
Gujarat, for export
to Europe, c.1700
Cotton embroidered
with silk
190.5 x 164 cm
V&A: IS.155–1953

SET OF BED HANGINGS

These Indian chintz furnishings for a four-poster bed were originally part of a complete room setting in Schloss Hof. This hunting castle in the Marchfeld near Vienna was bought in 1725 by Prince Eugene of Savoy (1663–1736), the Paris-born Habsburg military commander. In 1755 the castle was acquired by Maria Theresia for the imperial family.

Two single beds and six chair covers are remnants of an *en suite* room furnishing; the wall hangings have not survived. The material, cotton, suggests it was the summer furnishing of a room in the castle. The bed hangings consist of a tester, a headcloth, a counterpane, eight valances and three curtains. The lower parts of the dyed and painted Indian cotton panels used for the bed feature a strongly stylized rocky landscape populated by human figures and wild animals. Disproportionately large shoots grow out of the rocks and wind upwards, issuing fantastic, mainly red, flowers and coiled leaves in different shapes. Birds and insects fill the spaces between the individual flourishing branches. The design is strikingly similar to the so-called 'Ashburnham' hanging in the V&A (IS.156–1953) and is presumably contemporary with it and others in this design. The colours are somewhat faded from use, under the seams as well as on the surface, which suggests a different use of the textile before it was adapted for this bed. It is lined with blue silk and blue linen.

While building and furnishing his palaces, Prince Eugene acquired large numbers of textiles in England, the Netherlands and France. Among them were this bed, along with a surviving room-setting of appliqué Indian chintz in chinoiserie designs and a set of Indian embroidered bed furnishings. After the Prince's death in 1736 an inventory of Schloss Hof was drawn up. One room was explicitly mentioned as being decorated *en suite* with Indian printed cotton (room number 31). It included, among other things, a double bed and six ordinary chairs – the number matching with the surviving chair covers in the MAK. Evidence from

technical investigation suggests that the two single beds, now in the MAK, were originally a double bed. The inventory also matches with the surviving beds in the description of the blue and white braids and the blue lining. Thus an identification of the beds with the one mentioned in the inventory becomes quite likely. Most probably, the double bed was adapted for two single beds at the time of the latest documented alterations in the castle in the nineteenth century. **BK**

See further:
Haller 1903; Braubach 1963–5; Frantes 2005; Hanzl-Wachter 2005; Völker 2005; Völker 2007.

174 (above and detail opposite)
Bed with chintz hangings
Coromandel Coast, for export to Europe, c.1700; made up in Vienna early to mid-18th century
Height: approx. 250–80 cm; length: 220 cm; width: 110 cm
MAK, Vienna, T 9073

175
**Wall hanging or bedcover
(*palampore*)**
Coromandel Coast, for
export to Europe, c.1750–60
Cotton, mordant-dyed and
resist-dyed (chintz)
264 x 223 cm
V&A: IM.85–1937

176 (opposite)
**Wall hanging or bedcover
(*palampore*) with
Japanese designs**
Coromandel Coast, for
export to Europe, c.1725–50

Cotton, mordant-dyed
and resist-dyed (chintz)
279 x 204 cm
Duivenvoorde Castle,
Voorschoten

**Man's informal coat
(*japonse rok* or *banyan*)**
Coromandel Coast, for
export to Europe, *c.*1750
Cotton, mordant-dyed and
resist-dyed (chintz)
Length: 145 cm
Gemeentemuseum
Den Haag, The Hague,
K 139-1964

Satin stitch, more often associated with Chinese than Indian embroidery, was introduced into Indian trade textiles in the eighteenth century following the opening up of the China trade and the popularity of the so-called 'chinoiserie' style in Europe.

The textiles with the most enduring association with Britain's trade with India are undoubtedly chintz and muslin. In addition to the unaccustomed lightness of cotton cloth and the fastness of Indian dyes, Indian chintzes gave ordinary people the opportunity to wear and use colourful and richly patterned fabrics without having to pay the high price of woven silk. Their popularity and consequent threat to local weavers led to the prohibition, by Acts of Parliament of 1701 and 1721, of Indian plain and printed calico. Some of the dramatic stories in relation to this ban are well known, such as the mob of 5,000 protesting weavers marching on Parliament in 1697, and the shocking physical assaults on calico printers and women wearing chintz dresses in 1712.[109] Countless smaller individual stories reflect the effect of the Acts on ordinary people of the time, such as newspaper reports of smugglers arrested and banned goods seized, and of individuals fined £5 for wearing chintz dresses (a sum that was doubled to £10 in 1769 'to encourage the printed cotton and linen manufacturers of this kingdom'[110]). The chintz ban was lifted in 1774, by which time developments in spinning and, a little later, printing technology ensured that British and European imitations of Indian chintzes supplanted the originals.

Indian chintzes were relatively cheap to buy, but their fashionable status meant that they were popular at all levels of society in the eighteenth century. High-profile tastemakers such as Madame de Pompadour in France[111] or Prince Eugene of Savoy (pl.174) adopted it for dress or furnishing, as did middle-class ladies such as Barbara Johnson, a British parson's daughter.[112] Servants would sometimes be given chintz dresses by their mistresses, and some of the poorer women who were forced to give up their babies to the Foundling Hospital in London left tokens in the form of chintz pieces.[113]

Because of their relatively high status (although they never attained the elite associations of French or Italian silk) Indian chintzes tended to be preserved and are thus the most prominent surviving representatives of the textile trade. This is especially true in the Netherlands, where both public and private collections reflect the dominance of chintz furnishings, bedcovers and dress in eighteenth-century households (pls 176,

178 (opposite)
Jacket
Coromandel Coast, for
export to Europe, *c.*1750
Cotton, mordant-dyed and
resist-dyed (chintz), lined
with linen
Length: 84.4 cm
Given by G.P. Baker
V&A: IS.12-1950

Petticoat
Coromandel Coast, for
export to Europe, *c.*1725
Cotton, mordant-dyed and
resist-dyed (chintz)
Length: 111.7 cm
Given by G.P. Baker
V&A: IS.14-1950

177).[114] The Dutch also carried chintz, along with Bengali silk textiles and yarn, to Japan, trading first from Banten (Bantam) in Java and then from 1619 from Batavia (modern-day Jakarta). The imported chintz was, and still is, known in Japan as *sarasa* and was used in small pieces on garments and in tea ceremony paraphernalia, mainly because ordinary people were prohibited from wearing upper garments of colourful imported fabrics. A rare surviving chintz kimono, clearly made specifically as an inner kimono for a Japanese man of very high standing, survives in a private collection in Japan (pl.180). Indian striped and checked cotton fabrics (*shima-mono*, pl.179) also became immensely popular in Japan in the later seventeenth century, and by the mid-eighteenth century garments with vertical stripes 'began to occupy a central place in the fashion culture of the city [Edo: modern-day Tokyo]'.[115] Other export chintzes also found their way to Japan with the Dutch, including pieces clearly made with the Thai market in mind, which were recycled as fashionable kimonos (pl.181).

Muslins – fine, plain-woven cotton fabrics – were not prohibited in the eighteenth-century Acts, and their popularity lasted until the early nineteenth century, when spinning and weaving advances meant that mills in Scotland and Lancashire could supply fabrics almost as finely woven and considerably cheaper. Although fine muslin was made in several parts of India (Arni, in today's Tamil Nadu, for example, was a major producer – see pl.4),[116] it was Bengal that supplied most of the exported cottons, including fine muslin. From the 1760s onwards small numbers of expensive, finely woven Kashmir shawls were also imported as elegant accompaniments to loosely draped muslin dresses (pl.183).[117]

While cotton dominated Britain's trade with India, Bengali and Assamese silk also played an important role from the late seventeenth century onwards. Fine mulberry silk fabrics were already being imported into Britain from Iran and Syria, but the Indian imports were the less fine (and therefore cheaper) tasar and eri silks (see pl.7). *Arindi* (*endi* or *eri*) fabric in particular was considered 'a raw sort of cloth, neither silk nor cotton' on account of its rough texture, which was 'given … to poor people to wear and to lay in shops to be footed upon before 'tis fit to be sold'.[118] In 1679 a single bale of it was sent to England as a trial, but it was not a success. However, Job Charnock, the founder of Calcutta, persevered, as it was exceptionally strong and durable and he hoped that people would become 'acquainted to wearing of it', and

so imports of *arindi* cloth rose to 600 pieces in 1680 and 1,000 pieces in 1681.[119] Fabrics made of non-mulberry silk like these were often called 'herba' goods, while other Bengali silks, usually of mulberry silk mixed with cotton, were called 'taffeties' (from Persian *tafta*, meaning 'spun'). These were developed via advice in Company letters in the 1650s, with instructions to degum them before dyeing, a process that made them 'as glossy as Italian silks'.[120] By 1682 these 'taffeties' were described as 'a sure staple commodity … So great is the vent of that commodity for lyning all sorts of garments for Men and Women.'[121] Bengali mulberry silk continued to be a vital component of British-made mixed textiles into the nineteenth century: a minute of 1808 states that 'Bengal silk was become highly necessary in many branches of manufacture'.[122] A printed chart of 1817 lists the Bengali centres of silk production and the prices of their products (pl.182).[123]

In terms of quantity, the East India Company's trade in textiles from India reached its peak in the final years of the eighteenth century, when about 1.5 million pieces were exported.[124] Such quantities were achieved partly by means

179

Man's inner robe
Coromandel Coast, for export to Japan, c.1700–50
Cotton, warp and weft ikat field; mordant-dyed and resist-dyed (chintz) borders
Length: 143.9 cm
Kyushu National Museum, Dazaifu

180
Man's inner robe
Coromandel Coast, for
export to Japan, c.1720–30
Cotton, mordant-dyed and
resist-dyed (chintz)
Length: 137.5 cm
Private collection, Nagoya

181
Man's under-kimono
Coromandel Coast, for
export to Thailand; made
up into a robe in Japan,
c.1750–1800
Cotton, mordant-dyed
and resist-dyed (chintz)
Length: 137 cm
The Khalili Collection
of Kimono, KX 230

of severe exploitation of weavers by the Company in Bengal, Gujarat and south India.[125] Regulations were imposed that forced the weavers to work exclusively for the Company, which paid them less than all other buyers, including other nations' Companies. Weavers resorted to subterfuge in order to try to sell their goods elsewhere, but this led to threats and violence against them, carried out by Company sepoys. This kind of oppression may be the source of the stories of weavers having their thumbs cut off by the Company, which no authority has been able to verify.[126]

It was of course at precisely this time – the end of the eighteenth century – that advances were taking place in England that would reduce India's textile trade to a fraction of its former scale. By the 1850s cotton cloth was being sent from England to India (pls 186, 189),[127] and Britain's hope of making India a lucrative market for British-made cloth, an enterprise that had failed so miserably in the seventeenth century, had at last been realized. The effect of this reversal in the direction of trade went far beyond a purely economic impact on India's weavers – it was to affect the subsequent history of South Asia and the world as a whole.

182
Current prices of silk sold by the East India Company
1817
13.7 x 13.2 cm
V&A: IS.57A-1990

183
Dress
Probably Dhaka, made up in England, c.1810
Cotton, embroidered with cotton thread
Length: 177.8 cm
Given by Miss P.H. Rew
V&A: Circ.30-1958

Shawl
Kashmir, c.1750–60
Goat hair (pashmina), twill tapestry weave
288 x 128 cm
Given by Miss M. Davis
V&A: IM.17-1915

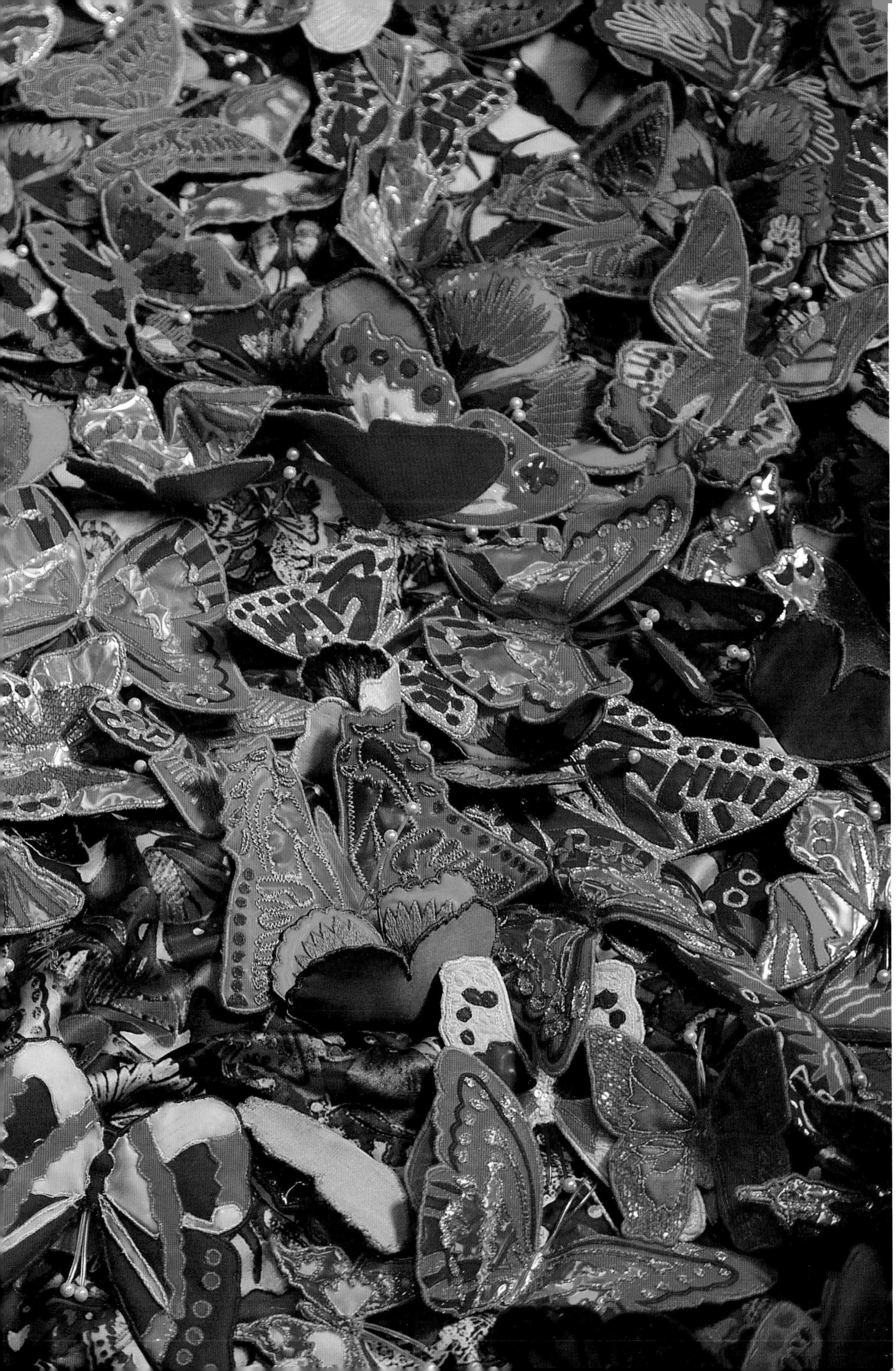

3 TEXTILES IN THE MODERN WORLD

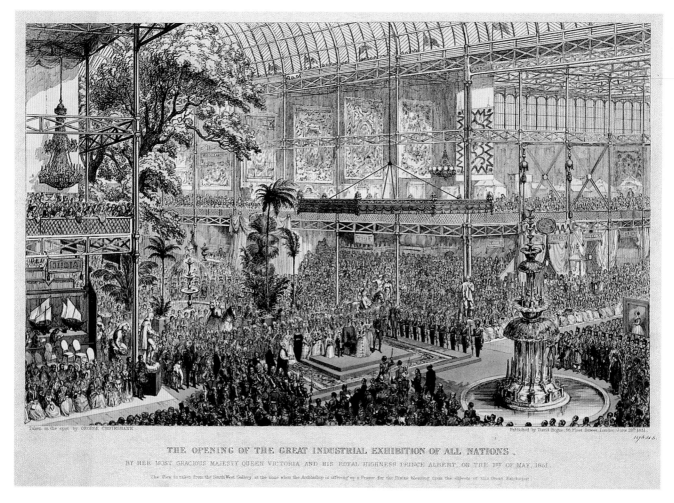

THE OPENING OF THE GREAT INDUSTRIAL EXHIBITION OF ALL NATIONS,
BY HER MOST GRACIOUS MAJESTY QUEEN VICTORIA AND HIS ROYAL HIGHNESS PRINCE ALBERT, ON THE 1ST OF MAY, 1851
The View is taken from the South West Gallery, at the time when the Archbishop is offering up a Prayer for the Divine blessing upon the objects of this Great Exhibition

The Great Exhibition of the Works of Industry of All Nations held in London in 1851 was hailed as a wonder of modern times. The vast glass and iron structure constructed to house it, spread across 19 acres of Hyde Park, demonstrated the marvels of industrial engineering. Inside this 'Crystal Palace' displays from across the world presented the progress of industrialized nations, the advantages of free trade and the possibilities of new technology. Within this international context of modernity, change and celebration, Indian textiles made a significant impact. They were at the centre of topical debates that focused on the effects of industrialization and mass production, design education, trade and empire (pl.184).[1]

Britain showcased its industrial prowess and imperial authority with the largest display in the building. Of this, the Indian court revealed the greatest riches and splendour of empire. An array of Indian textiles selected by the East India Company included fine gold and silk brocades from Ahmedabad (Gujarat), woollen shawls from Kashmir and diaphanous white muslins from Bengal.[2] Leading figures in the organization of the Great Exhibition, such as Henry Cole (1808–1882), Richard Redgrave (1804–1888) and Owen Jones (1809–1874),

184
**The Opening of the
Great Industrial Exhibition
of All Nations**
George Cruikshank, c.1851
Hand-coloured etching
25.3 × 40.3 cm
V&A: 19648

185

**Two lengths of furnishing
or dress fabric** (details)

(left) Ahmedabad, Gujarat,
c.1850
Silk and gold-
wrapped thread

268 x 79 cm
Purchased from the
Great Exhibition of 1851
V&A: 779–1852

(right) Probably
Ahmedabad, Gujarat, c.1850
Silk and gold-
wrapped thread

225 x 76.5 cm
Purchased from the
Great Exhibition of 1851
V&A: 788–1852

were advocates of the design reform movement and saw education in design as one of the objectives of the enterprise. Industrialization in Britain had caused a decline of traditional craftsmanship and an aesthetic confusion of ornamentation on mass-manufactured products. In seeking to educate manufacturers and the public about the principles of good design, they held up Indian textiles as worthy examples. The textiles were praised for their exquisite workmanship, richness of material and harmony of pattern with colour (pl.185).[3]

Another primary objective of the Great Exhibition, and subsequent exhibitions held across the world, was to facilitate trade between nations. For the East India Company, India was the main market for British goods, and the benefits of this were already evident in the growth of the Lancashire cotton mills since the 1780s, which by the 1830s were exporting up to 51 million yards of the fabric to India.[4] Thus India, the world's greatest producer of cotton textiles, was reduced to exporting raw cotton and importing foreign cloth, a process that had begun with the importation of yarn: by the late 1820s the price of Indian yarn was twice that of English yarn.[5] This is illustrated in a fine piece of cotton from Chanderi (Madhya Pradesh) – white with silver border, purchased from the 1867 Paris Exhibition – which is labelled as being 'made of English thread' (pl.186). The impact of this on an individual level is noted in a rare account by a Bengali widow dated to 1828:

> The weavers would come to my doorstep to buy the yarn thus spun ... Now for over three years, the mother and daughter-in-law are facing ricelessness again. Not only have the weavers stopped coming to buy my yarn, even when I send it to the hat [market place] they will not buy at one-fourth of the former price. I am completely at a loss to understand how this has come to pass. I made inquiries and have learned that the weavers are using English yarn now being extensively imported ... When I examined the yarn I indeed found it better than mine.[6]

The international exhibitions provided examples of textiles from which manufacturers could take inspiration and potentially reproduce and export. Another tool to advance commerce was a set of 18 volumes entitled *The Textile Fabrics of India*, which contained fabric samples from across

India, detailing their region of production, cost, weight and dimensions (pl.187). Under the leadership of John Forbes Watson (1827–92), Reporter on the Products of India at the India Office, these impressive sample books, which he regarded as 'trade museums', were distributed to chambers of commerce and schools of art across Britain to function as guides to aid British manufacturers wishing to expand into new markets.[7]

Displayed in the Paris Exhibition of 1867 was a bundle of 24 samples of cotton checked fabric labelled as 'trousering' from Visakhapatnam in southeast India (pl.188). The samples illustrate the variety of woven pattern of a utilitarian nature

186 (opposite)
Length of cotton cloth (detail)
England (yarn spun),
Chanderi, Madhya Pradesh
(woven), c.1867

Cotton and
silver-wrapped thread
900 x 77 cm
V&A: 0138 (IS)

187
***The Textile Fabrics
of India***
Album page,
vol.X, no.373,
c.1866

Printed cotton piece-
good sample
31 x 19.4 cm
V&A: Asia Department
Library

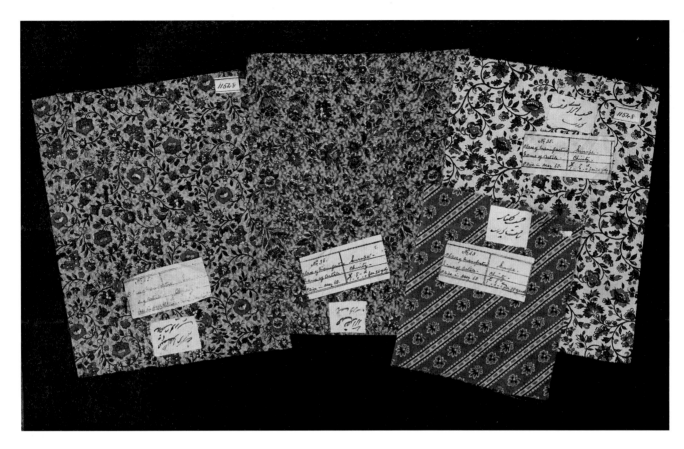

available in India, including one with a houndstooth design, a quintessentially British pattern. Forbes Watson notes that such designs were 'manufactured by the native weaver to suit European wants in India', drawing attention to the Indian weaver's ability to copy and adapt to a new market – a skill British manufacturers needed to emulate.[8] In India, these fabrics also catered for the new professional classes employed in government offices, who adopted western-style clothes.[9] European fabrics made inroads into the markets for mid-range and fine fabrics.[10] They appealed to the Indian population because of their low prices, quality, fastness of synthetic dyes, and the prestige of being able to dress in European cloth, which came to be regarded as cleaner and finer than homespun (pl.190).[11] Evidence of English cloth penetrating into the remoter regions, made possible by the railways, is illustrated

in samples purchased in Peshawar (in present-day Pakistan) in 1869 (pl.189).[12] These fabrics were intended to imitate the colours and patterns of Indian designs.

Indian weavers suffered because they were unable to compete with the quality and prices of imported fabric and were only able to maintain a hold on the market for either very coarse or extremely fine cloth. The amount of cloth woven in India between 1850 and 1880 fell by 40 per cent; but although there was also a marked decline in the variety of cloth being produced, the actual number of weavers did not decline.[13] At the same time, India too was beginning to industrialize its textile production. The first cotton mills were established in Bombay (Mumbai) and Ahmedabad from the late 1850s onwards.[14] This fledgling industry had difficulties establishing itself because of the British government's failure to protect the market with import duties.[15]

188 (opposite)
Trousering sample
swatches
Visakhapatnam,
Andhra Pradesh, c.1867
Cotton, 24 swatches
70 x 96 cm (each)
V&A: 5266 (IS)

189
Four fragments
of printed cotton
Woven and printed
in Europe, c.1869
Cotton

(left to right)
25 x 19.2 cm
V&A: 1738 (IS)
24.3 x 20.3 cm
V&A: 1734 (IS)

24 x 18.7 cm
V&A: 1735 (IS)
16.5 x 14.2 cm
V&A: 1731 (IS)

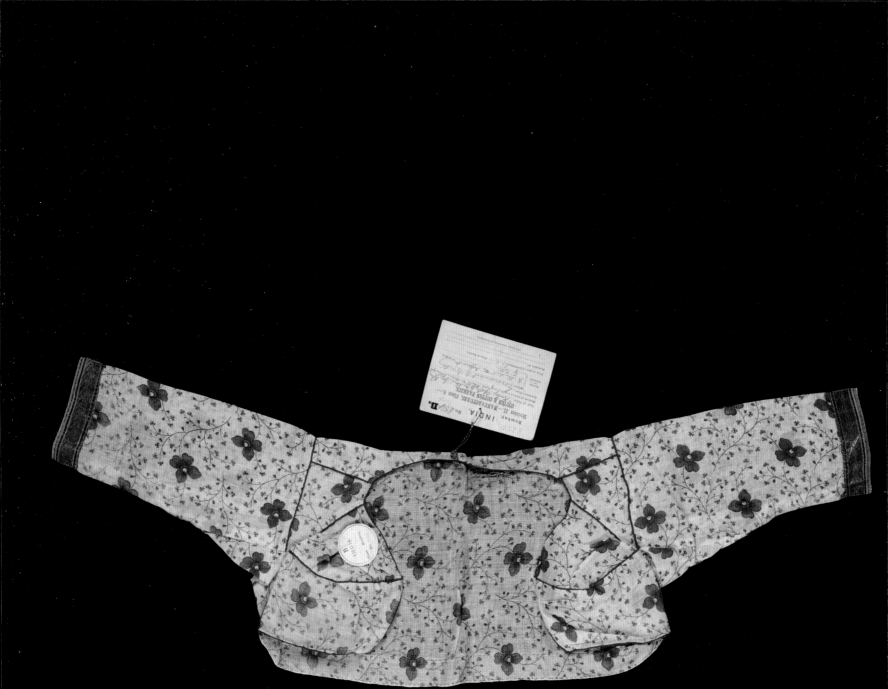

CHOLI (WOMAN'S BODICE)

This unassuming muslin choli is similar to other Indian garments in the V&A collections, but with significant differences in the origin and design of its fabric. Made in many styles and worn with either a skirt (*ghaghra*) or a sari, the choli evolved from ancient forms of wrapped breast-coverings for women; stitched versions may have been brought in from regions north of India in the early Christian era. The front-fastening choli, like this one, was probably a later development for wearing under a sari.[1]

The close-fitting shape, red seam bindings and bands of woven gold-wrapped thread on the sleeves of this particular bodice are typical of contemporary garments worn by Indian women, whether made from luxurious fabrics or pieced together from scraps of material. However, neither the violet motifs decorating the muslin nor their mauve colour is characteristic of Indian textiles. The original label attached to the garment describes it as 'Kutori Choley' (*katori* meaning 'cup'), either from Multan (then in Bombay Presidency, now in Pakistan) or in Multani style. It notes that the bodice is made from 'English Cloth'. This would have been machine-woven in England using imported long-staple cotton and printed in synthetic colours using a mechanical printing process.

The label is from the 1872 London International Exhibition. Cotton was a key theme of the Indian display, and this and many other cotton garments were also shown the following year at the Vienna Exhibition. A large number of cotton garments were exhibited alongside cotton seeds, raw cotton, and models and drawings of cotton manufacture. The inclusion of several cholis made from English-manufactured cotton illustrates the British government's contradictory efforts to improve Indian cotton production while supporting the attempts of the British cotton industry to penetrate the vast market of its Indian empire. Indian muslin – and particularly that from Bengal, made from local short-staple cotton – was a highly valued fabric both within India and in export markets, and had been a key commodity in the East India Company's trade. However, the success of this and other Indian cotton fabrics in the West had led to copying, and British cotton and muslin exports to India contributed to the near collapse of its traditional industries based on hand-weaving, notably in Bengal. **SA**

1   Goswamy 1993, pp.185–8.

190 (opposite)
Choli (woman's bodice)
Printed in Europe, made up
in western India, c.1871
Cotton with attached
borders of woven
gold-wrapped thread
Length: 31 cm
V&A: 8250 (IS)

KHADI AND THE SWADESHI MOVEMENT

The plight of the weavers and of the textile mills galvanized a political movement known as Swadeshi (meaning 'homeland'). Discontent with British rule had been steadily rising on many levels, with Indian mill owners and businessmen calling for action to support indigenous industries since the 1850s. Swadeshi urged the Indian population to boycott foreign goods, leading protesters in Dacca (Dhaka) and Bombay to publicly burn piles of foreign cloth in 1896.[16] The nation was encouraged to wear Indian fabric, an ideology that fuelled the nationalist movement in the ensuing years.

Khadi, a humble fabric, hand-woven from hand-spun yarn, was elevated into a symbol of defiance and freedom by Mohandas Karamchand Gandhi (1869–1948) in the 1920s. For him, *khadi* embodied moral, social, economic and political values. Informed by the Swadeshi boycotts and having read about the economic impact of the Lancashire mills on India's

Support and save your starving weavers
by the use of handloom products

192 (bottom)
Page from *Cartoon Booklet*
with 50 cartoons
on Swadeshi
1938
British Library, London,
P/T2978

191 (top)
Gandhi spinning cotton
in Ahmedabad, c.1931

34

193

Piece of *khadi* cotton (top)
Sadra, Gujarat
*c.*1867
112 x 63 cm
V&A: 0120 (IS)

Dhoti (bottom)
Ahmedabad, *c.*1867
Khadi cotton
352 x 94 cm
V&A: 5955 (IS)

textile industry, Gandhi lamented, 'it is difficult to measure the harm that Manchester has done to us'.[17] Furthermore, he declared that 'Foreign cloth must be totally banished from the Indian market, if India is to become an economically free nation, if her peasantry is to be freed from chronic pauperism ... Protection of her staple industry is her birthright.'[18] Inspired by the writings of John Ruskin (1819–1900) and his advocacy of an anti-industrial utopia, Gandhi argued that India's future lay not with western-style industrialization but in a village-led economy.[19] The resumption of hand-spinning and other village industries was a way of restoring meaningful labour to the masses, of achieving economic independence and ultimately self-rule. Gandhi called for the Indian people to take up spinning yarn, and weaving and wearing *khadi* (pls 191, 192). Furthermore, he also encouraged the boycotting of fabric from

India's mills. He disseminated his message by spinning in public while addressing gatherings, and simplified his dress so that he could identify with the masses and they could identify with him. The *khadi* cap he 'designed' became the iconic 'Gandhi cap'.[20] As the movement gained momentum, the visual impact of his clothing and the large crowds of supporters wearing *khadi* and Gandhi caps became a powerful tool of protest (pl.194).[21]

Gandhi chose to build his ashram in Ahmedabad in Gujarat, his home state, which had historically been associated with textile production. Gujarati examples of *khadi* had been collected by the India Museum (the forerunner of the V&A) long before Gandhi began his movement, including a white dhoti of fine cotton with simple red and blue borders, woven in around 1867 in Ahmedabad, and a much rougher cotton woven in Sadra in the Mahıkantha district of Gujarat (pl.193). The difference in

194
**Protesting the arrest
of Gandhi**
Bombay, 1930

195
**Jawaharlal Nehru,
President of India's
Congress Party, in his
library at home**
Photographed by
Margaret Bourke-White for
LIFE Magazine, 1946

quality between the two examples illustrates the contradictions of *khadi* that Gandhi had to deal with. Fine *khadi* was expensive and more costly than mill cloth, while cheaper versions were rough and had little appeal.[22] *Khadi* cloth was also often in short supply. Members of the Indian National Congress (INC), the main political party opposing British rule, began wearing it from 1921 as part of their official programme of resistance.[23] Recognizing *khadi* as central to their message of self-sufficiency, they incorporated the spinning wheel into the design of a flag for the nationalist movement. This firmly established *khadi* as a symbol of the nation.[24] Jawaharlal Nehru, leader of the INC and later to become India's first Prime Minister, used the symbolism of *khadi* in many ways, including tailoring it into a semi-fitted coat with a closed collar, which became an iconic piece of clothing known as the 'Nehru jacket' (pl.195).[25]

MODERNIZING THE HANDLOOM

Adapting artisan skills to meet new urban needs was the remit of several post-Independence institutions such as the All India Handloom Board and the All India Handicrafts Board, both set up in 1952, the Khadi and Village Industries Commission and the Weavers Service Centres, established in 1957 (pl.196). They had to modernize handloom production to revitalize it and give it a contemporary relevance while taking account of the simultaneous drive to further industrialize India's textile manufacturing (pl.197).[26] The founding in 1949 of the Calico Museum of Textiles in Ahmedabad was part of the new vision for education in India. Its modern exterior was matched by modern displays inside that gave a historical and technical overview of Indian textiles, taking the visitor through the economic background, raw materials, processes

196
**Advertisement for All India
Handloom Board**
Published in *Marg*, vol.XVII,
no.2, 1962

197
**Advertisement for
Raymond Woollen Mills**
Published in *Marg*, vol.III,
no.3, 1949

198 (left)
**Wedding of Indira
and Feroze Gandhi**
Anand Bhavan, Allahabad,
26 March 1942

199 (opposite
and detail above)
**Indira Gandhi's
wedding sari**
Delhi, c.1942
Khadi cotton with silk and
metal thread embroidery
Indira Gandhi Memorial
Trust Museum, New Delhi

INDIRA GANDHI'S WEDDING SARI

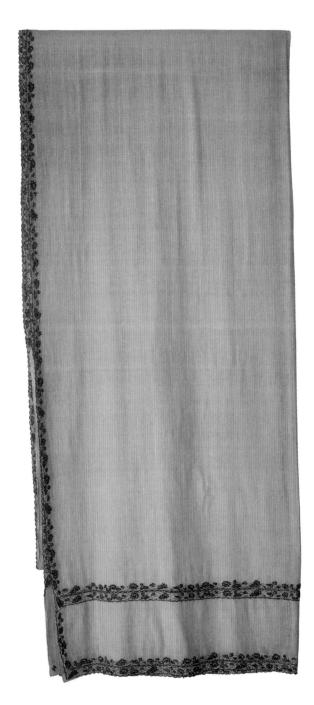

n 1920, following the non-cooperation movement against the British Raj, the Nehru family were among the first members of the Indian National Congress (INC) to adopt *khadi*. In 1921 and 1933, Motilal Nehru's daughters Vijay Lakshmi Pandit and Krishna Hutheesing wore *khadi* cotton saris at their weddings. A pearl-studded silk sari worn by young Kamala Kaul at her 1916 wedding to Jawaharlal Nehru was already a memory, albeit of a not-so-distant past.

By early 1942, Winston Churchill had sent Sir Stafford Cripps on a doomed mission to negotiate Indian support towards Britain's Second World War efforts. By then the Japanese Imperial Army had driven the British out of much of Southeast Asia and reached Rangoon, to the alarm of the Indian populace. It was against the backdrop of these stormy events that Indira Priyadarshini Nehru and Feroze Gandhi announced their wedding.

On 26 March 1942, Indira and Feroze Gandhi wed under the canopy-covered veranda of Anand Bhavan, Allahabad. The bride wore a pale pink *khadi* cotton sari hand-woven from thread spun by her father Jawaharlal Nehru while he was incarcerated during the still-ongoing struggle for India's freedom. The scallop-edged sari is embroidered all along its length with tiny silver and pink threads depicting lotus blooms, buds and leaves emerging from thin borders simulating running water. The utter simplicity of the *khadi* wedding sari was a deliberate choice, and a conscious reflection on Nehru's adherence to the Mahatma's constructive programme of Poorna Swaraj (complete independence). The movement aimed towards finding all the 'necessaries' of life within India, especially cloth. The Nehrus' use of the sari as a political statement thus captured the popular imagination and has been much mythologized. Today it is referenced as one among several hallowed symbols of India's long struggle for freedom.

> *The Charkha in the hands of a poor widow brings a paltry pice to her, in the hands of Jawaharlal it is an instrument of India's freedom. It is the office which gives the charkha its dignity. It is the office assigned to the constructive programme which gives it an irresistible prestige and power ... For my handling of civil disobedience without the constructive programme will be like a paralysed hand attempting to lift a spoon.*[1]   **PK**

1 'Constructive Programme: Its Meaning and Place', 13 December 1941, in *The Collected Works of Mahatma Gandhi*, vol.LXXV (New Delhi, 1941–2 [1994 reprint]), p.166.

and purpose of textiles. This survey was 'undertaken not in the spirit of an antiquarian revivalism but as a substructure of the future edifice of a living and modern Indian textile art'.[27] The museum's impressive collection was not intended to invite an imitation of the past, but was to be used to suggest ways of moving forwards with solutions appropriate for successive new generations. Influential cultural figures such as Mulk Raj Anand (1905–2004) and Pupul Jayakar (1915–1997) argued for the need to innovate in the handloom industry where tradition was not to be 'perceived as static, to be clung to blindly, rather progress required it to be adaptable and open to reinvention, within the spirit of the times to meet the "contemporary challenges of new functions, new technologies, new environment, and new relationships"'.[28] Adaptations in design to create more contemporary handloom fabrics was initiated by the Weavers Service Centres but with limited success.[29] The role of design in enabling innovation became more significant and more formalized after the founding of the National Institute of Design (NID) in 1961.[30]

The legacy of such post-Independence initiatives is apparent today. In the case of *khadi*, this fabric is still being produced, although partly mechanized spinning wheels have now come into use.[31] It is sold at heavily subsidized prices through government-run retail outlets called Khadi Gramodyog Bhavan situated across India stocked with dhotis, towels, saris and uncut fabric.[32] Its most recognizable item is the men's kurta, a collarless loose-fitting shirt that carries a patriotic symbolism often exploited by politicians during election times. *Khadi* also has an enduring romantic association with artisanal knowledge and handmaking traditions that appeals to contemporary fashion designers.

200
Sari by Taanbaan
Andhra Pradesh, 2014
Khadi cotton with *jamdani* brocading and metallic thread
564 x 116 cm
V&A: IS.14–2015

Many of them incorporate the fabric into their collections: Rajesh Pratap Singh has woven his own fine-count *khadi* in his studios to create beautifully diaphanous shirts, and Rashmi Varma has created a range of fashionable outfits using different textures and colours of *khadi*.[33] Taanbaan, a Delhi-based company run by Rta Kapur Chishti, is dedicated to sustaining handloom weaving and specializes in high-end saris and stoles (pl.200).[34] Recently emerging on the market is *khadi* denim, which has been developed by Arvind Limited in Ahmedabad and is being promoted by fashion designers.[35]

In between the Khadi Gramodyog Bhavan's outdated garments and high-end fashion is the clothing from Fabindia, a brand that built its reputation on Gandhian values and the sustaining of traditional fabrics by linking rural communities to urban markets. Since the 1990s a rising middle class has turned to Fabindia to buy tailored handloom garments, with *khadi* items available in more fashionable cuts, colours and designs. Fabindia was founded in the 1960s at a time when there was a post-Independence drive to promote crafts as an intermediary form of employment for a largely agrarian population to ease the way into full industrialization. The company was committed to creating a fair but profitable enterprise with the craft communities as the cornerstone, and it began by exporting furnishing fabrics, its most important client from 1965 being Terence Conran in London.[36] In the 1970s Fabindia fostered a domestic market for well-designed products with a set of ethical values attached. It cultivated a new generation of consumers who wanted Indian homespun fabrics with a modern aesthetic to furnish their homes, and to wear. Their simple kurta-pyjama suits were highly fashionable and remain a staple product today (pl.201).

201
Man wearing *khadi* kurta, waistcoat and dhoti
Jaipur, Rajasthan, 2014

ADAPTATION AND INNOVATION

The challenges facing handmade textile production were
complex and continue to be so. The decline and reinvention
of *chikankari* is a trajectory that is common to many textile
crafts. It illustrates the impact of government policies and the
commercial expansion of the 1960s and '70s on the adaptation
and innovation undertaken by designers in the 1980s through
to the present day. *Chikankari* is white embroidery on white
cotton produced mainly in Lucknow. High-quality work is
distinguished by extremely fine and even stitches, the variety of
which, when combined with delicate floral designs, trailing stems
and fine trellis patterns, creates the impression of lightness and
sophistication. There are myths surrounding its origins, and
surviving examples are traced to nineteenth-century Bengal,
where it appealed to European tastes, and to Lucknow, where
it was favoured by the ruling nawabs and their courts (pl.202).[37]

The decline of courtly patronage in the late nineteenth
century, followed later by post-Partition migration of wealthy
patrons out of Lucknow, led to a decline in demand and a
consequent deterioration in the quality of the embroidery. After
Independence, state-run enterprises promoted *chikankari* as a
means of generating employment for rural communities by both
producing for the domestic market and vigorously developing the
export industry. Increased commercialization in the 1960s saw
the demand for rougher, less precise work increase, and the

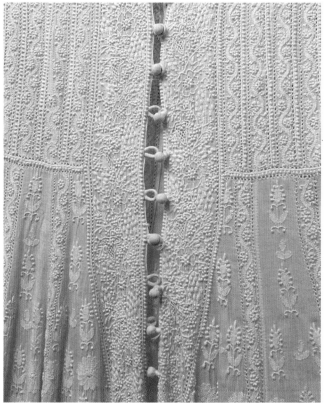

202 (top)
Sari (detail)
Lucknow, Uttar Pradesh,
c.1900
Cotton, embroidered with
cotton and tasar silk
532 x 119 cm
V&A: IS.5–2009

203 (bottom)
Detail of *anarkali*
(long dress)
Designed by Abu Jani
Sandeep Khosla
Lucknow, Uttar Pradesh,
2009

Cotton, embroidered
with cotton
Length: 134.7 cm
Collection of Abu Jani
Sandeep Khosla

demand for fine work, traditionally done by men, decline.[38] Men left the industry because of the fall in prestige and wages; women replaced them, but with less-developed skills. The production process was controlled by middlemen who orchestrated every stage of the making; they gave tailored garments marked with block-printed patterns to the women embroiderers who worked in their own homes and were paid according to the quality of their stitches. While this enabled women to earn extra income, it was also the source of much exploitation, as commercial demands for low-skilled work depressed wages. Over time, government schemes and non-governmental organizations (NGOs) have tried to create systems that 'empower' women by removing the middleman and providing a fairer wage, but few are as empowering as they might like to claim, and exploitation persists.[39]

The vast majority of *chikankari* consists of thick and rough stitches; it is ubiquitous in the shops of Lucknow today and readily available in most major cities (pl.207). Now produced in a range of coloured backgrounds or coloured threads, it has, for connoisseurs, lost its authenticity.[40] Superior *chikankari* consisting of more intricate stitches owes its revitalization and raised public profile to the input of designers in the 1980s. SEWA-Lucknow, an NGO set up in 1984, wished to provide a better livelihood for women by creating employment and paying higher wages. They were able to compete with the commercial sector through the aid of the designer and adviser Laila Tyabji,

founder of the craft development organization Dastkar. She created a very distinct aesthetic using Mughal-style silhouettes decorated with profuse embroidery – refined garments aimed at the fashion clientele of the metropolitan centres.[41]

Today some of the most sophisticated *chikankari* is to be found on the garments and saris designed by Abu Jani Sandeep Khosla (pl.203). Informed by the craft preservation initiatives of Pupul Jayakar, they place fine craftsmanship at the heart of their practice. Their work is inspired by the opulence of India's courtly cultures and they have recreated an impressive, elegant aesthetic that is favoured by Indian high society and celebrities, including Amitabh Bachchan, and those further afield, including Dame Judi Dench. Central to the making process are the printing blocks used for transferring the design onto the fabric: while it is common to use a few blocks on one piece, they have used up to 25, resulting in a wider range of stitches and taking up to 12 months to complete. The designers have innovatively introduced chiffon and organza as a base material, creating sheer pieces that drape easily (pl.204).[42] The appeal for *chikankari* is wide ranging and international, with exports reaching as far afield as America and Japan.[43] In 2010 the technique was chosen by Prada for its 'Made in India' range celebrating local craftsmanship,[44] and in 2014 the British supermarket chain Sainsbury's reproduced the aesthetic on summer shirts using machine embroidery also made in India.

204
Sari (detail)
Designed by Abu Jani
Sandeep Khosla
Lucknow, Uttar Pradesh,
2014
Silk chiffon, embroidered
with cotton, edged with
gold, silver metallic
crocheted border
450 x 114 cm
Collection of Abu Jani
Sandeep Khosla

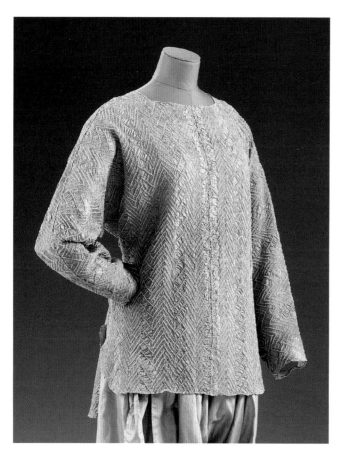

The revitalization of traditional techniques became the objective of many creative enterprises during the 1980s and '90s. Asha Sarabhai and Raag, her workshop based in Ahmedabad, began creating high-quality clothes and furnishings in 1976. Producing in limited numbers using appliqué, tie-dye and pintucking on naturally dyed or undyed hand-woven fabrics, the studio aimed to support traditional small-scale methods of production to counter the destructive forces of mass manufacturing. The garments have a restrained aesthetic with loose silhouettes based on *chogas* (loose robes) and kurtas and a focus on excellent craftsmanship. Their appeal is cross-cultural, not subject to short-term fashion trends, and encourages the wearability of understated luxury.[45] Following the 1993 V&A exhibition *Contemporary Traditions:*

205
Blouse and salwar
Designed by Asha
Sarabhai for Raag
Ahmedabad, Gujarat,
1994–5
Silk, tie-dyed
Length: 75 cm (blouse)
V&A: IS.13–1995

206
Coat by Brigitte Singh
Jaipur, Rajasthan, 2014
Cotton, block-printed
and quilted
Length: 110.5 cm
Given by Brigitte Singh
V&A: IS.15–2015

The Studio of Asha Sarabhai, a selection of pieces were acquired for the museum, including a striking chevron patterned tie-dye shirt for which the finest knotting was sourced from specialist tiers in Kutch (Gujarat), while dyeing was completed in the studio (pl.205).[46] The other garments include pieces that use machine embroidery as precisely as hand-stitching. Neeru Kumar emerged in the 1990s as a pioneer in experimenting with woven and textured textiles to create a contemporary aesthetic, with ikat weaving developing into one of her signature techniques. Her brand, Tulsi, is based in Delhi where she has centralized her production and brought ikat weavers from Odisha and other specialized craftspeople together. Tulsi is recognized for quality home furnishings as well as garments and has a thriving export market (pl.210).

Several studios have specialized in reviving particular techniques to a very high quality. Brigitte Singh has recreated fine block-printing in her workshops in Jaipur. Inspired by a fragment of the Mughal poppy design given to her by her father-in-law in the 1980s, she worked with master block-makers and printers to achieve the quality that had once graced the textiles of Mughal emperors.[47] Her studio specializes in reproducing historic motifs on garments and furnishings (pl.206).[48] An equally high-quality recreation of Kashmir shawls with Mughal designs has been achieved by Kashmir Loom, a company run by Jenny Housego and brothers Asaf, Hamid and Zahid Ali. From their workshops in Kashmir they also produce highly desirable contemporary pieces using simple stripes, block colours and metallic thread, which are popular in the West (pls 208, 209). Rahul Jain's woven silks have an opulent jewel-like aesthetic. His extensive study of Mughal and Safavid silks was essential to reproducing the complex weaving process for which he set up ASHA, his workshop of traditional drawlooms in Delhi in 1993. The attention to detail at every stage is remarkable and bestows a great level of authenticity to the finished piece: gold thread (98 per cent pure silver foil, plated with pure gold, wound over a cotton yarn) and the twistless silk yarn that gives clarity to the pattern had to be specially manufactured. . The weaving is so complex that it takes three craftsmen two days to weave 5 cm and about three and half months for the full piece, whereas a normal brocade sari of 5.5 metres would take the same weavers four weeks to produce (pl.211).[49] Initiatives such as these, of different scales and degrees of impact, keep traditional textile skills alive.

207
(clockwise from top left)
Woman's blouse
Purchased in Delhi, 2003
Cotton, embroidered with cotton
Length: 66 cm
Private collection

Woman's blouse
Designed by Prada
Lucknow, Uttar Pradesh, 2010
Cotton, embroidered with cotton
Length: 58 cm
Private collection

Woman's blouse
TU Collection, Sainsbury's
India, 2014
Cotton, machine embroidered with cotton
Length: 58.5 cm
Private collection

208
Shawl by Kashmir Loom
(detail)
Woven by Ali Mohd
Srinagar, Kashmir, 2011–13
Goat-hair (pashmina), twill
tapestry (*kani*) weave
230 x 115 cm
Kashmir Loom Collection

209 (opposite)
Shawl by Kashmir Loom
(detail)
Srinagar, Kashmir, 2012
Goat-hair (pashmina),
twill weave
198 x 99 cm
Private collection

210 (opposite)
Sari
Designed by Neeru Kumar
for Tulsi
Ikat tied and dyed by Bishwa
Meher in Sonepur, Odisha;
woven in Delhi, 2013
Silk, weft ikat
610 × 105 cm
V&A: IS.13–2015

211
Shawl (detail)
Delhi, 1996
Silk and silver-gilt thread,
samite weave
242 × 90 cm
British Museum, London
2001.0602.01

POPULARIZING TRADITIONAL TECHNIQUES

While the examples discussed above cater to an elite clientele, there are many ways in which traditional techniques are adapted to suit other groups. The most conspicuous way in which traditional techniques have become popularized is through wedding attire and cinema. At all levels of society, Indian wedding outfits aim to recreate an aesthetic that is associated with the opulence of the Maharajas, where *zardozi* (gold-thread work), beading, sequins and embroidery are profuse (pl.212).[50] The affluent woman will acquire her *lehnga* (bridal skirt or outfit) from a prestigious fashion designer, one of the most sought after of whom is Sabyasachi Mukherjee, who has built his reputation on reviving and raising awareness of India's textile heritage (pl.214).[51] The desirability of his sumptuously ornate wedding attire, and that of other top-end designers, has spawned a lucrative market in copying. Outfits

with similar designs and embellishments can be found in shops and markets at a range of prices (pl.215). Mukherjee believes that copying has led to a resurgence of *zardozi* skills in West Bengal, and though the quality differs widely it has led to increased employment. The splendour of bygone eras is also reinforced through film, where the historic epic becomes a vehicle for lavish sets and costumes. One of the finest examples of this is *Devdas*: remade in 2002 by Sanjay Leela Bhansali, it evokes an imagined era of lavish courtly culture. Abu Jani Sandeep Khosla, known for their reworking of traditional techniques as well as their skills in creating visually spectacular clothes, were responsible for designing a *lehnga* for the actress Madhuri Dixit. Taking their inspiration from Gujarati mirror-work, it was encrusted with large pieces of mirror but embroidered with gold thread instead of the traditional range of coloured threads (pl.213). The film was the most expensive Bollywood production to date

212
**Wedding ceremony
of Asha and Akil**
Kolkata, West Bengal, 2014

213
**Madhuri Dixit in costume
for the film *Devdas***
Mumbai, Maharashtra, 2002

Detail of *lehnga* worn
in the film *Devdas*
Mumbai, Maharashtra, 2002
Designed by Abu Jani
Sandeep Khosla
Silk, mirror-work,
embroidered with
gold thread, sequins
Length: 104 cm
Collection of Abu Jani
Sandeep Khosla

WEDGING ENSEMBLE

This unique wedding ensemble is a celebration of Indian textile heritage. It brings together multiple embroidery techniques, layers of hand-woven fabrics and skilled craftsmanship to create a romantic and opulent aesthetic. The clever use of pattern and embellishment with combinations of traditional and contemporary elements have made Sabyasachi Mukherjee one of the most sought-after designers for wedding attire.

The bridal outfit consists of four pieces: a choli (woman's bodice), an *anarkali* (long dress), a *lehnga* (skirt) and an *odhni* (large head-cover). The choli (not shown here) is made of hand-block-printed cotton fabric and is covered by the *anarkali*, which is textured and hand-embroidered with multiple *zardozi* techniques and embellished further with 'burnt' *zari* (gold-wrapped thread) and semi-precious beads. Mukherjee occasionally 'burns' his textiles by putting them through an acid bath. When this technique is used on gold embroidery it reduces the shine and gives an antique look, adding depth and richness of colour to the embellishment. The *lehnga* is typical of Mukherjee's layering technique: in all of his luxury pieces he uses *khadi* as a lining – it is the embodiment of all hand-woven fabrics and feels soft against the skin when it is of a fine thread count. The base of the *lehnga* is layered with hand-woven vintage Indian saris, overdyed in tones of rust and rose, which have been sourced from Laad Bazaar in Hyderabad, Peeli Kothi in Varanasi and Bhuj in Kutch. These are overlaid with *kantha* work (fine running

stitch) that has been done in Bolpur, Santiniketan, and is further embellished with heavy antique *zardozi* borders. To finish the outfit there is a tulle *odhni* detailed with *zardozi* (not shown here).

Mukherjee is based in Kolkata and has been nurturing the artisans in this region for many years, which has resulted in the revival of a high degree of craft skill. The *zardozi* on the *anarkali* and the *odhni* has been done by artisans in the villages of Barasat, Nodakhali and Daualpur, all in West Bengal. While sections of the outfits (such as the *zardozi* and *kantha* work) are made in a variety of locations, they are all brought together in Mukherjee's workshops in Kolkata.

The groom's attire consists of a *sherwani* (coat) made from cotton and hand embellished with *zardozi*. It is lined with an opulent silk sourced from Varanasi and paired with a silk kurta (not visible here) and brocade *churidar* (trousers). These have been teamed with a magnificent Kashmir shawl, hand embroidered with cotton thread in Srinagar and edged with *zardozi*-embellished borders from Bengal.

Sabyasachi Mukherjee is interested in raising the value and appreciation of textiles and techniques; in using *khadi* fabric and *kantha* work he aims to elevate them in the public perception, equating them to the luxury normally associated with *zardozi* and fine fabrics. The use of vintage saris celebrates the beauty of old craftsmanship and gives new life to them in a contemporary celebratory context. Each fabric and each stitch is associated with a story of skill and heritage. **DP**

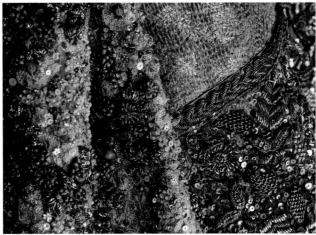

214 (opposite and
details above)
Wedding ensemble
Designed by Sabyasachi
Mukherjee
2014–15

Woven *khadi*, silk and
cotton; *kantha* and gold-
thread embroidery (*zardozi*)
Collection of Sabyasachi
Mukherjee

and the costumes reflected this. Images such as these feed the public imagination and create a demand for opulent dress. Another technique that has been popularized is block printing; People Tree, based in Delhi, is unusual in creating quirky prints for T-shirts and garments that have become cult items among the young and creative. The artists' collective responsible for their designs engages with social movements and activism, and the bold, playful nature of their garments reflects their alternative ethos (pl.216).[52]

INTERNATIONAL IMPACT

Constant adaptation of Indian skills continues to make an international impact. However, the emphasis has shifted from an appreciation of hand-woven fabrics and designs as seen in the pre-Independence period to a focus on handmade embellishment. The Belgian fashion designer Dries Van Noten started working with Kolkata-based craftsmen in 1987. For him, 'Made in India was a mark of prestige, synonymous with handmade', and his continued engagement with these craftsmen

is publicly acknowledged and celebrated.[53] Many western designers, including Karl Lagerfeld, Giorgio Armani, Jean Paul Gaultier and Marchesa, have created collections that are inspired by India's textiles and culture, and some use Indian craftsmanship on their designs. It is common, however, for designers to employ intermediary companies to supply them with hand-embellished details for their high-end garments. Shamina Talyarkhan runs Shameeza Embroideries in Mumbai, a company that has supplied Giorgio Armani, Ralph Lauren, Donna Karan, Calvin Klein and Jason Wu with embellishments for their gowns (pl.217).[54] Such gowns are worn by actresses at film premieres and appear on the front covers of international fashion magazines.[55] As the garments are not finished in India, though, there is no legal obligation to acknowledge the origin of the craftsmanship. Over the years, commercialization has resulted in Indian craftsmanship becoming associated with poor quality and mass manufacture, and while high-quality skills have been reinstated and are being utilized, as seen in the work of Shameeza Embroideries, still more needs to be done to reverse negative perceptions of 'made in India'. Vastrakala, based in Chennai, was started by Jean-François Lesage in 1993 and employs over 200 skilled embroiderers; it is now owned by the French fashion house Chanel and specializes in large-scale interior design projects.[56] Maximiliano Modesti's ARDY 2M design studio supplies embroidery to Hermès, Isabel Marant and others.[57] At a popular level today the desire for heavily beaded, sequined or embroidered garments is such that they are found on high streets across the globe in the retail stores of international companies such as Zara, Primark, New Look and H&M. Once again, though the label inside a garment states the country in which it is finished, the consumer may not be aware of the country of origin of its hand-embroidered decoration.

215 (above)
Sham Tex on Nai Sarak Marg, a street in an area of old Delhi specializing in wedding attire, 2014

216 (right)
T-shirt
Designed by Orijit Sen, produced for Bindaas Collective for People Tree Cotton, block-printed at

Chaubundi studio, Kaladera, Rajasthan Delhi, 2014 (purchased)
Length: 62 cm
Private collection

217 (opposite)
***Marie Claire*, May 2013, US edition**
Dolce and Gabbana dress embellished by Shameeza Embroideries

FLIP THIS ISSUE FOR MORE SCARLETT!

MAY 2013

marie claire

SCARLETT JOHANSSON
on her new man and
her raciest role ever

OUR
BIG
BEAUTY
ISSUE

287
Hair, Skin
& Body Tips
to Rock
Your World!

HOW TO
LOOK
HOT
NOW

Must-have shoes, killer bags,
and swimsuits for *every* body

JUICE
CLEANSES
How Healthy
Are They
Really?

$3.99

08530

0 279971 9

0 5 >

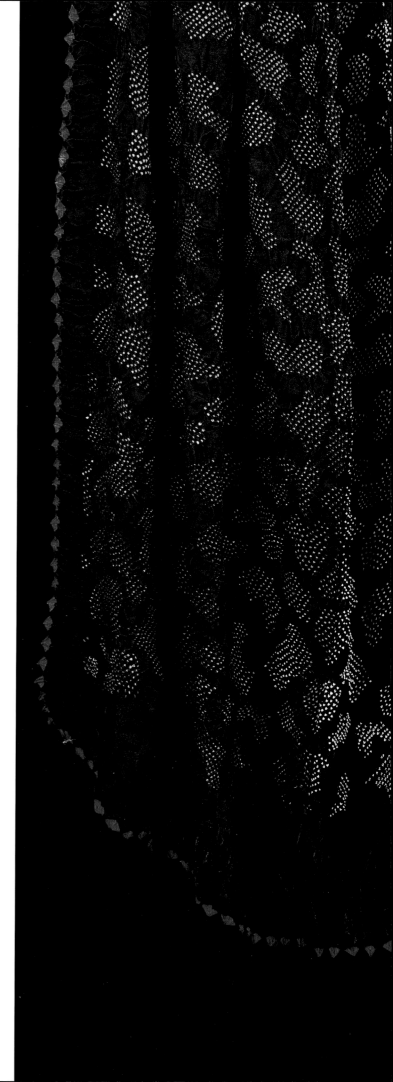

THE ROLE OF THE ARTISAN

Acknowledgement and authorship of skills within the
designer–artisan relationship is a contentious issue. Since
the 1960s designers have been promoted as central to the
survival of handmade textiles. However, the production of
such textiles involves a mutually dependent relationship:
while enterprising and creative designers innovate, raise
awareness and popularize crafts – and generate employment
for artisans – artisans are essential to designers in order to
create the aesthetics that make the designers' work unique.
Moreover, embedded in the artisans' skills are associations
with heritage and national identity that designers like to use
to promote their work. Undoubtedly inequalities exist: while
designers become recognized individuals, the artisan remains
anonymous. Occasionally, those makers who have received
national awards for excellence as master craftsmen are known
and acknowledged.[58] However, for the majority of artisans
it is uncertain whether employment in the crafts sector is as
empowering as some of these associations imply.[59] There is a
long tradition of NGOs working with textile communities across
India to develop artisanal skills and generate ways of making
an income, such as Dastakar, Sewa-Lucknow and Khamir. As
design education in colleges and universities is not accessible to
most artisans, a unique programme initially taught at the Kala
Raksha Vidhyalaya, and now at the newly formed Somaiya Kala
Vidya in Bhuj, teaches artisans about design and encourages
them to explore their traditions in a contemporary context.
The graduates call themselves artisan-designers and former
graduates include Aziz and Suleman Khatri, Dayalal Kudecha
and Khalid Amin Khatri (pls 218–20).[60]

Khalid Amin Khatri has learnt to innovate his
traditional skills of *ajrakh* printing. His bold and expressive
work has been shown in galleries and sold in metropolitan
boutiques (pl.219). India's growing economy, urbanization

218
Dupatta, *Kiri Makaudi*
(Ants)
Designed and made by
Aziz and Suleman Khatri
Bhadli, Kutch, Gujarat, 2012
Silk, tie-dyed
167 x 91 cm
V&A: IS.4-2015

219
Stole, *Haji Ali*
Designed and made by
Khalid Amin Khatri
Ajrakhpur, Kutch, Gujarat,
2012
Cotton, block- and resist-
printed, dyed
193 x 85 cm
V&A: IS.7-2015

220
Stole
Designed and made by
Dayalal Kudecha
Bhujodi, Kutch, Gujarat,
2014
Cotton
280 x 64 cm
V&A: IS.5-2015

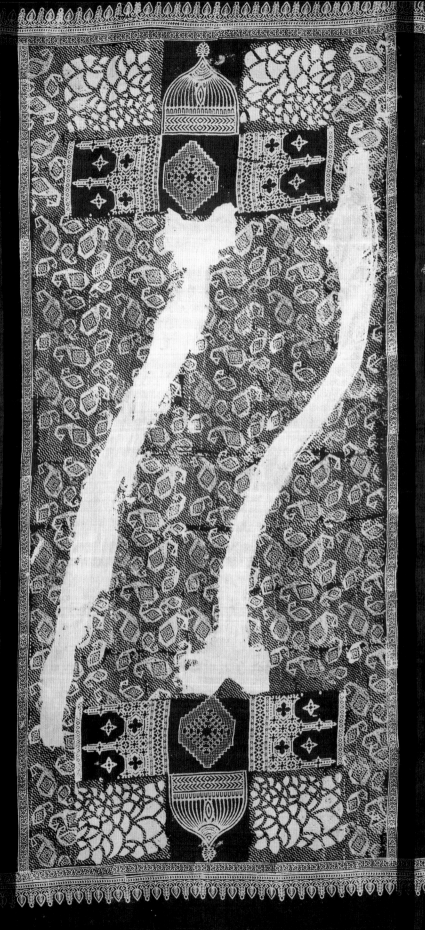

and affluence mean that textiles are increasingly being used for purely decorative purposes, to grace the walls of art galleries and smart cosmopolitan homes. Lavanya Mani uses the labour-intensive *kalamkari* technique to create immense wall hangings. A trained artist from the Sir J.J. School of Art in Mumbai, she references textile history, colonial interaction and female identity in her pieces (pl.221).[61] Ajit Kumar Das,

who is self-taught, uses natural dyes to paint compositions inspired by tantric motifs and natural forms (pl.223). Of particular note are his series of hangings in which pebbles, rocks and boulders balance gracefully on each other.[62] Swati Kalsi collaborates with artisans in Bihar to create works that use embroidery to great effect, layers of *sujni* (running stitch) and couching providing visual variation and texture (pl.222).[63]

221 (opposite, top)
Emperor's New Machine
By Lavanya Mani,
Vadodara, Gujarat, 2009
Natural dye and machine
embroidery on cotton
182.9 x 289.6 cm
Private collection

222 (opposite, bottom)
SHE LL (and detail)
Designed by Swati Kalsi
Embroidered by women
from Bihar, 2014
Silk, embroidered with *zari*

(metal-wrapped thread)
and red thread
Maximum length: 92 cm
Collection of the Devi
Foundation

223 (above)
**Prosthar Pokshi
('Stone Bird')**
By Ajit Kumar Das
Kolkata, West Bengal,
2012–13

Natural dye on cotton
250 x 160 cm
Collection of
Jenny Balfour-Paul

FASHION AND THE USE OF HAND-SKILLS

Alongside art, cosmopolitan culture is expressed through fashion. A pioneering role was played by Ritu Kumar, whose revival of block-printing in Kolkata in 1969 developed into a thriving fashion empire focused on the adaptation of textile crafts.[64] Today, most fashion designers have undergone their early training at the NID or the National Institute of Fashion Technology, where an understanding of textile traditions is integrated into their courses. For designers, using handloom fabric and traditional techniques is a way of giving their work a unique Indian identity and differentiating it from the homogeneity of global fashion.[65] Designers such as Rajesh Pratap Singh, Aneeth Arora and Rahul Mishra are notable for their integration of India's textile heritage with an international outlook. Arora and her label Péro create simple, loosely structured silhouettes from beautiful, understated, hand-woven fabrics (pl.224). Péro clothing displays an incredible attention to detail: buttonholes, seams, tassels, linings and fastenings are all meticulously crafted (pl.224, detail).[66] Mishra, known for his range of handloom fabrics with western silhouettes, won the highly acclaimed International Woolmark Prize in 2014. For this he used wool yarn to weave a translucent fabric and then embroidered densely detailed patterns with wool. Inspired by M.C. Escher's optical illusions, the patterns trace the transformation of a lotus into an urban landscape (pl.225).[67] Rajesh Pratap Singh, one of India's most respected designers, creates finely tailored, carefully detailed outfits for men and women that are both understated and elegant (pl.226). His ingenuity can be seen in the *Gamcha* jacket, which is inspired by the common *gamcha* cloth: a coarse

224
Dress layered over shirt
Designed by Aneeth Arora
for Péro, Spring/Summer 2010
Woven in West Bengal,
tailored in Delhi
Cotton, *jamdani* weave and
embroidery
Length: 105 cm
Given by Aneeth Arora
V&A: IS.10–2014

Detail from shirt
Designed by Aneeth Arora
for Péro, Spring/Summer
2010
Tailored in Delhi
Cotton, hand-stitched
details
Given by Aneeth Arora
V&A: IS.11–2014

225 (opposite)
Monochrome Dress
Designed by Rahul Mishra,
Spring/Summer 2014
Embroidered in West
Bengal
Tailored in Noida,
Uttar Pradesh, 2014
Merino wool, organza, jersey
Length: 85 cm
V&A: IS.10–2015

RAJESH PRATAP SINGH AJRAKH JACKET

This jacket is made from fabric that is inspired by a technique known as *ajrakh*, specific to artisan communities in western India and Pakistan (see p.43 and pl.42). Wax resists and mordants for blue and red dye are applied with carved wooden blocks to create a repeat pattern (see pl.43). At first glance the fabric appears to have a repeat floral design, one which is typical of traditional *ajrakh* patterns. However, on closer inspection it is possible to see that subtly integrated into the floral repeats are depictions of a human skull. The use of skull imagery on clothing in the West is today a familiar sight. It has its origins in rock music subculture which was incorporated into high fashion mainly through the designs of Alexander McQueen and then diffused into high-street culture. In India the skull is found in images of Hindu gods and retains its deathly associations.

Rajesh Pratap Singh is one of India's most important contemporary designers and is known for his adaptation of traditional techniques into contemporary forms. He has also been fascinated with the popular use of the human skull imagery. Excited by *ajrakh* printing, he tried to recreate a traditional design, but with the addition of the skull image. The process of *ajrakh* is long and time-consuming and takes up to 30 steps to complete. A key part of this is the carving of the wooden blocks that are used to print the pattern onto the fabric. In this instance the designer searched for a block-maker who was willing to carve the skull image, but many of the Muslim block-makers refused to do so because of their prohibition against creating representational figures, as well as the skull's associations with death. To realize his imagined article, Singh transferred the process to digital printing, making the jacket a creative fusion of tradition and technology. A couple of years later, Singh visited some Hindu woodcarvers who proceeded to make the blocks for him. He was thus able to print the fabric as initially envisioned, but it has not yet been made into any clothing. **DP**

226 (right and detail opposite)
Woman's jacket
Designed by Rajesh Pratap Singh, Delhi, Autumn/Winter 2010–11
Linen, digital print
Length: 71.5 cm
V&A: IS.27–2012

cotton checked towel, usually red and white but also found in other colour combinations, used by working men to wipe sweat from the body (pl.228). The cotton and silk fabric is hand-woven in Singh's workshops in Faridabad, Haryana, where he experiments with cloth (pl.227).[68] All these designers draw out the luxury of the handmade and its romantic association with ancient artisanal knowledge, creativity and skill.

By way of contrast, Rimzim Dadu experiments with creating intricate surface textures by using labour-intensive hand skills with her label, My Village. Simple silhouettes are constructed from a range of interesting techniques, such as heat-moulding fabric, to create three-dimensional effects; sequins are burnt by hand to create colour; and fine leather cord of different colours is assembled and stitched together to form a *patola* design (pl.229).[69] However, it is in the work of Manish Arora, India's most renowned designer, that elaborate craftsmanship and labour-intensive handicraft processes are used to incredible effect (pls 230, 231). His garments are distinguished by the exuberant clash of hyperreal colours with strong patterns and bold textures. He rethinks Indian embroidery, appliqué and beading by enlarging it or applying it with a breathtaking level of detail to create garments that celebrate handmaking skills.[70]

227
Men's *Gamcha* jacket
Designed by Rajesh
Pratap Singh, Delhi,
Spring/Summer 2009
Silk, cotton and linen blend
Length: 77 cm
V&A: IS.25–2012

228
**Rickshaw driver with
gamcha (checked cloth)**
Delhi, 2014

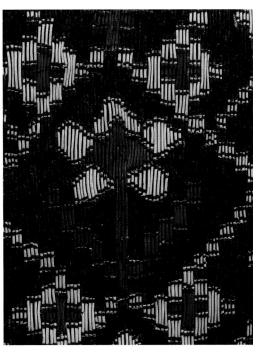

229
Skirt and blouse
Designed by Rimzim Dadu
for My Village
Autumn/Winter 2014
Skirt: cotton, appliqué
leather cords

Top: Wool with leather
cord details
Noida, Uttar Pradesh, 2014
Length: 76 cm (skirt),
69 cm (top)
V&A: IS.11–2015, IS.12–2015

230
Butterfly Dress
Designed by Manish Arora,
Spring/Summer 2008
Noida, Uttar Pradesh
Silk satin base with
reflective vinyl,

machine stitched and
embroidered butterflies,
appliqué silk and vinyl
Length: 167.5 cm (dress);
112 cm (train)
Manish Arora Collection

231
Skirt and top
Designed by Manish Arora
Noida, Uttar Pradesh,
Spring/Summer 2015
Skirt: Silk embellished with
metal appliqué, silk flowers,
crystal beads, pearls, sequins

Top: jersey, embellished
with iridescent strips,
metal, pearls
Length: 64 cm (skirt),
68.5 cm (top)
Manish Arora Collection

THE NEW SARI

Unstitched and elegantly draped, the sari is the most iconic item of Indian dress, a symbol of national identity that also reflects regional diversity. The sari as everyday attire for younger women has been in decline for many decades, particularly in urban centres where the variations of the salwar kameez (trouser and tunic) have become a more popular and versatile form of casual dress.[71] However, in recent years designers have been generating renewed interest in the sari by creating a more contemporary aesthetic, catering for a generation of affluent, cosmopolitan women and encouraging its wear beyond special occasions and weddings. Sanjay Garg and his brand Raw Mango have made a significant impact in this field by simplifying traditional motifs and experimenting with handloom weaving to make lighter, more wearable saris. One of his signature designs is that of the Indian crow, woven 108 times (108 being an auspicious number in India) in rows across the *pallu* (end), with just one bird woven in a contrasting colour (pl.233).[72] Jiyo!, an NGO working in Bihar and Andhra Pradesh, has created distinct contemporary pieces.[73] The Pebble Stream sari designed by Swati Kalsi consists of yellow running stitches that are varied in length and density to create organic forms (pl.235).[74] The ikat sari designed by Hitesh Rawat and Avinash Kumar for Jiyo! juxtaposes blocks of colour of varying sizes with apparent randomness to dynamic effect (pl.234). A

collaboration between artisan-designers Aziz and Suleman Khatri and designers NorBlack NorWhite has resulted in a design that evokes the moon (pl.232). It is made using a clamp-resist dyeing process with indigo. Handloom saris have taken on an edgier look under the well-established label of Abraham & Thakore (pl.236). Their aesthetic trademark is geometric forms in black, white or neutral shades, occasionally with splashes of yellow or red, which they also translate into their fashionable kurta-pyjama combinations (pl.237). Instead of the traditional choli, the saris are teamed with long-sleeved shirts and belts in a stylish contemporary fusion.[75] Kallol Datta provides an alternative aesthetic through bold, humorous and occasionally controversial prints with titles such as Roadkill, Landmine Lovers and Infestation. The showpiece that brought him to the public eye, called Suicide sari, uses silk-screen printing to transfer the monochrome illustration of a hanged man onto the fabric (pl.238). His sari blouses, deconstructed and loose fitting, add a further dimension to the overall look.[76] Emerging designer Rashmi Varma combines, in an innovative twist, tailoring with drape to create her *khadi* sari-dress. The enduring appeal of the sari and the handmaking process is such that it continues to inspire creativity and experimentation (pl.239).

Between the uplifting stories of adaptation and innovation, the stories of decline continue: cheap imitations of Banarasi silk saris from China and Surat are flooding the

232 (opposite and
details above)
Moon Sari
Designed and made by
Aziz and Suleman Khatri
with NorBlack NorWhite

Bhadli, Kutch, Gujarat, 2012
Tasar silk, clamp-resist dyed
560 x 110.5 cm
V&A: IS.3–2015

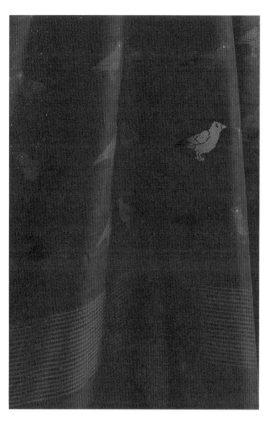

233
Sari with crow motif
Designed by Sanjay Garg
for Raw Mango
Chanderi, Madhya Pradesh,
2010
Silk and cotton
556 x 113 cm
V&A: IS.18-2001

234
Abstract sari
Designed by Hitesh Rawat
and Avanish Kumar for Jiyo!
Silk, ikat, hand-woven by
Jella Sudharkar in Guttapal,
Pochampally, Telangana,
2011–12
536 x 117 cm
V&A: IS.20–2012

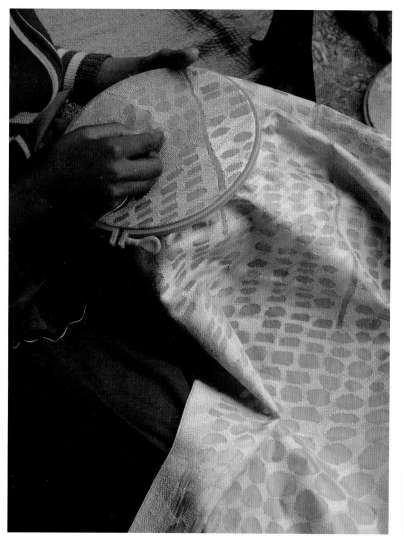

235 (opposite and
details above)
Pebble Stream sari
Designed by Swati Kalsi
for Jiyo!
Silk, embroidered by Guriya
Kumari, Rani Kumari, Anisa
Kumari and Khushboo
Kumari in Bihar, 2011–12
560 x 108 cm
V&A: IS.21–2012

HOUNDSTOOTH SARI

This sari consists of a black-and-white houndstooth pattern across two-thirds of the length, which then bleeds into a solid lime green section. A black border runs along the entire length of the sari, fusing the two sections. Designed by Abraham & Thakore, its production in silk using the double ikat technique is a result of their collaboration with the master weaver Shri Govardhana.

In their studio in Noida (Uttar Pradesh), the designers scaled up the houndstooth pattern on graph paper to the actual size so that the tied resists on the warp and weft could be calculated. In addition, a full-scale drawing of the sari was made to indicate where the patterned area should meet the solid area to enable the correct positioning of pleating and draping when worn. Govardhana's workshops in Puttapaka in Telangana (formerly Andhra Pradesh) then translated the paper designs into dyed yarn and woven fabric. With years of experience, a record of exhibiting internationally and a reputation for excellence, he is particularly responsive to new ideas and designs and was an ideal partner in this project. Four saris of this design were woven. Some supplementary houndstooth

fabric was tailored into a long-sleeved shirt at the designers' studio in Noida: only one of these was made, so the V&A's ensemble of sari and shirt is unique.

The houndstooth is a classic European design that was being woven in south India as early as the 1860s. A cotton sample in the V&A collection exhibited in Paris in 1867 is noted as being acquired from Visakhapatnam (see p.185) – the Indian weavers were catering for Europeans living in India at the time. In Britain houndstooth had developed from a lowly cloth worn by shepherds in Scotland, where it was known as shepherd's check, to a suiting fabric for gentlemen by the 1820s and to a luxury textile patronized by the Duke of Windsor in the 1930s.[1] When Christian Dior made his Café Anglais dress from it in the 1940s it became a part of women's fashion and has been subject to regular reinvention.[2] This sari is one further adaptation, which combines a contemporary aesthetic with multiple historic associations.

1 Stille 1970.
2 Font 2011.

236 (opposite and details above)
Houndstooth sari
Designed by Abraham & Thakore, woven in the workshop of Shri Govardhana Puttapaka, Telangana (sari), and Noida, Uttar Pradesh (shirt), 2013
Silk, double ikat
453 x 117 cm
Given by Abraham & Thakore
V&A: IS.3–2013

237
Jacket, kurta (tunic),
churidar **(trousers)**
Designed by Abraham
& Thakore
Tasar silk yarn and mulberry
silk, weft inlay (woven in
Varanasi, Uttar Pradesh
for Ekaya)

Tailored in Noida,
Uttar Pradesh, 2014
Length: 82 cm (jacket),
84.4 cm (kurta), 111.2 cm
(*churidar*)
V&A: IS.6–2015

238
**Suicide sari with Random
Suicide waistcoat and
Shoetread underskirt**
Suicide and Random
Suicide prints designed by
Kallol Datta and Indranil
Ram Kamath; Shoetread

print designed by
Kallol Datta
Kolkata, West Bengal,
Autumn/Winter 2011
Silk-screen print
Length: 600 cm (sari);
50.7 cm (blouse)

239
Bihar *Khadi* Indigo Dress
Designed by Rashmi Varma
Delhi, Spring/Summer 2015
Khadi cotton from West
Bengal, hand-embroidered
detail on *pallu*
Length: 145.5 cm
V&A: IS.9-2015

market and destroying the weaving communities of Varanasi.[77] At the same time, weavers in Assam are protesting against the copying of their designs by the weavers of Varanasi.[78] Such threats from within India and beyond, while typical of the complications that face handmade textiles today, also echo the moments of commerce and crisis that have formed the history of textiles in India. In 1867, in order to stimulate British exports, John Forbes Watson wrote about the qualities and survival of Indian textiles; although his statement can be read as a shocking reflection of a lack of modernity and progress, in its expression of India's mastery of handmaking skills it acknowledges that which is still true:

The hand-loom weaver still exists amongst us, nor is it likely that he will ever cease to do so. Less likely still is it that machinery will ever be able to drive him from the field in India. The very fine and the richly decorated fabrics of that country will probably always require the delicate manipulation of human fingers for their production.[79]

NOTES

INTRODUCTION

1 Throughout this book, 'India' refers to the undivided subcontinent as it was before 1947, when the majority of pieces discussed were made. Any reference to post-1947 history or objects uses the modern names of Pakistan and Bangladesh.

2 Annual Report 2013–14, ch.1, p.14. The Ministry's report for 2012–13 gave the figure as 6.8 million people. These figures do not include the great many people, mainly women, who embroider cloth at home for their own families' use rather than for sale, or those employed by NGOs in embroidery projects.

3 Kramrisch 1968, p.66.

4 See Bayley 1986 for a very useful overview of the role of cloth and weavers in Indian society.

5 Ibid., p.289.

6 Ibid., pp.301–2, source unidentified.

7 Thackston 1999, pp.80–1.

8 Abu'l Fazl 1977, vol.I, p.467, quoted in Pearson 1986–7, p.172.

9 Hambly 2003, pp.37–8.

10 London 2004, p.162.

11 See Desmond 1982.

12 Madras Central Committee 1855, p.xxxi.

13 Ibid., p.ii.

14 V&A Registry file MA/1/1620, 17 October 1947.

15 V&A Registry file MA/I/S839.

CHAPTER 1

1 Kenoyer 2004; Wild and Wild 2014.

2 Moulherat et al. 2002; Constantini 1983; Kenoyer 2004.

3 Gulati and Turner 1928 favour the earlier date of around 2600 BC; Marshall 1931, vol.I, pp.32–3; Mughal 1990; Watson 1983, p.163, note 10.

4 Betts et al. 1994.

5 It is possible that cotton textiles produced in India were exported as far as Iran, the Middle East and the Caucasus as early as pre-Harappan times. Cotton fibres which are very likely to be Indian have been excavated at a site belonging to the Maikop culture in the North Caucasus, dating from 3700–3200 BC. See Shishlina et al. 2003.

6 Santhanam and Hutchinson 1974, pp.89–99.

7 Pokharia et al. 2011; Jain 2002, p.33.

8 Chandra 1973, p.144.

9 Most Indian cotton thread being 'Z'-spun, it follows that when several individual 'Z'-twisted threads are combined to produce thicker warps, the bundle of 'Z'-spun threads is twisted in the opposite, 'S' direction. Probably because Indian weavers perfected the skills required to commercially mass-produce cotton textiles so early,

strong but thin multi-stranded cotton warps (Z6S, Z7S, Z8S, etc.) have always been associated with Indian carpets, which contrasts with neighbouring cultures such as Iran, whose cotton-warped carpets are typically composed of fewer, thicker, individual threads (for example, Z3S or Z4S).

10 The commercial export of 'mallow cloth' (Greek: molochine) from the Indus delta port of Barygaza is mentioned in the Periplus of the Erythraean Sea, but from which specific plant this fibre was extracted remains obscure and debated.

11 Ray 1917, pp.196–7.

12 See also V&A 05755 (IS) and IPN 1028 (dyed woven lengths), 05498 (IS), a single sock, and 05301 (IS), a carpet made from mudar floss: all were made at Shahpur Jail, Punjab. Several pieces were exhibited at the International Exhibition of 1862 in the 'Silk cotton' category. Mudar floss (and the related ak floss from Calotropis hamiltonii) were being experimented with for commercial production, but it proved impossible to produce cloth by means of machinery (Forbes Watson 1862, p.133). See also 'On the Cotton of the Calotropis Gigantea or Gigantic Nettle-Wort and on the Manufactures from the Same' in Madras 1858, pp.1–11.

13 Selk 2000.

14 Good, Kenoyer and Meadow 2009.

15 Gulati 1961.

16 Chowdhury 1982, pp.1–2.

17 The Silk Road in Southwest China 1992, p.169. By AD 69 the route from Sichuan to Burma was completed and under Han administrative control.

18 Balkrishna 1925; Chandra 1973.

19 Personal correspondence with Rahul Jain, 1 October 2014: 'In the silkweaving industry, mulberry silk is referred to as paat … Thus, the twistless silk weft characteristic of historical patterned silk is referred to as paat baana. In NE India, ONLY mulberry silk is referred to as paat.'

20 See Chandra 1973 for a survey of these accounts.

21 Abu'l Fazl 1977, vol.I, pp.97–100.

22 Exceptions include the yellow muga silk embroidery of the distinctive group of coverlets produced under Portuguese patronage in Satgaon, Bengal, for the European market from about 1600 to the 1630s (pl.166). Some of the Assamese Vrindavani vastra type lampas cloths are made of local tasar silk (pl.65 in the present volume; Jain 2013, p.62), and of course there have always been cloths woven entirely of muga, tasar and eri that have been marketed as such, for local use.

23 Cohen 2003; Cohen 2014.

24 Both Yusuf Ali (Ali 1974, pp.1–2) and

Rahul Jain (Jain 2013, p.17) add the rarely mentioned fact that mulberry silk worms other than Bombyx mori were native to India and were used commercially. These were primarily Bombyx textor (bar polu in Assam) and Bombyx croesi or sinensis (sar polu).

25 Gujarati weavers had been weaving complicated silks with metal thread for centuries but such textiles were limited in quantity and restricted to the very wealthy. Many authors without specialist knowledge of textiles believe that the weavers of Varanasi had been producing cloth with precious metal thread centuries before the modern industry began in the late eighteenth century (e.g. Das 1992, pp.10–25). Such authors assume that all early references to any cloth woven in Kashi/Varanasi are references to silks woven with metal thread, despite the fact that those sources never actually mention metal thread. If a text describes 'shining' or 'golden' cloth, this has been considered evidence of early silk weaving with metal thread. In fact, Varanasi was an important weaving centre famed for its fine woven cotton and silk, but no contemporary source before the late eighteenth century mentions it producing textiles with metal thread. The single exception is Niccolò (Niccolao) Manucci writing in the 1660s: 'In this city [Banaras; i.e. present-day Varanasi] is made much cloth worked in gold and silver, which is distributed hence all over the Mogul realm, and is exported to many parts of the world' (Manucci 1907, vol.II, p.83). If metal thread was really being used in Varanasi, it is inexplicable that his observations are not verified by any other authority. The next unambiguous observation of the use of metal-wrapped thread comes from Lord Valentia who visited Banaras in 1804 (see Chakraverty 2002, p.25; Chandra 1985, p.342). But that does not support the argument that textiles with metal thread were woven in Kashi/ Varanasi in the fourteenth century. None of the early Indian silk samite or lampas weave textiles from around the fifteenth to eighteenth centuries, which require a drawloom with naqshas, have metal threads. With the exception of Manucci, there is no evidence suggesting that Varanasi weavers used metal threads in their textiles until the late eighteenth century.

26 Watt 1903, pp.416–18.

27 Gleba 2008. Based on evidence from archaeological specimens as well as numerous references in both Greek and Roman literature, the craft was known by the fifth to the fourth centuries BC in the Greek colonies of Asia Minor, among

the barbarian tribes of Siberia and along the northern borders of China. It gradually spread further west so that by the first two or three centuries AD the Etruscans were weaving with metal-wrapped thread, and the Romans undoubtedly inherited their knowledge and skills from the Etruscans. By the fourth to the fifth centuries AD metal-wrapped thread was fairly widely used throughout much of Europe, the former Roman provinces of the Eastern Mediterranean, including the Byzantine Empire, and the rest of the Middle East and Iran.

28 Jain 1993–4, p.59; Bier 1987. In Bier's landmark exhibition all the examples from the Safavid dynasty have metal foil wrapped around a silk core in the 'S' direction. See also Kajitani 2001, note 37.

29 Karuppur saris and south Indian dhotis and turbans all have their metal-wrapped threads wrapped in the 'S' direction, for reasons that have yet to be satisfactorily explained.

30 See Cohen et al. 2012 and Rizvi 2001. Another, more coarse, type of goat under-hair known as kork was traditionally produced in Iran, especially near the towns of Kerman and Yazd (see Cohen 2010). This, rather than Kashmir, could have been the source of the pashmina identified by archaeologists at sites in Egypt and Syria. However, by the end of the nineteenth century the majority of pure pashmina and mixed pashmina/sheep's wool/Kermani goat-hair (kork) textiles were being woven by migrant Kashmiris who had fled Srinagar and were now settled in the Punjab. By the end of the twentieth century the vast majority of fine goat-hair pashmina was being produced in China and Mongolia.

31 For a pair of crocheted gloves, V&A: IM.145&A-1926 (formerly in the Hyderabad toshakhana or wardrobe store), see London 1982, cat.292 and Rutt 1987, pp.219–20. As with Kashmir shawls which were copied in Iran, gloves of this kind are sometimes identified as Iranian and made in Kerman. See also ibid., p.88, for eighteenth-century knitting in India including 'great quantities of cotton stockings' knitted at Pulicat.

32 The Antinoë textiles with pashmina wefts were first identified by Albert Gayet in 1898 and later by R. Pfister in 1934. See Martiniani-Reber and Bénazeth 1997, pp.68–70, 121; Pfister 1934, pp.61ff.

33 Schaller 2012, p.69.

34 Chandra 1973, p.55, where the term ranku (goat hair) is discussed; and Digby 2007, pp.408–12.

35 Raychaudhuri and Habib 1982, p.80; Chandra 1973, p.141, where various

translations of this famous passage are discussed. Kashmir shawls were not specifically mentioned, just goat-hair textiles in general. Thanks are due to Behnaz Atighi Moghaddam and Tim Stanley of the V&A for their help in researching this obscure term, which is presumably a loanword from another Semitic language.

36 Abu'l Fazl 1977, *A'in* 32, vol.I, pp.96–8.

37 See Cohen 2008, pp.179–81; and Rizvi and Ahmed 2009, p.25, where the term used is *khudrang* (self colour) for the natural goat-hair colours.

38 Irwin 1973, p.1; and Digby 2007.

39 Cohen et al. 2012, pp.20–1.

40 Wright and Kumar 1997.

41 Rizvi 2001, p.58. Janet Rizvi has used the posthumous records of the explorer William Moorcroft, which Moorcroft compiled in Kashmir in 1822–3.

42 Cardon 2007, pp.335–408.

43 Casson 1989, item 39.

44 Ashmolean Museum 1990.1099 (Barnes 1997, vol.II, cat.1092).

45 Lac remains a valuable natural product, but today most lac dye is considered a waste product since the shellac surrounding the insects has many more uses, primarily in the modern electronics industry (where, because it is inert, it does not conduct electricity and can be easily moulded into components) and food manufacture (for the hard outer casing of sweets, for instance). While still useful as a wood varnish, shellac has been largely replaced by cheaper synthetic substitutes. (Cochineal is also a common red food colouring.)

46 Though lac dye and cochineal dye are chemically close, lac contains laccaic acid while cochineal contains carminic acid. They can therefore be differentiated by chemical analysis.

47 Golikov 2001, pp.10–20.

48 Cardon 2007, pp.660–4.

49 Walker 1997, pp.24, 160–1.

50 Analysed by Ina Vanden Berghe of the Koninklijk Instituut voor het Kunstpatrimonium, Brussels, in June 2014, file number 2014.12306.

51 Ruth Barnes (Barnes 1997, vol.I, p.58) states that 30 of the Newberry Collection textiles recovered from Egypt were dye-tested and that of these 20 were found to have been dyed with madder (which would be *manjistha* in this context), 9 with *morinda* (*al*) and one with either *chay* or a synthetic alizarine dye.

52 Some dye experts call safflower 'Indian saffron', which is misleading as it is not saffron and has no relation to saffron.

53 A length of yellow-dyed cotton in the V&A – 5373 (IS) – has a note in its original acquisition record from the India Museum that it was dyed with

pomegranate rind, and analysis in 2014 by Prof. Richard Laursen of Boston University has confirmed this.

54 Our thanks to Professor Richard Laursen of Boston University for providing the dye analysis for this and other pieces.

55 Cardon 2007, pp.304–5.

56 Mohanty, Chandramouli and Naik 1987, pp.46–9.

57 The Chinese discovered a direct dye using buckthorn berries from two species (*Rhamnus utilis* and *Rhamnus chlorophora*), which produced a brilliant colourfast green, but the process was so complicated and expensive that it remains a unique exception to the rule. See Cardon 2007, pp.98–9.

58 The earliest surviving examples of Indian ikat textiles are two fragments excavated at Deir 'Ain 'Abata in Jordan, dating to the late seventh to early eighth century AD. One fragment is of cotton, the other of tasar silk, both materials adding to the strong likelihood of the fragments being of Indian origin. (Granger-Taylor 2012, pp.378–9, col.pl.47 and pl.95). Cotton ikat textiles of similar date (*c.* AD 650–810) and probable Indian origin have also been excavated at Nahal 'Omer in Israel (Shamir and Baginski 2014). While no early ikat textiles survive in India itself, evidence of its use by the fifth century is provided by its appearance in the wall paintings of the Ajanta caves in the Deccan.

59 Murphy and Crill 1991.

60 See, for example, Gittinger 1982, pp.24–5; Crill 2008, pp.12–13; Irwin and Brett 1970, pp.36–58.

61 Lamb 2005, pp.122–4.

62 Jain 1993–4; Lamb 2005, pp.206–39.

63 Samite contains an inner hidden warp separating the differently coloured multiple wefts within the same pass, allowing the textile to remain flat. The wefts required for the pattern are brought to the front of the cloth while those not used at that point remain at the back, all bound in a regular twill by the second set of binding warps.

64 When Varanasi drawloom weavers were interviewed in the twentieth century they claimed descent from Gujarati weavers or from a semi-mythical fourteenth-century Central Asian *naqshaband*, a drawloom pattern maker. See note 25 above; Watt 1903, pp.308–9.

65 Chaurasia 2008, p.299: 'The inscription is dated ... to 436. It records that a number of silk-weavers migrated from Lata (Central and Southern Gujarat) to Dasapura'; Agrawal 1989, p.252.

66 Jain 2011b.

67 The *Brahmajala Sutta*, a portion of the Buddhist *Digha Nikaya* (Long Discourses of the Buddha), lists many types of

embroidered textiles that are considered too luxurious to be used or owned by monks. Kashyap 1958, p.15; Singh and Ahivasi 1981, p.1, note 10; Rhys Davids and Rhys Davids 1899–1921, vol.1, pp.11–13.

68 Crill 1999; Irwin and Hall 1973; Elson 1979.

69 Irwin and Schwartz 1966, pp.18–19.

70 Crill 1999, pls 42, 43.

71 Crill 2012.

72 A group of metal-thread-embroidered textiles made for the court of Tipu Sultan of Mysore (d.1799) is a rare and possibly unique eighteenth-century survival (See Buddle 1990, pp.34–5, and Bonhams, 2015, lots 150–152 for examples).

73 Nabholz-Kartaschoff 1986, cats 79, 80.

CHAPTER 2

1 Madras Central Committee 1855, index numbers 2246–3269.

2 *Bombay Telegraph and Courier*, 1 March 1855, p.415, quoted in Hoffenberg 2001, p.103.

3 For example, V&A: 5570 (IS), which has a label reading 'Agra Central Prison' and giving the price of Rs 2-8-0 for a dozen dusters.

4 Today, as many male hand-weavers leave the profession to seek other employment, more women are taking up weaving. Some initiatives are actively encouraging this development, such as WomenWeave in Maheshwar (see http://www.thehindu.com/features/magazine/sally-holkar-handloom-weaving/article6646264.ece).

5 Mitra 1978, pp.173–4.

6 Subramaniam 2013, p.259.

7 For example, V&A: 5596 (IS), which has a label reading 'Mysore/Napkins (8)/Central Jail/Value Rs 2-"-"-'.

8 Bennett 1987, p.7 ; Madras 1857, vol.II, p.xvii.

9 Niaz Zaman, 'Women's Words/Women's Voices in the Kantha' in Philadelphia 2010, pp.114–37.

10 See Dallapiccola 2015 for a full account of these hangings.

11 Jayakar 1980, p.165.

12 Krishna and Talwar 2007, nos 3, 4.

13 Crill 1992.

14 See Crill 1995 for a discussion of the whole group.

15 Cohen et al. 2012, cat.103. A Kashmir shawl with the same inscription (*Kashi Vishvanath Ganga*) in the National Museum of India has additional woven images of Shiva and Parvati in the ends (Cohen et al. 2012, p.372).

16 Fischer and Pathy 1982.

17 Crill 1995, p.43, fig.4.

18 Fischer 2013.

19 Singh 1998.

20 London 1979, pp.34–5 and cats 52–63; Blurton 1998.

21 Klimburg-Salter 1997, pp.172–7; Wandl 1999.

22 Jain 2011a, p.7 and cats 10, 11.

23 Ahmed 2006; Graham 2006, fig.6.

24 Calico Museum Acc.no.983: Irwin and Hall 1973, cat.55; Mittal Museum Acc. no.76.1545: Mittal 2007, pp.244–5.

25 The latter suggestion is made by Valerie Berinstain in 'An early Jain embroidery' in Riboud 1989, pp.2–3.

26 Irwin and Hall 1973, cats 62–83.

27 Professor Nalini Balbir has commented that textiles of this type are also made to be presented to those about to complete fasts (personal email communication with Nick Barnard, March 2014).

28 See, for example, Brac de la Perrière 2008, pl.41; Losty 1982, pp.38–40, cat. nos 18–20. By far the closest comparison to the Indian talismanic shirts is a panel with the Quran written on cloth and decorated with very similar roundels to those on the shirts, illustrated in Sotheby's 'Arts of the Islamic World', 15 October 1998, lot 15. It was suggested in the catalogue that it carried a date expressed as a chronogram equivalent to AH 798/AD 1395, but this reading has been questioned.

29 Aslanian 2011.

30 See also a chintz curtain dated 1789, now in Armenia, reproduced in Guelton 2007, fig.2; also Evans 2014, figs 1 and 2, for a splendid chintz with a Deposition scene in the collection of the Holy See at Echmiadzin.

31 See 'Vestments' in Lisbon 2011, pp.80–91.

32 Probably the first person to adapt the life of Christ to the narrative *kalamkari* format was J. Gurappa Chetty, whose huge hanging made for the Festival of India in London in 1982 (V&A: IS.1-1983) may have been the inspiration for later versions. See Dallapiccola 2015, cat.19.

33 Quoted in Raychaudhuri and Habib 1982, pp.80–1.

34 Bernier 1914, pp.221–2, quoted in Raychaudhuri and Habib 1982, p.266.

35 Abu'l Fazl 1977, *A'in* 32, vol.I, pp.96–8.

36 The most detailed paintings of the period are those illustrating an imperial copy of the *Padshahnama*, the account of Shah Jahan's reign, which is now in the Royal Library at Windsor Castle. All the illustrations are published in Beach and Koch 1997.

37 Crill 1998, pp.87–103.

38 See, for example, Galloway 2011, cat.12.

39 For example, lot 154 of *Art of the Islamic and Indian Worlds*, Christie's, King Street, London, 9 October 2014.

40 Smart 1986.

41 Nagaswamy 1986; Anna L. Dallapiccola, 'Ceiling Paintings of Lepakshi' in

Dallapiccola et al. 2014, pp.92–107.

42 Illustrated in Debaine-Francfort and Idriss 2001, p.80, cat.22.

43 See above, pp.16–17.

44 Quoted in Warmington 2014, p.51.

45 Schoff 1974, pp. 42–5.

46 Wild and Wild 2005, p.13; ibid. 2014, p.225.

47 Ibid. 2005, pp.14–15 and figs 1b and c; ibid. 2014, pp.223–4.

48 See Barnes 1997, vol.I, pp.3–4, for an overview of the distribution of these fragments. Gittinger 1982, cats 9–44, illustrates an impressively varied selection from the Textile Museum's collection of over 100 pieces.

49 Barnes 1997, vol.I, p.31 and ills 5, 6.

50 One textile was excavated in another part of the site: Mackie 1989, pp.88–9, cited in Barnes 1997, vol.I, p.29.

51 See especially Ruth Barnes's work on the Newberry Collection in the Ashmolean Museum, Oxford (Barnes 1997).

52 See ibid., cats 238 and 296 respectively. 1990.259 (cat.250; pl.145 in the present volume) was Carbon-14 tested after publication.

53 Ibid., p.58. Thirty of the Newberry Collection textiles were dye-tested: 20 were dyed with a madder plant (probably *manjeet*), 9 with Morinda (*al*) and one with either *chay* or a synthetic alizarine.

54 For another example of similar fragments found in both Egypt and Indonesia, this time with goose (*hamsa*) design, see Guy 1998, figs 58, 59.

55 In his *Suma Oriental*, quoted in Pearson 1976, p.11.

56 Mas'udi 1861–77, vol.I, p.385.

57 Ibn Battuta 1983, p.229.

58 Ibid., p.110.

59 According to the French diplomat and natural historian Benoît de Maillet (1656–1738), quoted in Veinstein 1999, p.99.

60 Ibn Khurdadbih 1889, vol.VI, p.51.

61 Barbosa 1918–21, vol.2, p.146. For a very useful bibliographical survey of sixteenth-century travellers' accounts, see Bouchon 1999, pp.49–51.

62 See Veinstein 1999, esp. pp.113–15, for Indian textiles sent to the Ottoman Empire in the sixteenth to eighteenth centuries; also 'Textile Exports to Middle-East' in Sangar 1998, pp.221–5.

63 See Rizvi 2006 for an overview of this trade.

64 See Nabholz-Kartaschoff 1986, cat.111, for an illustration and discussion.

65 Crill 1998, pp.96–8; Nabholz-Kartaschoff 1986, cat.171.

66 See Bossert 1937, pls 37, 62.

67 Crill 1998, pl.126.

68 Horton 2004.

69 Ibid., p.73.

70 Stanley 1869, p.306.

71 Machado 2009a, p.165, note 26.

72 Machado 2009b, p.68.

73 Ibid., p.69.

74 Goswamy 2006.

75 Shokoohy 2006, p.159.

76 Machado 2009b, p.72.

77 See Fischer 2013.

78 Davies 1957.

79 Kriger 2009.

80 IOR/E/4/889, Madras Dispatches 1801–6, p.824, note 4.

81 Eicher 2006. The Kalabari also transform Madras handkerchiefs by removing selected threads to make a textile known locally as *pelete bite* (ibid.).

82 See Zurich 1997.

83 IOR/E/4/889, Madras Dispatches 1801–6, p.809.

84 Irwin and Schwartz 1966, pp.57, 60, 70.

85 Public Record Office, T.70/20, 1678–81; T.70/22, 1705–16; T.70/23, 1721–3; T.70/28, 1703–4. Typewritten list compiled by John Rhodes in Asian department archives, V&A.

86 Ibid., T.70/20.

87 PRO T.70/22, dated 3 December 1707.

88 Ibid., September 1709.

89 Wolters 1967, p.151, quoted in Barnes 1997, vol.I, p.110.

90 Christie 1993, p.199, quoted in Barnes 1997, vol.I, p.113.

91 Ibid.

92 See Guy 1998, fig.136, for an early twentieth-century photograph of the Sultan of Yogyakarta in ceremonial attire, including trousers of *patola* silk.

93 Crill 1998, pl.38.

94 Ibid., pl.39.

95 Guy 1998.

96 Quoted in Guy 1998, p.122.

97 Ibid.

98 Ibid., p.73.

99 Lemire 2009, pp.212–13.

100 North 2012, Appendix 25. I am grateful to Susan North for providing this information.

101 770,000 pieces of cotton and silk between 1600 and 1610 according to Riello 2009, p.264.

102 Crill 2006a, figs 7–11; London 1978, cat.6.

103 Serrano et al. 2008

104 Irwin and Hall 1973, p.35.

105 See, for example, New York 2013, cat.10B.

106 See Murphy 1990 for a fuller overview of the entry of Britain into the spice and textile trade.

107 Especially useful studies on the subject are Irwin and Schwartz 1966, Irwin and Brett 1970, Riello 2009, Riello 2013, Riello and Parthasarathi 2009, Riello and Roy 2009, Lemire 1991 and Lemire 1997.

108 See Crill 2008, figs 15, 16, for an English embroidery and its chintz counterpart.

109 See, for example, Lemire 1997, p.6.

110 *Archer's Bath Chronicle*, 7 September 1769.

111 See Crill 2008, fig.13, for a painting by François-Hubert Drouais (National Gallery, London, NG 6440) showing Madame de Pompadour in a chintz dress.

112 Rothstein 1978.

113 Styles 2010, fig.25.

114 See, for example, Hartkamp-Jonxis 1987 and Hartkamp-Jonxis 1994. An important Dutch family collection of chintzes amassed during the early twentieth century has been acquired by the Peabody Essex Museum, Salem, and awaits publication.

115 Kayoko 2009, p.191.

116 Watt 1903, p.289.

117 See, for example, Irwin 1973; Rizvi and Ahmed 2009; Cohen et al. 2012 for full accounts of the shawl trade to Europe.

118 Records of Fort St George, 16/9, quoted in Irwin and Schwartz 1966, p.59.

119 Master 1911, vol.II, pp.312–3, quoted in Sangar 1998, pp.58–9.

120 Letter Book II, 1658, fol.199 (John Irwin notes, Asian department, V&A).

121 Irwin and Schwartz 1966, pp.57–72. The articles and glossary in this work are a compilation of John Irwin's articles published in *The Journal of Indian Textile History* (Ahmedabad 1955–9), vols I–IV.

122 Ray 2005, p.27.

123 This chart accompanied the silk skeins shown in pl.9, p.22, together with an accompanying manuscript letter dated 7 February 1818 to a Mr Wardell 'with Mr Thompson's compliments' which states that the silk samples are 'of the good qualities of approved kinds' (V&A: IS.57–1990).

124 See the useful chart comparing textile exports of the East India Company (EIC) and the Dutch East India Company (VOC) between 1665 and 1834 in Riello 2013, p.328.

125 The Company official William Bolts, in his book *Consideration of Indian Affairs* of 1772, was highly critical of the Company's exploitation of Bengal in general, remarking that 'the Company's investment for Europe in a peculiar degree has been one continued scene of oppression' (quoted in Mitra 1978, p.48).

126 Bolts (ibid.) gives an account of Bengali silk-winders 'cutting their own thumbs' in order to avoid being forced into Company service, which may be closest to the thumb-cutting stories. There is a much earlier but similar reference to spinners' 'thumbs cut off' in an English translation of the *Arthashastra* of the fourth century BC, but this is discounted by a later commentator as a mistranslation of a punishment involving placing a tight-fitting ring around the thumb of spinners who transgress (Ray 1917, p.224, note 26).

127 See Ashmore 2009–10, fig.12, a Glasgow-printed cotton for the Indian market issued in 1851.

CHAPTER 3

1 See Greenhalgh 1988 and also Purbrick 2001.

2 See Kriegel 2001.

3 See Ashmore 2009–10.

4 Riello 2013, p.270.

5 Ibid.

6 Ibid., p.272.

7 Driver and Ashmore 2010, p.370.

8 Forbes Watson 1867, p.86.

9 Bayley 1986.

10 Ibid., p.308. See also Roy 1993, p.5.

11 Bayley 1986, pp.307–9.

12 Penetration of cloth into remoter regions of India is noted by Bayley 1986, p.308, and Riello 2013, p.270.

13 The effects of English imports on spinners and weavers were more complex than nationalist histories implied. See Roy 1993, p.11.

14 By 1865 there were 10 cotton textile mills, mostly in Bombay; by 1914 there were 211. See Roy 2012, p.190.

15 Bean 1989. pp.360–5.

16 Ibid., p.364.

17 Ibid., p.359.

18 *Young India*, 28 August 1924, 25, p.43. Quoted in Joshi 2002.

19 See Brantlinger 1996.

20 Tarlo 1996, pp.82–6.

21 For more on the importance of visual culture to the dissemination of Gandhi's message and the nationalist movement, see Trivedi 2007. Also, Brown 2010.

22 Tarlo 1996, p.88.

23 Bean 1989, p.355.

24 Roy 2006, pp.503–6.

25 Tarlo 1996, p.123. For the recent adaptation and use of the jacket by Narendra Modi, India's current Prime Minister, see Radha Sharma, 'The Nehru jacket, Now Modi Style', *The Times of India*, 21 September 2014, available online at http://timesofindia.indiatimes.com/india/The-Nehru-jacket-now-Modi-style/articleshow/43043940.cms (last accessed 29 October 2014).

26 For more on the development of post-Independence institutions, see McGowan 2009, pp.186–203.

27 Goetz 1949.

28 Jayakar 1962a.

29 Jayakar 1962b, p.66.

30 Balram 1998.

31 The use of semi-mechanized spinning wheels such as the *Ambar charkha* with its multiple steel spindles and hand-turned lever are now the norm and bring into question the use of the term *khadi* and what it constitutes. See Shefalee Vasudev, 'Wearing KHADI today?', *The Indian Express*, 15 August 2010, available online at http://indianexpress.com/article/news-archive/web/wearing-khadi-today/ (last accessed 29 October 2014). See also Jain 2002.

32 The All-India Khaddar Board was founded in 1922 to facilitate production and distribution. See McGowan 2009, pp.186–203. See also Trivedi 2007.

33 http://www.rashmivarma.com/ (last accessed 29 October 2014).

34 http://www.anandakhadi.com/ (last accessed 29 October 2014).

35 Sunita Ila Rao, 'Khadi x Denim', *Border & Fall* (2014), available online at http://www.borderandfall.com/karigar/khadi-denim-revolutionary-textile/ (last accessed 20 October 2014). For the use of *khadi* denim by contemporary designers, see Shefalee Vasudev, 'Trend Tracker: The Aam Fabric Party', Livemint, 24 January 2014, available online at http://www.livemint.com/Leisure/tzVBmtQdHBsE8ypP3xzcFM/Trend-Tracker--The-Aam-Fabric-Party.html (last accessed 20 October 2014).

36 For a history of Fabindia, see Singh 2010.

37 There is a lack of evidence concerning the origins and migration of *chikankari*. For an overview of the historical context, see Wilkinson-Weber 1999, pp.1–24. Also, Paine 1989.

38 Wilkinson-Weber 1999, pp.87–121, 157–82.

39 For personal accounts of the effects of commercialization in other textile crafts and initiatives to counter these effects, see Meeta and Sunny 2007. Also, Leonard 2006.

40 Manfredi 2007.

41 Wilkinson-Weber 1999, p.195.

42 Sinha 2012, pp.253–73.

43 Gargi Gupta, 'What Ails Lucknow *chikan*?', *Business Standard*, 14 May 2011, available online at http://www.business-standard.com/article/beyond-business/what-ails-lucknow-chikan-111051400003_1.html (last accessed 29 October 2014).

44 Tamsin Blanchard, 'Prada's New Range Is Made in Heaven', *Telegraph.co.uk*, 22 October 2010, available online at http://fashion.telegraph.co.uk/article/TMG8081394/Pradas-new-range-is-made-in-heaven.html (last accessed 29 October 2014). Also, Suzy Menkes, 'Throwing Down the Gauntlet', *The New York Times*, 28 September 2010, available online at http://www.nytimes.com/2010/09/29/fashion/29iht-rprada.html?_r=0 (last accessed 20 October 2014).

45 See Leonard 2006. See also Jane Mulvagh, 'Fashion: An Eastern legend and a magic word', *The Independent*, 27 January 1994, available online at http://www.independent.co.uk/life-style/fashion/news/fashion-an-eastern-legend-and-a-magic-word-ashas-minimal-indian-clothes-have-long-had-stylish-cerebral-devotees-her-new-shop-will-now-offer-some-enlightenment-to-the-rest-of-us-jane-mulvagh-reports-1402873.html (last accessed 31 October 2014).

46 This was a two-part exhibition held in different locations in the Museum. The other part, entitled *Design Now: RAAG Workshops*, was a display of soft furnishings and making processes. The acquisitions are numbered V&A: IS.4 to 29–1995 (garments) and V&A: IS.116 to 140–1993 (cushion covers). The reference file notes that the tie-dye knotting was completed outside the maker's studio.

47 Telephone interview with author, 10 November 2014.

48 Hellstrom 2012, pp.125–38.

49 Banalata Bipani, 'Salvaging a Lost Tradition', *Deccan Herald*, 9 October 2010, available online at http://www.deccanherald.com/content/103555/content/217452/F (last accessed 20 October 2014).

50 See Kuldova 2013c. For a detailed analysis of the social and cultural aspects of weddings and the new middle class, see Brosius 2010, pp.269–306.

51 Interview with designer at his studio in Kolkata, 24 March 2014. See also Catriona Luke, 'The Clothes Nationalist', *New Statesman*, 30 October 2008, available online at http://www.newstatesman.com/asia/2008/10/india-fashion-gandhi-designer (last accessed 31 October 2014); Malvika V. Kashyap, 'Sabyasachi Mukherjee', *Border & Fall* (2013), No.4, available online at http://www.borderandfall.com/journal/no-4-covenant/sabyasachi-mukherjee/ (last accessed 31 October 2014).

52 Meeta and Sunny 2007.

53 Frankel 2014, p.27.

54 Email correspondence between the author and Shamina Talyarkhan, and see Louis Werner, 'Mughal Maal', *Saudi Aramco World* (July/August 2011), vol.62, no.4, pp.24–33, available online at http://www.saudiaramcoworld.com/issue/201104/mughal.maal.htm (last accessed 20 October 2014). Also, Josh Patner, 'Women in Luxury: Shamina Talyarkhan', *Time*, available online at http://content.time.com/time/specials/packages/article/0,28804,1838865,1838857_1838729,00.html (last accessed 20 October 2014).

55 Interview with Shamina Talyarkhan in London, 30 August 2014.

56 For the ownership of Vastrakala by Chanel, see Elisabeta Tudor, 'Chanel acquires Indian atelier Vastrakala', *Style.Com/Arabia*, 4 June 2014, available at http://arabia.style.com/fashion/news/chanel-acquires-indian-atelier-vastrakala/ (last accessed 31 October 2014). For more on Vastrakala, see Christina Passariello, 'Heir to the House of Lesage Takes the Business to India', *The Wall Street Journal*, 10 October 2013, available online at http://online.wsj.com/news/articles/SB10001424052702304213904579095282167195254 (last accessed 31 October 2014).

57 Malvika V. Kashyap, 'Maximiliano Modesti', *Border & Fall* (2013), No.4, available online at http://www.borderandfall.com/journal/no-4-covenant/maximiliano-modesti/ (last accessed 20 October 2014).

58 Mastercraftsman awards are conferred by the Office of Development Commissioner for Handicrafts annually.

59 See Kuldova 2013b.

60 This design education programme has been devised by Judy Frater. She, along with named artisan-designers, was interviewed by the author in November 2014.

61 Mumbai 2009.

62 Singh 2014.

63 Swati Kalsi worked with the following group of women from Bihar: Anu Kumari, Rupa Kumari, Poonam Kumari, Komal Kumari, Kajal Kumari, Neha Kumari, Asmita Kumari, Amrita Kumari, Shalu Kumari, Sudhira Devi, Anita Devi, Juli Kumari.

64 Castelino 1994, pp.97–100.

65 For a more detailed look at contemporary Indian fashion, see Patel 2014.

66 Interview with Aneeth Arora and visit to studio in Delhi, 13 November 2010 and 25 January 2012.

67 'The Lotus Effect, Handmade with Love', International Woolmark Prize collection by Rahul Mishra, 2014.

68 Interview with Rajesh Pratap Singh and visit to studio in Faridabad, 19 November 2010.

69 Interview with Rimzim Dadu and visit to studio, 17 November 2010.

70 Visit to studio, 16 November 2010.

71 See Banerjee and Miller 2003, pp.79–87, 238–241. Also, Lynton 1995, pp.10–16.

72 Series of interviews with Sanjay Garg between 2010 and 2012 at his studio in Delhi.

73 Asian Heritage Foundation 2009. Interview with Jiyo!'s founder Rajeev Sethi and visit to studio, 15 February 2010 and 15 November 2010.

74 The piece was commissioned for the V&A (IS.21–2012) with design process and embroidery documented on file.

75 Interview with David Abraham and visit to studio in Delhi, 15 November 2010.

76 Interview with Kallol Datta in Kolkata, 22 November 2014.

77 Shefalee Vasudev, 'Ground Report: The Banaras bind', *Livemint*, 23 November 2013, available online at http://www.livemint.com/Leisure/5h1lnyORjhtn9PrOZ4wiXL/Ground-Report--The-Banaras-bind.html (last accessed 31 October 2014).

78 Samudra Gupta Kashyap, 'When the Looms Burned', *The Indian Express*, 7 April 2013, available online at http://archive.indianexpress.com/news/when-the-looms-burned/1098687/ (last accessed 31 October 2014).

79 Forbes Watson 1867, p.7.

BIBLIOGRAPHY

Abu'l Fazl 1977
Abu'l Fazl 'Allami, *The A'in-i Akbari*, trans. H. Blochmann, ed. D.C. Phillott (revised edn New Delhi 1977), 3 vols

Agrawal 1989
Ashvini Agrawal, *The Rise and Fall of the Imperial Guptas* (Delhi 1989)

Agrawal 2003
Yashodhara Agrawal, *Silk Brocades* (New Delhi 2003)

Ahmed 2006
Monisha Ahmed, 'Brocade for the Buddhists: The Textile Trade between Benaras and Tibet' in Rosemary Crill (ed.), *Textiles from India: The Global Trade* (Kolkata 2006), pp.9–26

Ali 1974
Abdullah Yusuf Ali, *A Monograph on Silk Fabrics Produced in the North-Western Provinces and Oudh* (Allahabad 1900, reprint Ahmedabad 1974)

Ames, forthcoming
Frank Ames, *Woven Gardens, Pashmina Jewels: Kashmir Shawls from the Samuel Josefowitz Collection* (London 2015), forthcoming

Archer, Rowell and Skelton 1987
Mildred Archer, Christopher Rowell and Robert Skelton, *Treasures from India: The Clive Collection at Powis Castle* (London 1987)

Ashmore 2008
Sonia Ashmore, 'Owen Jones and the V&A Collections', *V&A Online Journal* (London 2008), issue 01

Ashmore 2009–10
Sonia Ashmore, 'Colour and corruption: issues in the nineteenth century Anglo-Indian textile trade', *Text* (2009–10), vol.37, pp.11–18

Ashmore 2012
Sonia Ashmore, *Muslin* (London 2012)

Asian Heritage Foundation 2009
Asian Heritage Foundation, *Jiyo: Believe, Buy, Belong* (New Delhi c.2009)

Askari and Crill 1997
Nasreen Askari and Rosemary Crill, *Colours of the Indus: Costume and Textiles of Pakistan* (London 1997)

Aslanian 2011
Sebouh Aslanian, 'Julfa v. Armenians in India', *Encyclopaedia Iranica* (2011), vol.XV, fasc.3, pp.240–2

Balkrishna 1925
Balkrishna, 'The Beginnings of the Silk Industry in India', *Journal of Indian History* (April 1925), vol.IV, part 1, pp.42–52

Balram 1998
Singanapali Balram, *Thinking Design* (Ahmedabad 1998)

Banerjee and Miller 2003
Mukulika Banerjee and Daniel Miller, *The Sari* (Oxford 2003)

Barbosa 1918–21
Duarte Barbosa, *The Book of Duarte Barbosa: An Account of the Countries Bordering on the Indian Ocean and their Inhabitants, Written by Duarte Barbosa, and Completed about the Year 1518*, trans. and ed. Mansel Longworth Dames (London 1918–21), 2 vols

Barnes 1997
Ruth Barnes, *Indian Block-Printed Textiles in Egypt: The Newberry Collection in the Ashmolean Museum, Oxford* (Oxford 1997), 2 vols

Barnes, Cohen and Crill 2002
Ruth Barnes, Steven Cohen and Rosemary Crill, *Trade, Temple & Court: Indian Textiles from the TAPI Collection* (Mumbai 2002)

Bayley 1986
C.A. Bayley, 'The Origins of Swadeshi (home industry): Cloth and Indian Society, 1700–1930' in Arjun Appadurai, *The Social Life of Things* (Cambridge 1986), pp.285–321

Beach and Koch 1997
Milo Cleveland Beach and Ebba Koch, *The King of the World: The Padshahnama – An Imperial Mughal Manuscript from the Royal Library, Windsor Castle* (Washington DC 1997)

Bean 1989
S. Bean, 'Gandhi and Khadi, the Fabric of Indian Independence' in Annette B. Weiner and Jane Schneider (eds), *Cloth and Human Experience* (Washington DC 1989), pp.355–76

Bean 2006
S. Bean, 'Bengal Goods for America in the Nineteenth Century', in Rosemary Crill (ed.), *Textiles from India: the Global Trade* (Kolkata 2006) pp. 217–32

Bennett 1987
Ian Bennett, *Jail Birds: An Exhibition of 19th-Century Indian Carpets* (London 1987)

Bernier 1914
François Bernier, *Travels in the Mogul Empire, 1656-68*, trans. Irving Brock, revised V.A. Smith (London 1914)

Betts et al. 1994
A. Betts, K. van der Borg, A. de Jong, C. McClintock and M. van Strydonck, 'Early Cotton in Northern Arabia', *Journal of Archaeological Science* (1994), vol.21, pp.489–99

Bier 1987
Carol Bier (ed.), *Woven from the Soul, Spun from the Heart: Textiles Arts of Safavid and Qajar Iran, 16th–19th Centuries* (Washington DC 1987)

Bipani 2010
Banalata Bipani, 'Salvaging a Lost Tradition', Deccan Herald, 9 October 2010, http://www.deccanherald.com/content/103555/content/217452/F

Blanchard 2010
Tamsin Blanchard, 'Prada's New Range Is Made in Heaven', Telegraph.co.uk, 22 October 2010, http://fashion.telegraph.co.uk/article/TMG8081394/Pradas-new-range-is-made-in-heaven.html

Blurton 1998
T. Richard Blurton, 'The "Murshidabad" Pats of Bengal' in Jyotindra Jain (ed.), *Picture Showmen: Insights into the Narrative Tradition in Indian Art* (Mumbai 1998), pp.42–55

Bolts 1772
William Bolts, *Considerations on Indian Affairs* (London 1772)

Bonhams 2015
Bonhams, *Islamic and Indian Art* (sale catalogue), 21 April 2015

Bossert 1937
H.Th. Bossert, *Encyclopedia of Ornament: A collection of applied decorative forms from all nations and all ages* (London 1937)

Bouchon 1999
Geneviève Bouchon, 'Trade in the Indian Ocean at the Dawn of the Sixteenth Century' in Sushil Chaudhury and Michel Morineau (eds), *Merchants, Companies and Trade* (Cambridge 1999), pp.42–51

Brac de la Perrière 2008
Eloïse Brac de la Perrière, *L'art du livre dans l'Inde des sultanats* (Paris 2008)

Brand 1995
Michael Brand (ed.), *The Vision of Kings: Art and Experience in India* (Canberra 1995)

Brantlinger 1996
Patrick Brantlinger, 'A Postindustrial Prelude to Postcolonialism: John Ruskin, William Morris, and Gandhism', *Critical Inquiry* (Spring 1996), vol.22, pp.466–85

Braubach 1963–5
Max Braubach, *Prinz Eugen von Savoyen: Eine Biographie* (Vienna 1963–5), 5 vols

Brosius 2010
Christiane Brosius, *India's Middle Class: New Forms of Urban Leisure, Consumption and Prosperity* (New Delhi 2010)

Brown 2010
Rebecca M. Brown, *Gandhi's Spinning Wheel and the Making of India* (Abingdon 2010)

Buddle 1990
Anne Buddle, *Tigers Round the Throne* (London 1990)

Cardon 2007
Dominique Cardon, *Natural Dyes* (London 2007)

Casson 1989
Lionel Casson, *The Periplus Maris Erythraei: Text with Introduction, Translation, and Commentary* (Princeton 1989)

Castelino 1994
Meher Castelino, *Fashion Kaleidoscope* (New Delhi 1994)

Chakraverty 2002
Anjan Chakraverty, *The Master Naqshaband of Banaras Brocades: Ali Hasan alias Kalloo Hafiz* (New Delhi 2002)

Chandra 1973
Moti Chandra, *Costumes, Textiles, Cosmetics and Coiffure in Ancient and Mediaeval India* (New Delhi 1973)

Chandra 1985
Moti Chandra, *Kashi Ka Itihas* (Varanasi 1985)

Chaudhuri 1978
K. Chaudhuri, *The Trading World of Asia and the English East India Company 1660–1760* (Cambridge 1978)

Chaudhury and Morineau 1999
Sushil Chaudhury and Michel Morineau (eds), *Merchants, Companies and Trade* (Cambridge 1999)

Chaurasia 2008
Radhey Shyam Chaurasia, *History of Ancient India: Earliest Times to 1200 AD* (New Delhi 2008)

Chowdhury 1982
S.N. Chowdhury, *Muga Silk Industry* (Guwahati 1982)

Christie 1993
Jan W. Christie, 'Texts and Textiles in "Medieval" Java', *Bulletin de l'École française d'Extrême-Orient* (1993), vol.90, no.1, pp.181–211

Cohen 1999
Steven Cohen, 'The Earliest Indian Textile?', *Textile History* (1999), vol.30, no.1, pp.5–15

Cohen 2003
Steven Cohen, 'Assamese Lampas in the Riboud Collection and some proposed additions to the corpus of woven Assamese silks: double cloth and damask', *Bulletin du CIETA* (2003), no.80, pp.60–7

Cohen 2008
Steven Cohen, 'Textiles, Dress and Attire as Depicted in the Albums' in Elaine Wright, *Muraqqa: Imperial Mughal Albums from the Chester Beatty Library, Dublin* (Dublin 2008), pp.178–187

Cohen 2010
Steven Cohen, 'The Use of Fine Goat Hair for the Production of Luxury Textiles' in Jon Thompson, Daniel Shaffer and Pirjetta Mildh (eds), *Carpets and Textiles in the Iranian World 1400–1700* (Oxford and Genoa 2010), pp.124–41

Cohen 2014
Steven Cohen, 'Two Outstanding Mughal *Qanat* Panels in the David Collection', *Journal of the David Collection* (2014), vol.4, pp.170–201

Cohen et al. 2012
Steven Cohen (ed.), Rosemary Crill, Jeffrey B. Spurr and Monique Lévi-Strauss, *Kashmir Shawls: The TAPI Collection* (Mumbai 2012)

Constantini 1983
Lorenzo Constantini, 'The Beginning of Agriculture in the Kachi Plain: The Evidence of Mehrgarh' in B. Allchin (ed.), *South Asian Archaeology* (Cambridge 1983), pp.29–33

Crill 1992
Rosemary Crill, 'Vrindavani Vastra: Figured Silks from Assam', *Hali* (1992), issue 62, pp.76–83

Crill 1993
Rosemary Crill, 'Embroidered Topography', *Hali* (1993), issue 67, pp.90–5

Crill 1995
Rosemary Crill, 'Vaishnavite Silks: The Figured Textiles of Assam' in Jasleen Dhamija (ed.), *The Woven Silks of India* (Mumbai 1995), pp.37–48

Crill 1998
Rosemary Crill, *Indian Ikat Textiles* (London 1998)

Crill 1999
Rosemary Crill, *Indian Embroidery* (London 1999)

Crill 2006a
Rosemary Crill (ed.), *Textiles from India: The Global Trade* (Kolkata 2006)

Crill 2006b
Rosemary Crill, 'The Earliest Survivors? The Indian Embroideries at Hardwick Hall' in Rosemary Crill (ed.), *Textiles from India: The Global Trade* (Kolkata 2006), pp.245–60

Crill 2008
Rosemary Crill, *Chintz: Indian Textiles for the West* (London 2008)

Crill 2012
Rosemary Crill, 'Embroidery in Kashmir Shawls' in Steven Cohen (ed.), Rosemary Crill, Jeffrey B. Spurr and Monique Lévi-Strauss, *Kashmir Shawls: The TAPI Collection* (Mumbai 2012), pp.290–319

Dallapiccola 2015
Anna L. Dallapiccola, *Kalamkari Temple Hangings* (Ahmedabad 2015)

Dallapiccola et al. 2014
Anna L. Dallapiccola et al. (eds), *Rayalaseema: The Royal Realm, Architecture and Art of Southern Andhra Pradesh* (Mumbai 2014)

Das 1992
Sukla Das, *Fabric Art* (Delhi 1992)

Davies 1957
K.G. Davies, *The Royal African Company* (London 1957)

Debaine-Francfort and Idriss 2001
C. Debaine-Francfort and A. Idriss, *Keriya: Mémoires d'un fleuve* (Paris 2001)

Desmond 1982
Ray Desmond, *The India Museum 1801–1879* (London 1982)

Dhamija 2004
Jasleen Dhamija (ed.), *Asian Embroidery* (New Delhi 2004)

Digby 2007
Simon Digby, 'Export Industries and Handicraft Production under the Sultans of Kashmir', *Indian Economic and Social History Review* (2007), vol.44, issue 4, pp.407–23

Dowleans 1851
A.M. Dowleans (ed.), *Catalogue of East Indian Productions Collected in the Presidency of Bengal and Forwarded to the Exhibition of Works of Art and Industry to be Held in London in 1851* (Calcutta 1851)

Driver and Ashmore 2010
Felix Driver and Sonia Ashmore, 'The Mobile Museum: Collecting and Circulating Indian Textiles in Victorian Britain', *Victorian Studies* (2010), vol.52, no.3, pp.353–85

Edwards 2011
Eiluned Edwards, *Textiles and Dress of Gujarat* (Ahmedabad 2011)

EIC Correspondence 1802
East India Company Commercial Correspondence (Madras 1802), British Library IOR/E/4/889

Eicher 2006
Joanne B. Eicher, 'Kalabari Identity and Indian textiles in the Niger Delta' in Rosemary Crill (ed.), *Textiles from India: The Global Trade* (Kolkata 2006), pp.153–71

Elson 1979
Vickie Elson, *Dowries from Kutch* (Los Angeles 1979)

Evans 2014
Ben Evans, 'The Armenian Knot', *Hali* (Spring 2014), issue 179, pp.93–6

Finn 2014
Patrick J. Finn, *Quilts of India* (New Delhi 2014)

Fischer 2013
Eberhard Fischer, *Temple Tents for Goddesses in Gujarat, India* (Zurich 2013)

Fischer and Pathy 1982
Eberhard Fischer and Dinanath Pathy, 'Gita Govinda Inscribed Ikat-textiles from Orissa', *Journal of the Orissa Research Society* (April 1982), vol.1, no.2, pp.7–15

Font 2011
Lourdes Font, 'Dior Before Dior', *West 86* (Spring/Summer 2011) vol.18, no.1, pp.26–49

Forbes Watson 1862
John Forbes Watson, *The International Exhibition of 1862. A Classified Descriptive Catalogue of the Indian Department* (London 1862)

Forbes Watson 1866
John Forbes Watson, *The Textile Fabrics of India*, 1st series (London 1866), 18 vols

Forbes Watson 1867
John Forbes Watson, *The Textile Manufactures and the Costumes of the People of India* (London 1867)

Frankel 2014
Susannah Frankel, 'The Fabric of the Story' in Pamela Golbin et al., *Dries Van Noten* (Tielt 2014), pp.13–35

Frantes 2005
Harald Frantes, *Die vollständige Ausstattung der Schlösser Hof an der March und Niederweiden von 1736: Das Nachlaßinventar von Prinz Eugen von Savoyen* (Vienna 2005)

Fukuoka 2014
Ages of Sarasa, exh. cat., Fukuoka Art Museum, Fukuoka 2014

Galloway 2011
Francesca Galloway, *Islamic Courtly Textiles & Trade Goods: 14th to 19th Century* (London 2011)

Gittinger 1982
Mattiebelle Gittinger, *Master Dyers to the World: Technique and Trade in Early Indian Dyed Cotton Textiles* (Washington DC 1982)

Gittinger 1989
M. Gittinger, 'Ingenious Techniques in Early Indian Dyed Cotton' in K. Riboud (ed.), *In Quest of Themes and Skills – Asian Textiles* (Bombay 1989), pp.4–15

Gleba 2008
Margarita Gleba, 'Auratae vestes: Gold Textiles in the Ancient Mediterranean' in C. Alfaro and L. Karali (eds), *Vestidos, Textiles y Tintes: Estudios sobre la producción de bienes de consumo en la Antigüedad, Actas del II Symposium Internacional sobre Textiles y Tintes del Mediterráneo en el mundo antiguo (Atenas, 24 al 26 noviembre, 2005), Purpureae Vestes II: Textiles and Dyes in Antiquity* (Valencia 2008), pp.61–77

Goetz 1949
H. Goetz, 'The Calico Museum of Textiles at Ahmedabad', *Marg* (1949), vol.3, no.4, p.61

Gole 1989
Susan Gole, *Indian Maps and Plans* (New Delhi 1989)

Golikov 2001
Valery Golikov, 'The technology of silk dyeing by cochineal. II. The experimental investigation of the influences of types and concentrations of cations' and 'The technology of silk dyeing by cochineal. III. The influences of pH, water quality, cream of tartar and oak galls' in Jo Kirby (ed.), *Dyes in History and Archaeology* (2001), vol.16/17, pp.10–33

Good, Kenoyer and Meadow 2009
I.L. Good, J.M. Kenoyer and R.H. Meadow, 'New Evidence for Early Silk in the Indus Civilization', *Archaeometry* (2009), vol.51, no.3, pp.457–66

Goswamy 1993
B.N. Goswamy, *Indian Costumes in the Calico Museum of Textiles* (Ahmedabad 1993)

Goswamy 2006
B.N. Goswamy, 'Occupying Some Spaces, Darkly: Sidis in Paintings from Kutch' in Kenneth X. Robbins and John McLeod (eds), *African Elites in India: Habshi Amarat* (Ahmedabad 2006), pp.234–43

Graham 2006
Joss Graham, 'The Contemporary Use of Gyasar Brocade in Qinghai Province, China (Amdo, Tibet)' in Rosemary Crill (ed.), *Textiles from India: The Global Trade* (Kolkata 2006), pp.27–38

Granger-Taylor 2012
Hero Granger-Taylor, 'The Textiles' in K.D. Politis, *The Sanctuary of Lot at Deir 'Ain 'Abata in Jordan: Excavations 1988–2003* (Amman 2012) section V.10d, pp.378–91

Great Exhibition 1851
Official and Descriptive Catalogue of the Great Exhibition of the Works of Industry of All Nations 1851 (London 1851), 4 vols

Great Exhibition 1852
A Catalogue of the Articles of Ornamental Art selected from the Exhibition of the Works of Industry of All Nations in 1851, and purchased by the Government prepared at the desire of the Lords of the Committee of Privy Council for Trade (London 1852)

Greenhalgh 1988
Paul Greenhalgh, *Ephemeral Vistas* (Manchester 1988)

Guelton 2007
Marie-Hélène Guelton, 'De l'Inde à l'Arménie: la fabrication des rideaux de chœur peints et imprimés', in *Ors et trésors d'Arménie* (Lyon 2007)

Gulati 1961
A.N. Gulati, 'A Note on the Early History of Silk in India' in J. Clutton Brock, K. Vishnu-Mittre and A.N. Gulati (eds), *Technical Reports on Archaeological Remains* (Poona 1961), pp.53–9

Gulati and Turner 1928
A.N. Gulati and A.J. Turner, 'A Note on the Early History of Cotton', *Technical Laboratory Bulletin* (1928), no.17, pp.1–10

Gupta 2011
Gargi Gupta, 'What Ails Lucknow *chikan*?', *Business Standard*, 14 May 2011, http://www.business-standard.com/article/beyond-business/what-ails-lucknow-chikan-111051400003_1.html

Guy 1992
John Guy, 'Indian Textiles for the Thai Market – A Royal Prerogative', *Textile Museum Journal* (1992), pp.82–96

Guy 1998
John Guy, *Woven Cargoes: Indian Textiles in the East* (London 1998)

Guy and Swallow 1990
John Guy and Deborah Swallow (eds), *Arts of India, 1550–1800* (London 1990)

Hadaway 1917
W.S. Hadaway, *Cotton Painting and Printing in the Madras Presidency* (Madras 1917)

Haller 1903
Max Haller, *Geschichte von Schlosshof: Cultur-historische Skizze des k. u. k. Lustschlosses Schloßhof a. d. March* (Vienna 1903)

Hambly 2003
Gavin R.G. Hambly, 'The Emperor's Clothes: Robing and "Robes of Honour" in Mughal India' in S. Gordon (ed.), *Robes of Honour: Khil'at in Pre-Colonial and Colonial India* (Oxford 2003), pp.31–49

Hanzl-Wachter 2005
Lieselotte Hanzl-Wachter (ed.), *Schloss Hof: Prinz Eugens tusculum rurale und Sommerresidenz der kaiserlichen Familie* (Vienna 2005)

Hartkamp-Jonxis 1987
Ebeltje Hartkamp-Jonxis (ed.), *Sits: Oost-West Relaties in Textiel* (Zwolle 1987)

Hartkamp-Jonxis 1994
Ebeltje Hartkamp-Jonxis, *Sitsen uit India: Indian Chintzes* (Amsterdam 1994)

Hellstrom 2012
Krystyna Hellstrom, *Jaipur Quilts* (New Delhi 2012)

Hoffenberg 2001
Peter H. Hoffenberg, *An Empire on Display* (Berkeley 2001)

Horton 2004
Mark Horton, 'Artisans, Communities and Commodities: Medieval Exchanges between Northwestern India and East Africa', *Ars Orientalis* (2004), vol.34, pp.63–80

Ibn Battuta 1983
Ibn Battuta, *Travels in Asia and Africa 1325–1354*, trans. and ed. H.A.R. Gibb (London 1929, reprint 1983)

Ibn Khurdadbih 1889
Ibn Khurdadbih, *Kitab al-Masalik wa'l-Mamalik*, ed. M.J. de Goeje (Leiden 1889)

Irwin 1952
John Irwin, 'Indo-Portuguese Embroideries of Bengal', *Journal of Royal India, Pakistan and Ceylon Society* (1952), vol.XXVI, no.2, pp.65–73

Irwin 1973
John Irwin, *The Kashmir Shawl* (London 1973)

Irwin and Brett 1970
John Irwin and Katharine B. Brett, *Origins of Chintz* (London 1970)

Irwin and Hall 1973
John Irwin and Margaret Hall, *Indian Embroideries* (Ahmedabad 1973)

Irwin and Schwartz 1966
John Irwin and P.R. Schwartz, *Studies in Indo-European Textiles History* (Ahmedabad 1966)

Jain 1993–4
Rahul Jain, 'The Indian Drawloom and its Products', *Textile Museum Journal* (1993–4), vols 32–3, pp.50–81

Jain 2002
Rahul Jain et al., *Khadi: The Fabric of Freedom* (New Delhi 2002)

Jain 2011a
Rahul Jain, *Rapture: The Art of Indian Textiles* (New Delhi 2011)

Jain 2011b
Rahul Jain, *Woven Textiles: Technical Studies Monograph No.2: Mughal Velvets in the Collection of the Calico Museum of Textiles* (Ahmedabad 2011)

Jain 2013
Rahul Jain, *Woven Textiles: Technical Studies Monograph No. 3, Indian Lampas – Weave Silks* (Ahmedabad 2013)

Jayakar 1962a
Pupul Jayakar, 'Homage to Handloom' (editorial), Marg (1962), vol.15, no.4, p.3

Jayakar 1962b
Pupul Jayakar, 'Weaver's Service Centres of the All India Handloom Board', *Marg* (1962), vol.15, no.4, pp.64–71

Jayakar 1980
Pupul Jayakar, *The Earthen Drum: An Introduction to the Ritual Arts of Rural India* (New Delhi 1980)

Joshi 2002
Divya Joshi (ed.), *Gandhiji on Khadi*, (Mumbai 2002)

Kajitani 2001
Nobuko Kajitani, 'A Man's Caftan and Leggings from the North Caucasus of the Eighth to Tenth Century: A Conservator's Report', *Metropolitan Museum Journal* (2001), vol.36, pp.85–124

Kashyap 1958
Bhikkhu Jagdish Kashyap (ed.), *Digha Nikaya: vol.I, Silakkhanda-vagga* (Nalanda 1958)

Kashyap 2013a
Malvika V. Kashyap, 'Maximiliano Modesti', *Border & Fall* (2013), No.4, http://www.borderandfall.com/journal/no-4-covenant/maximiliano-modesti/

Kashyap 2013b
Malvika V. Kashyap, 'Sabyasachi Mukherjee', *Border & Fall* (2013), No.4, http://www.borderandfall.com/journal/no-4-covenant/sabyasachi-mukherjee/

Kashyap 2013c
Samudra Gupta Kashyap, 'When the Looms Burned', *The Indian Express*, 7 April 2013, http://archive.indianexpress.com/news/when-the-looms-burned/1098687/

Kayoko 2009
Fujita Kayoko, 'Japan Indianized: The Material Culture of Imported Textiles in Japan, 1550–1850' in Giorgio Riello and Prasannan Parthasarathi (eds), *The Spinning World: A Global History of Cotton Textiles, 1200–1850* (Oxford 2009), pp.181–203

Kenoyer 2004
Jonathan Mark Kenoyer, 'Ancient Textiles of the Indus Valley Region' in Noorjehan Bilgrami (ed.), *Tana Bana: The Woven Soul of Pakistan* (Karachi 2004), pp.18–31

Klimburg-Salter 1997
Deborah Klimburg-Salter, *Tabo: A Lamp for the Kingdom* (Milan 1997)

Kramrisch 1968
Stella Kramrisch, *Unknown India: Ritual Art in Tribe and Village* (Philadelphia 1968)

Kriegel 2001
Laura Kriegel, 'Narrating the Subcontinent in 1851: India at the Crystal Palace' in Louise Purbrick (ed.), *The Great Exhibition of 1851: New Interdisciplinary Essays* (Manchester 2001), pp.146–78

Kriger 2009
Colleen Kriger, 'Guinea Cloth: Production and Consumption of Cotton Textiles in West Africa before and during the Atlantic Slave Trade' in Giorgio Riello and Prasannan Parthasarathi (eds), *The Spinning World: A Global History of Cotton Textiles, 1200–1850* (Oxford 2009), pp.105–26

Krishna and Krishna 1966
Anand Krishna and Vijay Krishna, *Banaras Brocades* (New Delhi 1966)

Krishna and Talwar 2007
Kalyan Krishna and Kay Talwar, *In Adoration of Krishna: Pichhwais of Shrinathji. TAPI Collection* (Mumbai 2007)

Kuldova 2013a
Tereza Kuldova (ed.), *Fashion India: Spectacular Capitalism* (Oslo 2013)

Kuldova 2013b
Tereza Kuldova, 'Laughing at Luxury: Mocking Fashion Designers' in Tereza Kuldova (ed.), *Fashion India: Spectacular Capitalism* (Oslo 2013), pp.167–92

Kuldova 2013c
Tereza Kuldova, '"The Maharaja Style" Royal Chic and Double Vision' in Tereza Kuldova (ed.), *Fashion India: Spectacular Capitalism* (Oslo 2013), pp.53–4

Lamb 2005
Venice Lamb, *Looms Past and Present: Around the Mediterranean and Elsewhere* (Hertingfordbury 2005)

Lefèvre 2006
Vincent Lefèvre, 'A propos d'une célèbre toile peinte (kalamkari) de la collection Riboud au musée Guimet' in H. Chambert-Loir and B. Dagens (eds), *Anamorphoses, Hommage à Jacques Dumarcay* (Paris 2006), pp.127–39

Lemire 1991
Beverly Lemire, *Fashion's Favourite: The Cotton Trade and the Consumer in Britain, 1660–1800* (Oxford 1991)

Lemire 1997
Beverly Lemire, *Dress, Culture and Commerce: The English Clothing Trade before the Factory, 1660–1800* (London 1997)

Lemire 2009
Beverly Lemire, 'Revising the Historical Narrative: India, Europe and the Cotton Trade, c.1300–1800' in Giorgio Riello and Prasannan Parthasarathi (eds), *The Spinning World: A Global History of Cotton Textiles, 1200–1850* (Oxford 2009), pp.205–26

Leonard 2006
Polly Leonard, 'The Accidental Purist', *Selvedge* (2006), issue 9, pp.68–70

Lisbon 2011
Museum of Christian Art: Convent of Santa Monica, Goa, India, exh. cat., Lisbon 2011

London 1978
Embroidered Quilts from the Museu Nacional de Arte Antiga, Lisboa, exh. cat., Kensington Palace, London 1978

London 1979
Arts of Bengal. The Heritage of Bangladesh and Eastern India, exh. cat., Whitechapel Art Gallery, London 1979

London 1982
The Indian Heritage: Court Life and Arts under Mughal Rule, exh. cat., Victoria and Albert Museum, London 1982

London 2004
Encounters: The Meeting of Asia and Europe 1500–1800, exh. cat., Victoria and Albert Museum, London 2004

Los Angeles 1974
Fabric and Fashion, ed. Mary Hunt Kahlenberg, exh. cat., Los Angeles County Museum of Art, Los Angeles 1974

Losty 1982
Jeremiah P. Losty, *The Art of the Book in India* (London 1982)

Luke 2008
Catriona Luke, 'The Clothes Nationalist', *New Statesman*, 30 October 2008, http://www.newstatesman.com/asia/2008/10/india-fashion-gandhi-designer

Lynton 1995
Linda Lynton, *The Sari* (London 1995)

Machado 2009a
Pedro Machado, 'Awash in a Sea of Cloth: Gujarat, Africa, and the Western Indian Ocean, 1300–1800' in Giorgio Riello and Prasannan Parthasarathi (eds), *The Spinning World: A Global History of Cotton Textiles, 1200–1850* (Oxford 2009), pp.161–79

Machado 2009b/2013 (pb)
Pedro Machado, 'Cloths of a New Fashion: Indian Ocean Networks of Exchange and Cloth Zones of Contact in Africa and India in the Eighteenth and Nineteenth Centuries' in Giorgio Riello and Tirthankar Roy (eds), *How India Clothed the World: The World of South Asian Textiles, 1500–1850* (Leiden and Boston 2009), 2013, pp.53–84

Mackie 1989
Louise Mackie, 'Textiles' in G.T. Scanlon and W. Kubiak, *Fustat Expedition Final Report: vol.2, Fustat-C* (Winona Lake 1989), pp.81–97

Madras Central Committee 1855
List of Madras Products transmitted by the Madras Central Committee for the Universal Exhibition to be held at Paris in 1855 (Madras 1855)

Madras 1857
Madras Exhibition 1857, *I. Juries Reports on the subjects in the 30 Classes into which the Exhibition was divided* (Madras 1857)

Madras 1858
Madras Exhibition of 1859 of the Raw Products of Southern India (Madras 1858)

Mahalingam 2012
A. Mahalingam, *The Vijayanagara-Nayakas: Art and Culture* (New Delhi 2012)

Mahmood 1989
Tahir Mahmood, 'The Dargah of Sayyid Salar Mas'ud Ghazi in Bahraich: Legend, Tradition and Reality' in Christian W. Troll (ed.), *Muslim Shrines in India: Their Character, History and Significance* (New Delhi 1989), pp.24–43

Manfredi 2007
Paola Manfredi, 'In Search of Perfection: *Chikankari* of Lucknow' in Laila Tyabji (ed.), *Threads & Voices: Behind the Indian Textile Tradition* (Mumbai 2007), pp.19–29

Manucci 1907
Niccolao Manucci, *Storia do Mogor, or Mogul India 1653–1708*, trans. William Irvine (London 1907), 4 vols

Marshall 1931
J. Marshall, *Mohenjo-Daro and the Indus Civilisation* (London 1931), 3 vols

Martiniani-Reber and Bénazeth 1997
Marielle Martiniani-Reber and Dominique Bénazeth, *Textiles et mode sassanides: les tissus orientaux conservés au Département des antiquités égyptiennes, Musée du Louvre* (Paris 1997)

Master 1911
Streynsham Master, *The Diaries of Streynsham Master, 1675–1680, and other contemporary papers relating thereto*, ed. Sir Richard Carnac Temple (London 1911), 2 vols

Mas'udi 1861–77
Al-Mas'udi, *Murudj al-Dhahab, Les Prairies d'Or*, trans. and ed. Ch.A.C. Barbier de Meynard and A.J.B. Pavet de Courteille (Paris 1861–77), 9 vols

McGowan 2009
Abigail McGowan, *Crafting the Nation in Colonial India* (New York 2009)

Meeta and Sunny 2007
Meeta and Sunny, 'Chippas of Rajasthan . . . Bindaas Unlimited' in Laila Tyabji (ed.), *Threads & Voices: Behind the Indian Textile Tradition* (Mumbai 2007), pp.31–43

Menkes 2010
Suzy Menkes, 'Throwing Down the Gauntlet', *The New York Times*, 28 September 2010, http://www.nytimes.com/2010/09/29/fashion/29iht-rprada.html?_r=0

Mitra 1978
Debendra Bijoy Mitra, *Cotton Weavers of Bengal* (Calcutta 1978)

Mittal 2004
Jagdish Mittal, 'Indian Embroidery through the Ages: Some Masterpieces' in Jasleen Dhamija (ed.), *Asian Embroidery* (New Delhi 2004), pp.25–44

Mittal 2007
Jagdish Mittal, *Sublime Delight through Works of Art from Jagdish and Kamla Mittal Museum of Indian Art* (Hyderabad 2007)

Mohanty, Chandramouli and Naik 1987
B.C. Mohanty, H.D. Chandramouli and H.C. Naik, *Natural Dyeing Processes of India* (Ahmedabad 1987)

Moulherat et al. 2002
C. Moulherat, M. Tengberg, J.F. Haquet and B. Mille, 'First Evidence of Cotton at Neolithic Mehrgarh, Pakistan: Analysis of Mineralised Fibres from a Copper Bead', *Journal of Archaeological Science* (2002), vol.29, no.12, pp.1393–401

Mughal 1990
Mohammed Rafique Mughal, 'Further Evidence of the Harappan Culture in the Greater Indus Valley: 1971–90', *South Asian Studies* (1990), no.6, pp.175–99

Mulvagh 1994
Jane Mulvagh, 'Fashion: An Eastern Legend and a Magic Word', *The Independent*, 27 January 1994, http://www.independent.co.uk/life-style/fashion/news/fashion-an-eastern-legend-and-a-magic-word-ashas-minimal-indian-clothes-have-long-had-stylish-cerebral-devotees-her-new-shop-will-now-offer-some-enlightenment-to-the-rest-of-us-jane-mulvagh-reports-1402873.html

Mumbai 2009
In Praise of Folly: Lavanya Mani, ed. Annapurna Garimella, exh. cat., Chemould Prescott Road, Mumbai 2009

Murphy 1990
Veronica Murphy, 'Europeans and the Textile Trade' in John Guy and Deborah Swallow (eds), *Arts of India, 1550–1800* (London 1990), pp.152–71

Murphy and Crill 1991
Veronica Murphy and Rosemary Crill, *Tie-Dyed Textiles of India* (Ahmedabad and London 1991)

Nabholz-Kartaschoff 1986
Marie-Louise Nabholz-Kartaschoff, *Golden Sprays and Scarlet Flowers* (Kyoto 1986)

Nagaswamy 1986
R. Nagaswamy, 'Mughal cultural influence in the Setupati murals in the Ramalinga Vilasam at Ramnad' in R. Skelton et al. (eds), *Facets of Indian Art* (London 1986), pp.203–10

New York 2013
Interwoven Globe: The Worldwide Textile Trade, 1500–1800, ed. Amelia Peck, exh. cat., Metropolitan Museum of Art, New York 2013

North 2012
Susan North, *Dress and Hygiene in Early Modern England: A Study of Advice and Practice*, PhD thesis, Queen Mary College, University of London, 2012

Paine 1989
Sheila Paine, *Chikan Embroidery: The Floral Whitework of India* (Princes Risborough 1989)

Passariello 2013
Christina Passariello, 'Heir to the House of Lesage Takes the Business to India', *The Wall Street Journal*, 10 October 2013, http://online.wsj.com/news/articles/SB10001424052702304213904579095282167195254

Patel 2014
Divia Patel, *India: Contemporary Design: Fashion, Graphics, Interiors* (New Delhi 2014)

Patner n.d.
Josh Patner, 'Women in Luxury: Shamina Talyarkhan', *Time*, http://content.time.com/time/specials/packagesarticle/0,28804,1838865_1838857_1838729,00.html

Pearson 1976
M.N. Pearson, *Merchants and Rulers in Gujarat* (New Delhi 1976)

Pearson 1986–7
M.N. Pearson, 'The Mughals and the Hajj', *Journal of the Oriental Society of Australia* (1986-7), vols 18-19, pp.164-79

Pfister 1934
R. Pfister, *Textiles de Palmyre* (Paris 1934)

Philadelphia 2010
Kantha: The Embroidered Quilts of Bengal from the Jill and Sheldon Bonovitz Collection and the Stella Kramrisch Collection of the Philadelphia Museum of Art, ed. Darielle Mason, exh. cat., Philadelphia Museum of Art, Philadelphia 2010

Pokharia et al. 2011
Anil K. Pokharia et al., 'Archaeobotany and Archaeology at Kanmer, a Harappan Site in Kachchh, Gujarat: Evidence for Adaptation in Response to Climatic Variability', *Current Science* (June 2011), vol.100, no.12, pp.1833-46

Possehl 1990
Gregory L. Possehl, 'Revolution in the Urban Revolution: The Emergence of Indus Urbanization', *Annual Review of Anthropology* (1990), vol.19, pp.261-82

Purbrick 2001
Louise Purbrick (ed.), *The Great Exhibition of 1851: New Interdisciplinary Essays* (Manchester 2001)

Rao 2014
Sunita Ila Rao, 'Khadi x Denim' in *Border & Fall* (2014), http://www.borderandfall.com/karigar/khadi-denim-revolutionary-textile/

Rao, Shulman and Subrahmanyam 1998
V.N. Rao, D. Shulman and S. Subrahmanyam, *Symbols of Substance: Court and State in Nayaka Period Tamil Nadu* (New Delhi 1998)

Ray 1917
J.C. Ray, 'Textile Industry in Ancient India', *Journal of the Bihar and Orissa Research Society* (1917), vol.III, part II, pp.180-238

Ray 2005
Indrajit Ray, 'Long waves of silk price in Bengal during 17th-18th centuries'. Paper given at GEHN conference no.8, Pune, 2005 http://www.lse.ac.uk/economicHistory/Research/GEHN/GEHNPDF/PUNERay.pdf

Raychaudhuri and Habib 1982
T. Raychaudhuri and I. Habib (eds), *The Cambridge Economic History of India, c.1200-c.1750* (Cambridge 1982)

Rhys Davids and Rhys Davids 1899–1921
T.W. Rhys Davids and C.A.F. Rhys Davids (trans.), *Dialogues of the Buddha* (Oxford 1899-1921), 3 vols

Riboud 1989
Krisha Riboud (ed), *In Quest of Themes and Skills: Asian Textiles* (Mumbai 1989)

Riello 2009
Giorgio Riello, 'The Globalisation of Cotton Textiles' in Giorgio Riello and Prasannan Parthasarathi (eds), *The Spinning World: A Global History of Cotton Textiles, 1200-1850* (Oxford 2009), pp.261-87

Riello 2013
Giorgio Riello, *Cotton: The Fabric that Made the Modern World* (Cambridge 2013)

Riello and Parthasarathi 2009
Giorgio Riello and Prasannan Parthasarathi (eds), *The Spinning World: A Global History of Cotton Textiles, 1200-1850* (Oxford 2009)

Riello and Roy 2009
Giorgio Riello and Tirthakar Roy (eds), *How India Clothed the World: The World of South Asian Textiles, 1500-1850* (Leiden and Boston 2009)

Rizvi 2001
Janet Rizvi, *Trans-Himalayan Caravans: Merchant Princes and Peasant Traders in Ladakh* (Oxford and Delhi 2001)

Rizvi 2006
Janet Rizvi, 'The Asian Trade in Kashmir Shawls' in Rosemary Crill (ed.), *Textiles from India: The Global Trade* (Kolkata 2006), pp.81-98

Rizvi and Ahmed 2009
Janet Rizvi and Monisha Ahmed, *Pashmina* (Mumbai 2009)

Robbins and McLeod 2006
Kenneth X. Robbins and John McLeod (eds), *African Elites in India: Habshi Amarat* (Ahmedabad 2006)

Rockey 1913
N.L. Rockey, 'Progress of Islam in Oudh', *Muslim World* (1913), vol.3, pp.250-6

Rothstein 1978
Natalie Rothstein, *Barbara Johnson's Album of Styles and Fabrics* (London 1978)

Roy 2006
Srirupa Roy, '"A symbol of Freedom": The Indian Flag and the Transformations of Nationalism, 1906-2002', *The Journal of Asian Studies* (August 2006), vol.65, no.3, pp.495-527

Roy 1993
Tirthankar Roy, *Artisans and Industrialization: Indian Weaving in the Twentieth Century* (Oxford 1993)

Roy 2012
Tirthankar Roy, *India and the World Economy* (Cambridge 2012)

Rutt 1987
Richard Rutt, *A History of Hand Knitting* (London 1987)

Sangar 1998
S.P. Sangar, *Indian Textiles in the Seventeenth Century* (New Delhi 1998)

Santhanam and Hutchinson 1974
V. Santhanam and J.B. Hutchinson, 'Cotton' in J.B. Hutchinson (ed.), *Evolutionary Studies in World Crops: Diversity and Change in the Indian Subcontinent* (New York 1974)

Schaller 2012
George B. Schaller, *Tibet Wild: A Naturalist's Journeys on the Roof of the World* (Washington DC 2012)

Schoff 1974
Wilfred H. Schoff (trans. and ed.), *The Periplus of the Erythraean Sea* (New York 1912, reprint New Delhi 1974)

Schwerin 1984
Kerrin Graefin V. Schwerin, 'Saint Worship in Indian Islam: The Legend of the Martyr Salar Masud Ghazi' in Imtiaz Ahmad (ed.), *Ritual and Religion among Muslims in India* (New Delhi 1984), pp.143-61

Selk 2000
Karen Selk, 'Journeys in the Wild Silk Jungles of India', *Spin-Off* (Spring 2000), pp.57-76

Sen Gupta 2010
Subhadra Sen Gupta, *Hampi: Discover the Splendours of Vijayanagar* (Delhi 2010)

Serrano et al. 2008
Carmo Serrano, Teresa Pacheco Pereira, Ana Isabel Seruya and Ana Lopes, 'Dyes in Indo-Portuguese bedspreads of 16th to 18th centuries', *CIETA Bulletin* (2007-8), vols 84-5, pp.76-91

Shamir and Baginski 2014
Orit Shamir and Alisa Baginski 'The Earliest Cotton Ikat Textiles from Nahal 'Omer Israel 650-810 CE', in M.L. Nosch, Z. Feng and L. Varadarajan (eds), *Global Textile Encounters. Ancient Textiles*, Series 20 (Oxford 2014), pp.65-73

Sharma 1992
I.K. Sharma, 'Royal Devotee' in *Art and Culture around 1492: 1992 Seville Universal Exposition*, exh. cat., Seville 1992

Sharma 2014
Radha Sharma, 'The Nehru Jacket, Now Modi Style', *The Times of India*, 21 September 2014, http://timesofindia.indiatimes.com/india/The-Nehru-jacket-now-Modi-style/articleshow/43043940.cms

Shishlina et al. 2003
N.I. Shishlina, O.V. Orfinskaya and V.P. Golikov, 'Bronze Age Textiles from the North Caucasus: New Evidence of Fourth Millennium BC Fibres and Fabrics', *Oxford Journal of Archaeology* 22(4), pp.331-44 (2003)

Shokoohy 2006
Mehrdad Shokoohy, 'The Sidi Sayyid – or Sidi Said – Mosque in Ahmedabad' in Kenneth X. Robbins and John McLeod (eds), *African Elites in India: Habshi Amarat* (Ahmedabad 2006), pp.144-61

Singh 1998
Kavita Singh, 'To Show, To See, To Tell, To Know: Patuas, Bhopas, and their Audiences' in Jyotindra Jain (ed.), *Picture Showmen: Insights into the Narrative Tradition in Indian Art* (Mumbai 1998), pp.100-15

Singh 2010
Radhika Singh, *The Fabric of Our Lives: The Story of Fabindia* (New Delhi 2010)

Singh 2014
Martand Singh, *Ajit Kumar Das, Natural Dye Artist* (Kolkata 2014)

Singh and Ahivasi 1981
Chandramani Singh and Devaki Ahivasi, *Woollen Textiles and Costumes from Bharat Kala Bhavan* (Varanasi 1981)

Sinha 2012
Gayatri Sinha, *Abu Jani Sandeep Khosla: India Fantastique* (London 2012)

Sivaramamurti 1985
Calambur Sivaramamurti, *Vijayanagara Paintings* (New Delhi 1985)

Smart 1986
Ellen Smart, 'A Preliminary Report on a Group of Important Mughal Textiles', *Textile Museum Journal* (1986), vol.25, pp.5-23

Spuhler 1978
Friedrich Spuhler, *Islamic Carpets and Textiles in the Keir Collection* (London 1978)

Stanley 1869
Henry E.J. Stanley (trans. and ed.), *The Three Voyages of Vasco da Gama, and His Viceroyalty: From the Lendas da India of Gaspar Correa* (London 1869)

Stein 1907
Marc Aurel Stein, *Ancient Khotan I and Ancient Khotan II* (Oxford 1907)

Stille 1970
T.A. Stille, 'The Evolution of Pattern Design in the Scottish Woollen Textile Industry in the Nineteenth Century,' *Textile History* (December 1970), vol.1.3, pp.309–31

Stronge 2002
Susan Stronge, *Painting for the Mughal Emperor* (London 2002)

Stronge 2008
Susan Stronge, 'The Minto Album and its Decoration, c.1612–40' in Elaine Wright, *Muraqqa: Imperial Mughal Albums from the Chester Beatty Library, Dublin* (Dublin 2008), pp.82–105

Stronge 2009
Susan Stronge, *Tipu's Tigers* (London 2009)

Styles 2010
John Styles, *Threads of Feeling: The London Foundling Hospital's Textile Tokens, 1740–1770* (London 2010)

Subramaniam 2013
Lakshmi Subramaniam, 'The Political Economy of Textiles in Western India: Weavers, Merchants and the Transition to a Colonial Economy' in Giorgio Riello and Tirthakar Roy (eds), *How India Clothed the World: The World of South Asian Textiles, 1500–1850* (Leiden and Boston 2009), pp.253–80

Suvorova 2004
Anna Suvorova, *Muslim Saints of South Asia: The Eleventh to Fifteenth Centuries* (Abingdon 2004)

Tarlo 1996
Emma Tarlo, *Clothing Matters: Dress and Identity in India* (London 1996)

Temple 1884
R.C. Temple, 'The Marriage of Ghazi Salar' in *The Legends of the Punjab* (Bombay 1883–5), vol.2

Thackston 1999
W.M. Thackston (trans.), *The Jahangirnama: Memoirs of Jahangir, Emperor of India* (Washington DC 1999)

The Silk Road in Southwest China 1992
The Silk Road [in] Southwest in [sic] China, Bashu Culture Picture Album Series (Chengdu 1992)

Trivedi 2007
Lisa Trivedi, *Clothing Gandhi's Nation: Homespun and Modern India* (Bloomington, IN 2007)

Tudor 2014
Elisabeta Tudor, 'Chanel Acquires Indian Atelier Vastrakala', *Style.Com/Arabia*, 4 June 2014, http://arabia.style.com/fashion/news/chanel-acquires-indian-atelier-vastrakala/

Tulloch 1999
Carole Tulloch, 'That Little Magic Touch: The Headtie', in A. de la Haye and E. Wilson (eds), *Defining Dress: Dress as Object, Meaning and Identity* (Manchester 1999), pp.63–78

Tyabji 2007
Laila Tyabji (ed.), *Threads & Voices: Behind the Indian Textile Tradition* (Mumbai 2007)

Varadarajan, Filliozat and Gittinger 1986
L. Varadarajan, V. Filliozat and M. Gittinger, *Study of a Painted Textile from the A.E.D.T.A. Collection*, preface by Krishna Riboud (Paris 1986)

Vasudev 2010
Shefalee Vasudev, 'Wearing *Khadi* Today', *The Indian Express*, 15 August 2010, http://indianexpress.com/article/news-archive/web/wearing-khadi-today/

Vasudev 2013
Shefalee Vasudev, 'Ground Report: The Banaras Bind', *Livemint*, 23 November 2013, http://www.livemint.com/Leisure/5h1lnyORjhtn9PrOZ4wiXL/Ground-Report--The-Banaras-bind.html

Vasudev 2014
Shefalee Vasudev, 'Trend Tracker: The Aam Fabric Party', *Livemint*, 24 January 2014, http://www.livemint.com/Leisure/tzVBmtQdHBsE8ypP3xzcFM/Trend-Tracker--The-Aam-Fabric-Party.html

Veinstein 1999
Gilles Veinstein, 'Commercial Relations between India and the Ottoman Empire (late 15th to late 18th centuries)' in Sushil Chaudhury and Michel Morineau (eds), *Merchants, Companies and Trade* (Cambridge 1999), pp.95–115

Devi and Kapur 1987
Pria Devi and Ritta Kapur (eds), *Visvakarma Ksetra: 4 Zones in Traditional Textile Development and the Visvakarma II, 1987 Collection* (New Delhi 1987)

Völker 2005
Angela Völker, 'Ausstattungstextilien aus Schloss Hof im MAK' in Lieselotte Hanzl-Wachter (ed.), *Schloss Hof: Prinz Eugens tusculum rurale und Sommerresidenz der kaiserlichen Familie* (Vienna 2005), pp.110–19

Völker 2007
Angela Völker, 'An Indian Chinoiserie from an Austrian Palace: The Textile Furnishings of Prince Eugene's State Bedroom in Schloss Hof' in A. Jolly (ed.), *A Taste for the Exotic: Foreign Influences on Early Eighteenth-century Silk Designs* (Riggisberg 2007), pp.57–76

Vyas and Daljeet 1988
Chintamani Vyas and Dr Daljeet, *Paintings of Tanjore and Mysore* (Jhansi 1988)

Walker 1997
Daniel Walker, *Flowers Underfoot* (New York 1997)

Wandl 1999
Erna Wandl, 'Painted Textiles in a Buddhist Temple', *Textile History* (1999), vol.30, no.1, pp.16–28

Warmington 2014
E.H. Warmington, *The Commerce between the Roman Empire and India* (Cambridge 1928, reprint 2014)

Watson 1983
A.M. Watson, *Agricultural Innovation in the Early Islamic World* (Cambridge 1983)

Watt 1903
George Watt, *Indian Art at Delhi 1903* (Calcutta 1903)

Watt and Wardwell 1997
James Watt and Anne Wardwell, *When Silk Was Gold: Central Asian and Chinese Textiles* (New York 1997)

Welch 1985
S.C. Welch, *Indian Art and Culture: 1300–1900* (New York 1985)

Werner 2011
Louis Werner, 'Mughal Maal', *Saudi Aramco World* (July/August 2011), vol.62, no.4, pp.24–33, http://www.saudiaramcoworld.com/issue/201104/mughal.maal.htm

Wild 2006
John Peter Wild, 'Berenike, Archaeological Textiles in Context' in Sabine Schrenk (ed.), *Textiles in situ: Their Findspots in Egypt and the Neighbouring Countries in the First Millennium CE* (Riggisberg 2006), pp.175–84.

Wild and Wild 2005
John Peter Wild and Felicity Wild, 'Rome and India: Early Indian Cotton Textiles from Berenike, Red Sea Coast of Egypt' in Ruth Barnes (ed.), *Textiles in Indian Ocean Societies* (London and New York 2005), pp.10–15

Wild and Wild 2014
John Peter Wild and Felicity Wild, 'Through Roman Eyes: Cotton Textiles from Early Historic India' in Sophie Bergerbrant and Solvi Helene Fossoy (eds), *A Stitch in Time: Essays in Honour of Lise Bender Jørgensen* (Gothenburg 2014), pp. 209–36

Wilkinson-Weber 1999
Clare M. Wilkinson-Weber, *Embroidering Lives: Women's Work and Skill in the Lucknow Embroidery Industry* (New York 1999)

Wilson 1995
Verity Wilson, 'Early Textiles from Central Asia: The Stein Loan Collection', *Textile History* (1995), vol.26, no.1, pp.23–52

Wolters 1967
O.W. Wolters, *Early Indonesian Commerce: A Study of the Origins of Srivijaya* (Ithaca and Oxford 1967)

Wright 2008
Elaine Wright, *Muraqqa: Imperial Mughal Albums from the Chester Beatty Library, Dublin* (Dublin 2008)

Wright and Kumar 1997
Belinda Wright and Ashok Kumar, *Fashioned for Extinction: An Exposé of the Shahtoosh Trade* (New Delhi 1997)

Zurich 1997
Kreuz und Quer der Farben: Karo- und Streifenstoffe der Schweiz für Afrika, Indonesien und die Türkei, ed. Sigrid Barten, exh. cat., Museum Bellerive, Zurich 1997

GLOSSARY

Asavali G
Gujarati sari of silk and metal-wrapped thread. Woven on a drawloom, the ground is almost always metal-wrapped thread bound in twill with polychrome silk continuous and discontinuous pattern wefts.

Avatara S
incarnation of the Hindu god Vishnu

Bandhna/bandhni H
to tie/tie-resist dyeing

Banyan E
an informal robe for a western man

Charkha H
spinning wheel

Chhap H
print, stamp

Chikan/chikankari P
white-work embroidery on cotton

Choga H, T
loose-fitting robe for a man

Choli H
woman's bodice

Chunri/chunari H
tie-resist dyeing; a tie-dyed head-cover

Churidar H
lit. 'with bangles'; trousers with extra-long legs that fit tightly to the calves and are worn wrinkled

Darzi P
tailor

Dhoti H
man's garment, wrapped around the hips and between the legs

Gamcha/gamusa H, A
cotton all-purpose cloth, often red-and-white checked

Ghaghra H
gathered skirt worn in western India

Gopi H
one of the female cowherds who fell in love with Krishna in Vrindavan

Gota H
ribbon made of silver strip woven with silk thread

Hat H
local village market

Jama H
man's robe with ties fastening at either the left or right side of the body

Kachha H
'raw'; fugitive (of dyes)

Kalabattun H
thread made of thin metal wrapped around a silk core

Kalam Ar, P
bamboo pen used for drawing the outlines and some dyed areas on *kalamkari* (qv) textiles

Kalamkari P
'pen work'; technique in which the designs are drawn by hand with a *kalam* (qv). Later, printed textiles using the same designs as those formerly hand-drawn

Kambal H
blanket

Kantha B
quilt made of recycled old saris and dhotis

Karkhana P
workshop, especially those attached to royal courts

Khadi H
fabric of hand-spun and hand-woven cotton

Khilat Ar, P
robe of honour or set of clothes given by a ruler to a favoured courtier or visitor

Kurta H
long, loose shirt for a man

Lahariya H
lit. 'wavy'; form of tie-resist dyeing in which diagonal patterns are produced by wrapping folded cloth

Lampas F
A fully integrated complex weave producing two visibly contrasting weave structures – for example, a combination of a twill ground with polychrome patterns woven in satin weave; a plain weave ground with twill patterns; or a ground in small-scale plain weave with patterns in larger-scale plain weave. There are two types of warp – a main or foundation warp and a binding warp – and two types of weft: a ground or foundation weft and pattern wefts. Such a complex weave, first developed in the early tenth or eleventh century, possibly in Iran, can only be produced on a drawloom or its modern mechanized equivalent. The earliest surviving Indian examples of lampas date from the fifteenth to seventeenth centuries.

Lehnga/lehenga H
skirt for a wedding outfit; sometimes used for the whole outfit

Lungi H
man's garment, wrapped around the hips

Masnad P
couch or seat, especially that of a ruler

Mata ni chandarvo/ mata ni pachedi G
canopy or hanging in honour of the Goddess made by the Vagri community of Gujarat

Namabali B
'Row of names'; textiles decorated with repeated names, usually of deities

Naqshband P
'pattern tier'; an expert craftsman who makes the pattern designs for drawloom weaving

Odhni/odhani H
large rectangular textile that covers a woman's head and upper body

Palampore E
anglicized form of *palangposh* 'bed-cover'. A bed- or wall-hanging exported from India to Europe, usually in chintz or embroidery.

Pashmina H
soft under-hair from the Kashmir shawl goat, used for weaving shawls

Patka P
man's decorative waist-sash

Patolu (sing.)/patola (pl.) G
Gujarati double-ikat silk textile

Peshwaz P
woman's front-opening robe

Phulkari P, H
lit. 'flower work'; embroidery in floss silk in surface darn stitch, associated with Punjab and neighbouring areas

Pichhwai H
lit. 'that goes behind'; a textile hung behind the image of Krishna in a shrine

Qanat T
lit. 'wing'; movable fabric screen made of decorative panels

Rumal P
lit. 'face wipe'; a small cloth or decorative coverlet

Saf Ar, P
a row, especially of conjoined prayer mats in a mosque

Salwar kameez P, H
outfit of trousers and long shirt

Samite F
Weft-faced compound twill in Iran, western Europe, Central Asia and India, warp-faced compound twill in China. There are two warps, a visible main binding warp and an unseen inner warp that separates several differently coloured wefts, allowing one coloured weft at a time to be brought to the front to produce the pattern, while keeping all the other differently coloured wefts flat and unseen at the back. Samite was first developed between the first and second centuries AD, reaching its most technically advanced state by the eighth to ninth centuries, although the earliest surviving Indian examples date from the thirteenth to fifteenth centuries AD.

Sar o pa P
'head and foot'; an alternative term in India for *khilat* (qv)

Saraparda P
'main curtain'; an alternative term in India for *qanat* (qv)

Sarasa J
textiles imported into Japan

Sattra A
Assamese monastery

Shela M
a large shawl worn by Maratha women

Sherwani P, H
a formal, tailored men's coat

Sujni/sujani H
embroidery, especially a type of running stitch done in Bihar; applied to the quilts made in Bihar in this technique

Taqueté F
Weft-faced compound plain weave in the West, warp-faced compound plain weave in China. There are two warps, a main binding warp and an unseen inner warp that separates several differently coloured wefts, allowing one coloured weft at a time to be brought to the front to produce the pattern, while keeping all the other differently coloured wefts flat and unseen at the back. Taqueté was first developed in western or central Asia in the last few centuries BC, but in India we find it combined with other weaves in *patkas* dated as late as the seventeenth and eighteenth centuries.

Telia rumal H
'oily rumal'; ikat textiles formerly used in Hyderabad and exported to the Middle East

Tojli K
small spool used to insert extra pattern wefts in Kashmir shawls

Tus/tush P
the fine hair of the *chiru*, the Tibetan antelope *Parthenops hodgsonii*

Zanjir P
'chain'; the side borders of a Kashmir shawl

Zardozi P
'gold embroidery'; embroidery or couching done with *kalabattun* (qv) and other metallic yarns

Zari P
'golden'; general term for metallic yarn, strip, etc. used to adorn textiles

A   Assamese
Ar Arabic
B   Bengali
E   English
F   French
G   Gujarati
H   Hindi
J   Japanese
K   Kashmiri
M   Marathi
P   Persian
S   Sanskrit
T   Turkish

INDEX

PICTURE CREDITS
(by plate number)

108 Courtesy of York Museums Trust
114 TAPI Collection, India
115 © 2015 Museum of Fine Arts, Boston
116 TAPI Collection, India
118 Photo Scala, Florence/bpk, Bildagentur fuer Kunst, Kultur und Geschichte, Berlin
120 © The Trustees of the Chester Beatty Library, Dublin
121 © 2015 Museum of Fine Arts, Boston
122 Photo © RMN-Grand Palais (musée Guimet, Paris)/Thierry Ollivier
128 Photography by Erik Gould, courtesy of the Museum of Art, Rhode Island School of Design, Providence
129 Courtesy National Museum, New Delhi.
131 © National Trust Images/Erik Pelham
133 Photography by Erik Gould, courtesy of the Museum of Art, Rhode Island School of Design, Providence
134 Virginia Museum of Fine Arts, Richmond. Robert A. and Ruth W. Fisher Fund, Photo: Katherine Wetzel © Virginia Museum of Fine Arts
135 National Gallery of Victoria, Melbourne
136 Photo © RMN-Grand Palais (musée Guimet, Paris)/Jean-Gilles Berizzi
141 Photo © RMN-Grand Palais (musée Guimet, Paris)/Thierry Ollivier
142 © 2015. Image copyright The Metropolitan Museum of Art/Art Resource/Scala, Florence
144 ullstein bild / Getty Images
145 © Ashmolean Museum, University of Oxford
146 © Ashmolean Museum, University of Oxford
147 © Trustees of the British Museum
148 RGS/IBG
154 Courtesy of National Library of Jamaica
155 Joanne B. Eicher
161 TAPI Collection, India
167 Philadelphia Museum of Art. Gift of the Friends of the Philadelphia Museum of Art, 1988
170 © Tate, London 2015
172 © The British Library Board
174 ÖNB/Vienna, L 4314-D Pos
174 © MAK/Georg Mayer
176 Photograph by Maragereta Svensson, Amsterdam
177 Collection of the Gemeentemuseum Den Haag
179 Photograph by YAMASAKI Shinichi Kyushu National Museum
180 Matsuzakaya collection, Courtesy of General Foundation J.Front Retailing Archives
181 © Nour Foundation, Courtesy of the Khalili Family Trust
191 Mary Evans Picture Library
192 © The British Library Board
194 © Bettmann/CORBIS
195 Photo by Margaret Bourke-White/The LIFE Picture Collection/Getty Images
198 Courtesy Sonia Gandhi, Chairperson, Indira Gandhi Memorial Trust Photograph by Ishan Tankha
200 Courtesy of Taanbaan

201 Photograph by Divia Patel
206 Courtesy of Brigitte Singh
208 Courtesy of Kashmir Loom
209 Courtesy of Kashmir Loom
211 © Trustees of the British Museum
212 Arjun Kartha Photography
213 Courtesy of Abu Jani Sandeep Khosla
213 DAMFX/THE KOBAL COLLECTION
214 Courtesy of Sabyasachi
215 Photograph by Divia Patel
217 Courtesy of People Tree
217 Txema Yeste/Trunk Archive
219 © Khalid Amin
221 Image Courtesy of Chemould Prescott Road and the artist, Photograph by Anil Rane, From a Private collection, Mumbai
222 Courtesy of the Lekha and Anupam Poddar Collection
223 © Ajit Kumar Das www.ajitkumardas.com
224 White Jamdani dress with quilting details by Aneeth Arora for p é r o
225 Courtesy of Rahul Mishra
226 © Rajesh Pratap Singh
227 © Rajesh Pratap Singh
228 © Asis Kumar Chatterjee
229 Courtesy of 'my village' by Rimzim Dadu
230 Courtesy of Manish Arora
231 Courtesy of Manish Arora
232 © Aziz and Suleman Khatri
235 © Jiyo!
237 FDCI – Fashion Design Council of India
238 Courtesy of Kallol Datta
239 Prarthna Singh

CONTRIBUTORS

SA Sonia Ashmore, Textile Historian

SC Steven Cohen, Independent Textile Historian

RC Rosemary Crill, Senior Curator, Asian Department, Victoria and Albert Museum

AF Avalon Fotheringham, Fabric of India Exhibition Research Assistant, Victoria and Albert Museum

BK Barbara Karl, Curator, Textiles and Carpets Collection, Museum für angewandte Kunst/Gegenwartskunst

PK Pramod Kumar KG, Independent Scholar, Managing Director of Eka Archiving Services PVt. Ltd.

DP Divia Patel, Curator, Asian Department, Victoria and Albert Museum

AP Anamika Pathak, Curator, Decorative Art, National Museum – New Delhi

AS Aurelie Samuel, chargée des collections textiles, Musée national des arts asiatiques Guimet

ACKNOWLEDGEMENTS

The exhibition *The Fabric of India* and this accompanying book would not have been possible without the help and support of a great many people, both within the V&A and outside.

Good Earth India kindly supported the exhibition and special thanks are due to Simran and Anita Lal for all their enthusiasm and encouragement. We are also grateful to Experion and Nirav Modi for their support of the exhibition.

Teams of colleagues within the V&A have been central to the creation of both the exhibition and book, especially those in Conservation and Collections Management, Asian Department, Exhibitions Department, V&A Publishing and the Photographic Studio. My colleague Divia Patel, the exhibition's co-curator, brought the exhibition and book up to the present day with her judicious selection of modern and contemporary pieces, and has expertly conveyed the crucial role of textiles in India's more recent history. Our Research Assistant, Avalon Fotheringham, has been invaluable throughout the development of the exhibition and has also contributed essays to this book. The exhibition's designer Gitta Gschwendtner and her team provided a fittingly elegant setting for the textiles and Jason Singh created an innovative soundscape.

While many of the pieces in the exhibition were drawn from the V&A's own collection, key loans allowed a fuller story to be told. The lenders to the exhibition, both public institutions and private individuals, have been extremely generous in allowing their pieces to be shown. In India, we thank The National Museum of India, New Delhi, and especially Dr Venu Vasudevan for all his help throughout; CSMVS (former Prince of Wales Museum), Mumbai; Devi Art Foundation, Haryana; the Tapi Collection, Surat; Manish Arora; Asaf Ali and Jenny Housego; Abu Jani and Sandeep Khosla, and Sabyasachi Mukherjee. In the United States: The Metropolitan Museum of Art, New York; The Museum of Fine Arts, Boston; Los Angeles County Museum of Art and Rhode Island School of Design Museum, Providence. In Europe and the UK: Musée National des Arts Asiatiques Guimet, Paris; Staatliche Museen zu Berlin; Gemeentemuseum Den Haag, the Hague; Duivenvoorde Castle, Voorschoten; MAK – Austrian Museum of Applied Arts, Vienna; the Nasser D. Khalili Collection of Islamic Art, London; the British Museum, London; the National Trust, Powis Castle; York Art Gallery and Museum; the Ashmolean Museum, University of Oxford; Royal Botanic Gardens, Kew; Natural History Museum, London; Karun Thakar; Dr Jenny Balfour-Paul; Her Majesty The Queen, and three anonymous lenders.

We are immensely grateful to Aneeth Arora, David Abraham, Rakesh Thakore and Kevin Nigli, Brigitte Singh and Karun Thakar, who have generously given pieces in the exhibition to the V&A. For help in sourcing contemporary pieces, thanks are due to Khalid Amin, Chemould Gallery, Rimzim Dadu, Kallol Datta, Judy Frater, Sanjay Garg, Rta Kapur Chishti, Swati Kalsi, Aziz and Suleman Khatri, Dayalal Kudecha, Neeru Kumar, Lavanya Mani, Mayank Mansingh Kaul, Rahul Mishra, Lekha Poddar, Anupam Poddar, Rajesh Pratap Singh, Rashmi Varma and Malika Verma Kashyap. We are also grateful to Manou for giving us access to his images of street fashion.

Like the exhibition, this book has also benefited from the knowledge, expertise and support of many people. I am especially grateful to Steven Cohen for his deeply researched contributions and for many discussions about the historic material in the book. Divia Patel and the other contributors provided excellent material which included much new research, and sincere thanks are due to them for their essays. I am also deeply grateful to Rahul Jain in Delhi, who was endlessly patient in answering a barrage of questions about weaving, both historic and contemporary. Pramod Kumar KG was very generous with information and advice. Others who kindly provided information on specific topics were Peter Andrews, who shared his valuable findings on Tipu's Tent, Nalini Balbir, Ruth Barnes, Crispin Branfoot, Dominique Cardon, John Gillow, Hero Granger-Taylor, Lynda Hillyer, Mark Kenoyer, Richard A. Laursen, Alexander McCarter, Margaret Makepeace, Susan North, Lisa Trivedi, Carol Tulloch, Ina Van den Bergh and Junnaa Wroblewski. For their help with sourcing images for the book, we are grateful to Anna Dallapiccola, Harsha Dehejia, Ben Evans, Dickran Kouymjian, Jyotindra Jain, Jutta Jain-Neubayer, Charllotte Kwon, Tim McLaughlin and Shamina Talyarkhan.

I would also particularly like to thank my former colleagues Robert Skelton and Veronica Murphy, whose encouragement and inspiration set me on my museum career many years ago. Without them, this exhibition and this book could not have existed.

Rosemary Crill